THE EUROPEAN UNION SERIES

General Editors: Neill Nugent, William E. Paterson

CW00435228

The European Union series provides an authorita[tive] [li]brary on the European Union, rang-ing from general introductory texts to definitive [assessments of key institutions and] actors, issues, policies and policy processes, and t[he role of member states.]

Books in the series are written by leading scholars in their fields and reflect the most up-to-date research and debate. Particular attention is paid to accessibility and clear presen-tation for a wide audience of students, practitioners and interested general readers.

The series editors are **Neill Nugent**, Emeritus Professor of Politics at Manchester Metropolitan University, UK, and **William E. Paterson**, Honorary Professor in German and European Studies, University of Aston. Their co-editor until his death in July 1999, **Vincent Wright**, was a Fellow of Nuffield College, Oxford University.

Feedback on the series and book proposals are always welcome and should be sent to Stephen Wenham, Palgrave, 4 Crinan Street, London N1 9XW, or by e-mail to **s.wenham@palgrave.com**

General textbooks

Published

Laurie Buonanno and Neill Nugent **Policies and Policy Processes of the European Union**

Desmond Dinan **Encyclopedia of the European Union**
[Rights: Europe only]

Desmond Dinan **Europe Recast: A History of the European Union (2nd edn)**
[Rights: Europe only]

Desmond Dinan **Ever Closer Union: An Introduction to European Integration (4th edn)**
[Rights: Europe only]

Mette Eilstrup Sangiovanni (ed.) **Debates on European Integration: A Reader**

Simon Hix and Bjørn Høyland **The Political System of the European Union (3rd edn)**

Dirk Leuffen, Berthold Rittberger and Frank Schimmelfennig **Differentiated Integration**

Paul Magnette **What is the European Union? Nature and Prospects**

John McCormick **Understanding the European Union: A Concise Introduction (6th edn)**

Brent F. Nelsen and Alexander Stubb **The European Union: Readings on the Theory and Practice of European Integration (4th edn)**
[Rights: Europe only]

Neill Nugent (ed.) **European Union Enlargement**

Neill Nugent **The Government and Politics of the European Union (7th edn)**

John Peterson and Elizabeth Bomberg **Decision-Making in the European Union**

Ben Rosamond **Theories of European Integration**

Sabine Saurugger **Theoretical Approaches to European Integration**

Ingeborg Tömmel **The European Union: What it is and How it Works**

Esther Versluis, Mendeltje van Keulen and Paul Stephenson **Analyzing the European Union Policy Process**

Hubert Zimmermann and Andreas Dür (eds) **Key Controversies in European Integration**

Forthcoming

Magnus Ryner and Alan Cafruny **A Critical Introduction to the European Union**

Also planned

The European Union and Global Politics
The Political Economy of European Integration

The major institutions and actors

Published

Renaud Dehousse **The European Court of Justice**
Justin Greenwood **Interest Representation in the European Union (3rd edn)**
Fiona Hayes-Renshaw and Helen Wallace **The Council of Ministers (2nd edn)**
Simon Hix and Christopher Lord **Political Parties in the European Union**
David Judge and David Earnshaw **The European Parliament (2nd edn)**
Neill Nugent and Mark Rhinard **The European Commission (2nd edn)**
Anne Stevens with Handley Stevens **Brussels Bureaucrats? The Administration of the European Union**
Wolfgang Wessels **The European Council**

Forthcoming

Ariadna Ripoll Servent **The European Parliament**
Sabine Saurugger and Fabien Terpan **The European Court of Justice and the Politics of Law**

The main areas of policy

Published

Karen Anderson **Social Policy in the European Union**
Michael Baun and Dan Marek **Cohesion Policy in the European Union**
Tom Delreux and Sander Happaerts **Environmental Policy and Politics in the European Union**
Michele Chang **Monetary Integration in the European Union**
Michelle Cini and Lee McGowan **Competition Policy in the European Union (2nd edn)**
Wyn Grant **The Common Agricultural Policy**
Martin Holland and Mathew Doidge **Development Policy of the European Union**
Jolyon Howorth **Security and Defence Policy in the European Union (2nd edn)**
Johanna Kantola **Gender and the European Union**
Stephan Keukeleire and Tom Delreux **The Foreign Policy of the European Union (2nd edn)**
Brigid Laffan **The Finances of the European Union**
Malcolm Levitt and Christopher Lord **The Political Economy of Monetary Union**
Janne Haaland Matláry **Energy Policy in the European Union**
John McCormick **Environmental Policy in the European Union**
John Peterson and Margaret Sharp **Technology Policy in the European Union**
Samuel Schubert, Johannes Pollak and Maren Kreutler **Energy Policy of the European Union**

Forthcoming

Sieglinde Gstöhl and Dirk de Bievre **The Trade Policy of the European Union**
Christian Kaunert and Sarah Leonard **Justice and Home Affairs in the European Union**
Paul Stephenson, Esther Versluis and Mendeltje van Keulen **Implementing and Evaluating Policy in the European Union**

Also planned

Political Union

The member states and the Union

Published

Carlos Closa and Paul Heywood **Spain and the European Union**
Andrew Geddes **Britain and the European Union**
Alain Guyomarch, Howard Machin and Ella Ritchie **France in the European Union**
Brigid Laffan and Jane O'Mahoney **Ireland and the European Union**

Forthcoming

Simon Bulmer and William E. Paterson **Germany and the European Union**
Brigid Laffan **The European Union and its Member States**

Issues

Published

Senem Aydın-Düzgit and Nathalie Tocci **Turkey and the European Union**
Derek Beach **The Dynamics of European Integration: Why and When EU Institutions Matter**
Christina Boswell and Andrew Geddes **Migration and Mobility in the European Union**
Thomas Christiansen and Christine Reh **Constitutionalizing the European Union**
Robert Ladrech **Europeanization and National Politics**
Cécile Leconte **Understanding Euroscepticism**
Steven McGuire and Michael Smith **The European Union and the United States**
Wyn Rees **The US–EU Security Relationship: The Tensions between a European and a Global Agenda**

Forthcoming

Graham Avery **Enlarging the European Union**
Thomas Christiansen, Emil Kirchner and Uwe Wissenbach **The European Union and China**
Tuomas Forsberg and Hiski Haukkala **The European Union and Russia**

Environmental Policy and Politics in the European Union

Tom Delreux
and
Sander Happaerts

 palgrave

First published 2016 by
PALGRAVE

Palgrave in the UK is an imprint of Macmillan Publishers Limited, registered in England, company number 785998, of 4 Crinan Street, London, N1 9XW.

Palgrave Macmillan in the US is a division of St Martin's Press LLC, 175 Fifth Avenue, New York, NY 10010.

Palgrave is a global imprint of the above companies and is represented throughout the world.

Palgrave® and Macmillan® are registered trademarks in the United States, the United Kingdom, Europe and other countries.

ISBN 978–0–230–24425–2 hardback

ISBN 978–0–230–24426–9 paperback

This book is printed on paper suitable for recycling and made from fully managed and sustained forest sources. Logging, pulping and manufacturing processes are expected to conform to the environmental regulations of the country of origin.

A catalogue record for this book is available from the British Library.

A catalog record for this book is available from the Library of Congress.

Printed in China

Contents

List of figures, tables and boxes

Figures

Tables

Boxes

List of abbreviations

ACEA	European Automobile Manufacturers Association
AIA	Advance Informed Agreement
ALDE	Alliance of Liberals and Democrats for Europe
AOSIS	Alliance of Small Island States
BASIC	Brazil, South Africa, India and China
BAT	best available technology
CAN-E	Climate Action Network Europe
CBD	Convention on Biological Diversity
CDM	Clean Development Mechanism
CEFIC	European Chemicals Industry Council
CITES	Convention on International Trade in Endangered Species
CLIM Committee	Temporary Committee on Climate Change
CLRTAP	Convention on Long-Range Transboundary Air Pollution
COEX-NET	Network Group for the Exchange and Coordination of Information Concerning Coexistence of Genetically Modified, Conventional and Organic Crops
COP	Conference of the Parties
COPA/COGECA	Committee of Professional Agricultural Organisations/General Committee for Agricultural Cooperation in the European Union
COREPER	Committee of Permanent Representatives
DG	Directorate-General
DG CLIMA	Directorate-General Climate Action
DG ENER	Directorate-General Energy
DG ENV	Directorate-General Environment
DG MARE	Directorate-General Maritime Affairs and Fisheries
DG SANTE	Directorate-General Health and Food Safety

DSB	Dispute Settlement Body
EAP	Environmental Action Programme
EBRD	European Bank for Reconstruction and Development
EC	European Community
ECHA	European Chemicals Agency
ECI	European Citizens Initiatives
ECoB	European Coexistence Bureau
ECOFIN	Economic and Financial Affairs Council
ECPA	European Crop Protection Association
ECR	European Conservatives and Reformists Group
EEA	European Environment Agency
EEB	European Environmental Bureau
EEC	European Economic Community
EFDD	Europe of Freedom and Direct Democracy Group
EFSA	European Food Safety Authority
EFTA	European Free Trade Association
EIA	Environmental Impact Assessment
EIB	European Investment Bank
EIONET	European Environment Information and Observation Network
EMA	European Medicines Agency
EMAS	Eco-Management and Audit Scheme
ENF	Europe of Nations and Freedom
ENP	European Neighbourhood Policy
ENVI Committee	Environment, Public Health and Food Safety Committee
EP	European Parliament
EPI	environmental policy integration
EPP Group	Group of the European People's Party
ERDF	European Regional Development Fund
ETS	Emissions Trading Scheme
EU	European Union
EUETS	European Union Emissions Trading Scheme
EUROPIA	European Petroleum Industry Association
EUSDS	European Union Sustainable Development Strategy
F-gas	fluorinated gas
FAO	Food and Agriculture Organization

FoEE	Friends of the Earth Europe
G20	Group of Twenty
GDP	gross domestic product
GMO	genetically modified organism
Greens/EFA	Greens/European Free Alliance
GUE/NGL	Confederal Group of the European United Left/Nordic Green Left
HEAL	Health and Environment Alliance
ICAO	International Civil Aviation Organization
ICPDR	International Commission for the Protection of the Danube River
IMCO Committee	Internal Market and Consumer Protection Committee
IMPEL	European Union Network for the Implementation and Enforcement of Environmental Law
IPCC	Intergovernmental Panel on Climate Change
ITRE Committee	Industry, Research and Energy Committee
JI	Joint Implementation
LIFE (and LIFE+)	Financial Instrument for the Environment
MEA	multilateral environmental agreement
MEF	Major Economies Forum
MEP	Member of the European Parliament
MOP	Meeting of the Parties
MSR	market stability reserve
NFI	Naturefriends International
NGO	non-governmental organization
OECD	Organisation for Economic Co-operation and Development
OLP	ordinary legislative procedure
PMEM	post-market environmental monitoring plan
QMV	qualified majority voting
REACH	Registration, Evaluation, Authorisation and Restriction of Chemicals
REFIT	Regulatory Fitness and Performance
REIO	Regional Economic Integration Organization
RoHS	Restriction of Hazardous Substances
S&D	Group of the Progressive Alliance of Socialists & Democrats

SCoFCAH	Standing Committee of Food Chain and Animal Health
SEA	Single European Act
SEA	Strategic Environmental Impact Assessment
SEIS	Shared Environmental Information System
SOER	The European environment – state and outlook
SPA	Special Protection Area
SPS Agreement	Sanitary and Phytosanitary Agreement
T&E	Transport and Environment
TEC	Treaty establishing the European Community
TEEC	Treaty establishing the European Economic Community
TEU	Treaty on European Union
TFEU	Treaty on the Functioning of the European Union
TRAN Committee	Transport and Tourism Committee
TTIP	Transatlantic Trade and Investment Partnership
UK	United Kingdom
UNCCD	United Nations Convention to Combat Desertification
UNCED	United Nations Conference on Environment and Development
UNCHE	United Nations Conference on the Human Environment
UNECE	United Nations Economic Commission for Europe
UNFCCC	United Nations Framework Convention on Climate Change
US	United States
WCED	World Commission on Environment and Development
WEEE	Waste of Electrical and Electronic Equipment
WPE	Working Party on the Environment
WPIEI	Working Party on International Environmental Issues
WTO	World Trade Organization
WWF	World Wide Fund for Nature
WWF-EPO	World Wide Fund for Nature European Policy Office

Preface

This book is the result of a long journey that spanned several years and encompassed interactions with various people who all deserve our sincerest thanks.

First of all, our warmest gratitude goes out to Hans Bruyninckx, professor of global environmental politics at the University of Leuven before he was designated as the Executive Director of the European Environment Agency in 2013. Hans had been part of this book project from the very start, but when he exchanged academia for the EEA he had to withdraw as an author. While it is unfortunate that he could not continue to work with us until this book was completed, we are very grateful for exciting discussions about the design of the manuscript and for his contribution to earlier drafts of several chapters. Above all, we are indebted to Hans for the way he inspired us and shaped our thinking about environmental policy and global governance during many years as a colleague and a mentor.

We are grateful to our publishers at Palgrave, Stephen Wenham and Steven Kennedy, as well as the 'European Union Series' editors, Neill Nugent and William Paterson, and the anonymous reviewers for their constructive suggestions and their enduring patience. We would also like to thank our colleagues at the *Institut de sciences politiques Louvain-Europe* at the University of Louvain (Louvain-la-Neuve, Belgium), the *Leuven International and European Studies Institute* and the *Research Institute for Work and Society* (both at the University of Leuven, Belgium) for their encouragements and intellectual input. Bart Van Ballaert, François Randour, Thomas Laloux, Tom Creten and Björn Koopmans provided us with excellent research assistance and critical comments. Many thanks also go to Anne Stevens for proofreading the manuscript.

Gaining deeper understanding of the processes and substance of EU environmental policy and politics was possible only through our discussions with many European and national policy-makers whom we have met in recent years in the framework of a variety of research projects. We thank all the practitioners we have interviewed for their insights and for even giving us the opportunity to witness EU environmental policy-making from the inside. Our thanks also go out to our colleagues from other universities and research institutes across the globe who indirectly contributed to this book through stimulating discussions and constructive remarks on our work.

Our final thanks are for our friends and families, and particularly to Marjan, Marte and Stien (for Tom) and to Annelien, Lauranne and Oliver (for Sander), for their continued support and welcome distraction while we wrote this book and kept the chapters up to date.

Tom Delreux
Sander Happaerts

Introduction

Objectives and approach of the book

The European Union (EU) has developed one of the world's most stringent sets of environmental policies in the course of a couple of decades. A complex framework of regulatory standards aiming to improve the state of the environment is in force in all major areas of environmental policy, including water or air pollution, chemicals regulation or the fight against climate change. The dense collection of environmental policy measures that are binding on twenty-eight European countries, their populations and their industries shows that a relatively high level of environmental protection can be combined with an equally high level of economic development and growth. These policies are shaped, adopted and implemented through a complex governance system including various actors, different legal procedures and political practices, and multiple levels of governance.

This book analyses the state of play of the EU's environmental policies and the political dynamics behind them. It discusses the development of the EU's environmental policy, the main institutions and actors that are formally and informally involved in the policy-making processes, the EU's activities in the traditional and the 'new' environmental subdomains, and the role of the EU in global environmental politics. Paying particular attention to the driving forces and dynamics that have made environmental policy and politics what they are today, the book examines issues including the evolution from narrow environmental concerns (protecting plants and animals and focus on air and water quality) to environmental policy integration, the EU's contribution to global environmental governance and the shift from traditional regulatory policies to new governance arrangements. The approach followed throughout the book is built around two axes: a focus on both policies and politics, and an emphasis on the interdependence between what happens at the EU level and at the international level.

First, the book deals with both environmental policy and environmental politics. On the one hand, *policies* are the actual measures that are adopted to deal with a particular environmental problem. In the EU, they include the entire range of binding environmental legislation (EU regulations, directives and decisions) as well as a number of non-binding pieces of soft law. In analysing EU environmental policies, the book discusses the policies' content, underlying rationales, instruments and actual impact. It reviews both traditional EU environmental policies that are focused on fighting pollution and on protecting nature (such as waste, water, air or biodiversity policy) and more specific policy initiatives to promote sustainable development and environmental policy integration. Particular attention is paid to the EU's policies with regard to the contentious issues of genetically modified organisms (GMOs) and climate change. Alongside an analysis of the EU's internal environmental policy framework, the EU's external environmental policies will also be considered by focusing on the EU's contribution to global environmental governance.

On the other hand, *politics* refers to what happens in the policy-making processes where various actors – EU institutions, national authorities, interest groups – negotiate and finally achieve compromises about the environmental policy choices of the EU. In other words, it is through politics that policies are produced. This book's analysis of EU environmental politics addresses questions such as: who are the main actors in EU environmental policy-making?; where is the balance of power in the EU when deciding upon environmental policies?; is the policy-making process dominated by technocratic experts or rather by elected politicians?; through which institutional (formal) rules and (informal) practices are policies adopted and implemented?; and what is the role and power of interest groups in the policy-making process?

Second, arguing that there is a close relationship between environmental policy and politics at the EU level and at the global level, the book considers the interaction between the EU and developments in global environmental governance as a vital explanation for the state of play of EU environmental policy and politics. As EU environmental policies are not developed in an international vacuum, the book pays close attention to the international context and the way it is interlinked with the processes and outcomes of environmental policy-making in the EU. A twofold dynamic characterizes this interaction. On the one hand, European policy initiatives are to a varying degree driven by global environmental governance as they implement international commitments of the EU or as they apply principles or policy paradigms that have been developed at the international level. On the other hand, the EU is also a co-shaper of international environmental policies. It plays an important role in many international environmental negotiation processes where it is usually among those actors which make the greatest demands for stronger environmental protection at the global level. These two levels continuously interact, which explains why this book aims to put EU environmental policy and politics in the broader perspective of global environmental governance.

EU environmental policy matters

Environmental policy as a major area of EU activity

The quantity and scope of environmental policy have grown in the last decades and they are still expanding. Nowadays environmental policy is one of the largest areas of EU activity, with more than 400 pieces of environmental legislation in force in the EU. They form a comprehensive regulatory system with a major impact on the member states, thereby considerably limiting the remaining room for manoeuvre of national policy-makers. Moreover, through the principle of environmental policy integration, environmental concerns have spilled over to other policy fields, such as energy, agriculture, transport or industrial policy. The environment is thus a deeply Europeanized policy area with important transversal effects. Why are environmental issues so extensively dealt with at the European level?

First, many environmental phenomena are transboundary in nature and the policies addressing them need to be so as well. It is a classic observation in many textbooks on environmental policy that air pollution does not stop at national borders, that river systems do not recognize territorial boundaries or that the worst consequences of climate change are not necessarily felt in the region where they are caused. Adequate solutions for transboundary problems require international cooperation, i.e. cooperation between the states where the causes and/or the effects of the problem occur. This not only explains why environmental issues are addressed at the European level, but also why the environment is often addressed by other regional organizations and agreements in the world as well as through global environmental governance.

Second, the EU provides a particularly fertile ground for the development of a dense environmental protection system. The economic foundations of the European integration project are based on the liberalization of trade among the European member states and the creation of a common market. Multiple and potentially different national environmental policy frameworks would undermine free trade in the EU and are thus incompatible with the economic purposes of European integration. As a result, the harmonization of environmental norms at the European level is the only way to combine the common market purpose of the integration project with the desire to protect the environment.

Third, although the adoption of regulatory environmental policies is essential for a well-functioning common market, such policies go beyond an economic logic as they also serve environmental objectives. Economic competition between states can cause a so-called race to the bottom, which implies that governments lower their environmental standards to create a more attractive economic context for industries operating in a competitive system. However, the EU has been able to resist that race to the bottom as an increase in regulatory competition has not led to a decrease in environmental protection in the EU. The reason is that, through the harmonization of environmental standards at the European level, member states have found an escape route from the race to the bottom, which allows for the combination of strong environmental policies and market liberalization. In that sense, the 'race to the bottom' risk has been countered by a 'race to Brussels' (Holzinger and Sommerer 2011).

Public opinion data shows that European citizens care about the environment (or at least say they care about the environment) and that they prefer action to protect the environment to be carried out at the EU level. The Special Eurobarometer survey of 2011, which examines the attitudes of European citizens towards the environment, revealed that 95 per cent of European citizens feel that protecting the environment is important, with 58 per cent of them finding it 'very important' (European Commission 2011a). In no single member state do less than 90 per cent of the respondents consider the environment (very) important. Moreover, two thirds of European citizens consider that environmental policies should be developed at the European level, where of course national governments continue to play an important role. The overall level of support for EU-wide action is high, notwithstanding national differences with, for instance, strong societal support in Cyprus and in Spain and the lowest levels of support for tackling environmental problems through EU policies in a number of Central and Eastern European member states, Finland, Austria and the United Kingdom (UK).

A final reason why analysing EU environmental policy and politics is important is that it is a policy area where several fascinating dynamics of supranational EU policy-making come together. Hence, exploring how the EU works and what kind of policies it produces in the environmental field also offers us broader insights about the EU in general. Environmental policy-making involves multiple levels of governance. The traditional so-called 'Community method' at the European level steers environmental policy-making, but national, and in many cases subnational levels too, are responsible for implementation of the policies – and thus for ensuring that European policies have an actual impact in practice. As mentioned before, the global level matters too.

Environment is also an interesting area as the major EU institutions are involved in the policy-making process. The traditional institutions of the 'Community method' – the European Commission, Council, European Parliament and Court of Justice – play a key role in initiating, formulating, adopting and interpreting environmental policies, but they increasingly do so by relying on and interacting with, for instance, European agencies or committees with member state officials. Moreover, environmental policy is a field where, in the lobbying activities by non-state actors, two types of interests may come into conflict. Whereas business lobby groups defend the specific and concentrated interests of particular economic sectors or individual firms, environmental non-governmental organizations (NGOs) advocate the diffuse interest of protecting the environment. These two types of interests are additionally revealing for understanding the mobilization potential of societal interests in European policy-making and they shed light on the impact of private actors on European policies. Analysing environmental policy and politics in the EU also reveals insights about the role of policy paradigms, such as the 'green economy' mantra in the development of specific policy measures in recent years. But simultaneously, environmental policy-making in the EU shows that translating ambitious discourses and policy goals into actual policies that make a difference on the ground remains a major challenge.

Impact of environmental policy on Europe's environment

EU environmental policy matters not only because of the political dynamics mentioned above, but also because it has a considerable impact on the state of the environment in Europe. Environmental policy has very concrete effects. It directly affects the living context, and thereby also the health, of more than half a billion Europeans. The actual impact of EU environmental policies on the environmental state of affairs in Europe is assessed by the European Environment Agency (EEA) in its five-yearly report 'The European environment – state and outlook' (SOER). The report published in 2015 presents a double message (European Environment Agency 2015). On the one hand, EU environmental policy has unquestionably improved the overall state of the environment and the quality of life in Europe. But on the other hand, major environmental problems remain in several environmental subdomains and the EU is facing significant challenges in each of these areas.

First the good news: environmental policy makes a difference as it has contributed to an improvement of the quality of ecosystems and of the health and living standards of European citizens. The 2015 SOER summarizes that 'in many parts of Europe, the local environment is arguably in as good a state today as it has been since the start of the industrialization' (European Environment Agency 2015: 9). In other words: environmental policies have delivered. Air and water quality have considerably improved, the use of hazardous industrial pollutants has decreased, recycling rates have increased in almost all member states, and material resources and energy are now used in a more efficient way. Likewise, greenhouse gas emissions, responsible for climate change, have been reduced by almost 20 per cent compared to 1990 levels in a period when the European economy grew by more than 45 per cent.

However, the news is not that bright as the 2015 SOER concludes that 'despite the environmental improvements of recent decades, the challenges that Europe faces today are considerable. European natural capital is being degraded by socio-economic activities such as agriculture, fisheries, transport, industry, tourism and urban sprawl. And global pressures on the environment have grown at an unprecedented rate since the 1990s, driven not least by economic and population growth, and changing consumption patterns' (European Environment Agency 2015: 9–10). For instance, air and noise pollution continue to have negative effects on human health, particularly in the densely populated areas in Europe. Although the use of many chemicals is strictly regulated in the EU, the intensified use of a number of these substances in consumer products is considered to pose health risks. The continuing threat on the conservation of protected species and habitats is another area of remaining concern. And even though the developed policy framework has an effect, 'the level of ambition of existing environmental policy may be inadequate to achieve Europe's long-term environmental goals', as for instance the current policy measures to combat climate change are not sufficient to keep the EU on the path to achieve its self-imposed greenhouse gas emission reduction objective of 80–95 per cent by 2050 (European Environment Agency 2015: 12).

Outline of the chapters

This book is structured around ten chapters, which can be grouped in three clusters. The first two chapters *sketch the scene* of the EU's environmental policy and politics by portraying the historical developments as well as the evolving global context within which European environmental policies are embedded. The three following chapters focus on EU environmental *politics* by examining the policy-making process and which actors and institutions are involved. The final five chapters adopt a *policy* perspective by discussing the content, drivers and effects of the EU's environmental *acquis*.

Chapter 1 provides a historical overview of the development of European environmental policy from the early days of European integration to today. It also presents the main principles and the legal bases of today's EU environmental policy. The chapter discusses the remarkable growth of this policy area and the evolution from a rather incoherent set of measures towards a comprehensive environmental policy framework. Analysing five phases of environmental policy-making, the chapter shows that measures related to the environment were initially taken to serve the creation of the common market, but were gradually characterized by an environmental protection logic. Environmental competences were established at the European level and the EU's powers in this field expanded further from the end of the 1980s. Simultaneously, environmental policy-making became more and more institutionalized at the EU level and supranational decision-making became the rule.

The chapter ends by discussing the most recent developments since the late 2000s, when the 'green economy' paradigm and the calls for better (and less) regulation and enhanced implementation left their mark more and more on environmental policy-making.

Chapter 2 situates the evolution of EU environmental policies and politics in a global context. It makes it clear that the EU has been influenced by global dynamics and is not developing its policies in splendid isolation. This chapter provides an overview of the formation and institutionalization of global environmental governance as well as the role of the EU in these global processes. It pays particular attention to the end of the Cold War and the profound consequences of processes of economic, political and environmental globalization. The EU's interaction with the United States (US) and the emerging powers is discussed, as well as the challenges that recent changes in global governance pose to the EU. The chapter shows that these global dynamics do need to be taken into consideration to fully understand environmental politics at the EU level.

Chapter 3 presents an in-depth analysis of the main actors and institutions that develop environmental policy in the EU. It explains how they function internally and which political dynamics determine their role in environmental policy-making. The following main actors are successively examined: the European Commission (the EU's main executive, playing an important role in proposing policies and monitoring their implementation), the European Parliament (directly elected by the European citizens), the Council of the EU (where environment ministers, diplomats and experts of the twenty-eight member states meet and which is together with the Parliament responsible for adopting environmental legislation), the European Council (bringing together the heads of state and government of the member states, who determine the broad strategies of environmental policies), the Court of Justice (providing judicial oversight) and some agencies outside the traditional institutional framework (the European Environment Agency and the European Chemicals Agency).

Chapter 4 proceeds by analysing the policy-making process that takes place between the actors and institutions presented in the previous chapter. It first analyses how environmental policies are formulated. The chapter demonstrates that the formal policy-making procedure only reveals one part of the story and that to a large extent actual policy-making practice deviates from what one would expect on the basis of the formal rules. Particular attention is therefore paid to the increased importance of so-called early agreements in environmental policy-making, which increase its efficiency but also raise questions about its transparency and democratic nature. In its second section, this chapter looks at the implementation of environmental policy. It discusses implementation at the EU level, where rather complex comitology procedures allow member states to monitor the implementation powers of the Commission, and implementation at the member state level. One of the main problems of European environmental policy today is its considerable implementation deficit. The chapter also explores the main reasons for the poor implementation record of member states.

Chapter 5 demonstrates that environmental policy-making in the EU is characterized by a dense patchwork of lobby activities by interest groups. Whereas environmental NGOs by and large defend general environmental and ecological interests and concerns, business lobby groups represent particular interests of a certain economic sector, economic activity or single company. The chapter successively discusses the functions, strategies and actual impact of interest groups in EU environmental policy-making. It argues that interest groups can provide legitimacy and expertise to the policy-making process and that their input is often explicitly demanded by the European institutions. These interest groups apply a range of strategies to get their voices heard, combining activities at different levels and in different stages of the policy-making process.

Chapter 6 takes stock of the various types of environmental policy instruments. It shows that the EU applies a broad range of policy instruments and that the combination of instruments has evolved over time. The chapter discusses and evaluates four types of instruments employed in EU environmental policy: regulatory instruments (imposing obligations and introducing standards), planning instruments (orienting policy-making), market-based instruments (sanctioning or rewarding behaviour through market mechanisms) and information instruments (stimulating changes and generating policy-relevant information). For each of these instruments, the political rationale, the advantages and disadvantages, and the way they have been applied by the EU are assessed. The chapter makes it clear that the EU is constantly trying to strike a balance between, on the one hand, direct regulation with an interventionist logic embodied in binding legislation and, on the other hand, policy instruments that grant more flexibility and involve a softer way of governing.

Chapter 7 gives an overview of the main issue-based environmental policies, which are primarily aimed at fighting pollution and protecting nature: waste, air, water, biodiversity, soil and noise policy. These were the first environmental policies developed by the EU and they have evolved into comprehensive, well-developed and far-reaching policy frameworks. Rather than presenting a comprehensive overview of all existing policy measures, the chapter discusses the origins and basic characteristics of the policies, their main political developments and their interplay with global environmental politics. Their major achievements, as well as the principal challenges the EU is still facing in these domains, are evaluated. Two transversal strategies for sustainable development that the EU has initiated since the 1990s receive particular attention here: environmental policy integration and the EU Sustainable Development Strategy.

Chapter 8 focuses on the EU's policy with regard to genetically modified organisms (GMOs). It examines a central principle in EU environmental policy, namely the precautionary principle, which underlies the way the EU regulates GMOs and which distinguishes the European approach considerably from the approach of many other countries in the world, notably the United States. GMOs are subject to an intense societal debate in Europe, which has led to major controversies and has affected the current state of the European policy framework. The chapter also demonstrates that the EU is placed in a somewhat isolated position internationally, facing fierce opposition from countries with large agricultural and food industries. This international situation has resulted in trade disputes between the EU and its main agricultural and food trading partners, pressurizing the EU to adapt its restrictive GMO policies.

Chapter 9 analyses the EU's climate change policy in detail. The major impact that this policy has on the transitions in economic systems has made climate change the most salient environmental issue in the EU as well as worldwide. Despite internal controversies about the level of ambition of its climate policy, the EU has succeeded in adopting an encompassing set of policy measures to fight climate change, which is today one of the world's most ambitious regulatory frameworks in this field. The chapter describes the main choices that the EU has made in this area, what their implications are and how they are linked with developments in international climate change governance. It discusses in depth the EU's emissions trading scheme (ETS), a number of pieces of regulatory climate legislation and the EU's attempts to steer policies in the medium and the long term by adopting climate and energy targets for 2020, 2030 and 2050. The chapter also critically assesses the achievements and the effectiveness of EU climate change policy.

Chapter 10 then shifts the focus from internal environmental policies towards the external dimension of these policies by examining the EU as an actor in international environmental politics. It analyses the active engagement of the EU in shaping the global process of environmental policy formation. After having discussed the EU's status in these international negotiations, the chapter explores if and how the EU manages to reach a common position and the way that position is then represented externally. Furthermore, it examines the EU's role in international environmental politics by focusing on its leadership ambitions, the extent to which these are achieved and the effectiveness of the EU as a global actor in the environmental field. Linking the analysis to the previous chapter, particular attention is paid to the role of the EU in multilateral climate change negotiations, which have been the most politicized international environmental negotiations.

Chapter 1

The Evolution of EU Environmental Policy

The environmental policy of the European Union has undergone remarkable development. The founding fathers of the European integration project did not mention environmental policy in the first European treaties, as a result of which the legal basis for environmental protection was extremely limited. Nowadays, however, environmental policy is one of the largest and most important policy domains of the EU. Moreover, whereas the first steps of the development of EU environmental policy were a side effect of economic integration, it has evolved into a fully-fledged policy domain. The EU today has 'the most comprehensive regional environmental protection regime in the world' (Axelrod et al. 2011: 224).

This evolution in the growth of EU environmental policy can be illustrated by examining the number of pieces of environmental legislation that were in force each year from 1957 onwards. By presenting the evolution in the number of pieces of environmental legislation that are applicable across the entire EU (i.e. regulations and directives, see Box 6.1), Figure 1.1 shows the increase in EU environmental policies since 1957. Not only has the quantity of environmental legislation increased considerably, also 'an enormous growth in the scope and ambitiousness of the environmental *acquis*' has taken place (Jordan et al. 1999: 376). European environmental policy has had a considerable impact on various policies at the level of the member states and the policy autonomy of national policy-makers in the environmental field has been increasingly limited by the growing regulatory framework at the EU level. Furthermore, environmental considerations need to be taken into account by other policy domains. All these elements result in environmental policy currently occupying a central place in the EU's sphere of action.

FIGURE 1.1 *The evolution of the number of pieces of European environmental legislation (regulations and directives) in force*

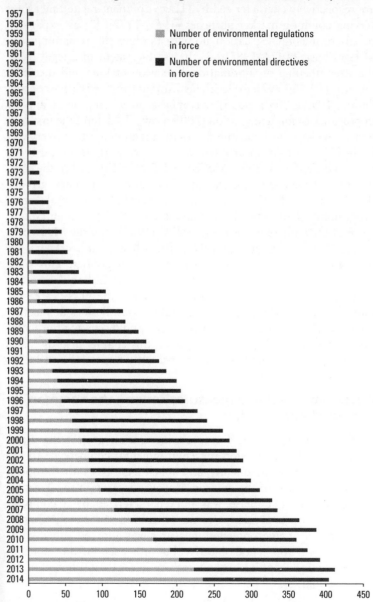

Source: based on Eurlex data

Analysing the history and evolution of European environmental policy, this chapter analytically distinguishes five phases, which are respectively characterized by (1) environment-related measures serving common market purposes (1957–1972); (2) an expansion of environmental legislation notwithstanding the remaining lack of legal basis (1972–1987); (3) the establishment of a legal basis, the strengthening of supranational decision-making and the 1992 impetus (1987–1992); (4) legal, institutional and legislative consolidation (1992–2009); and (5) an emphasis on 'green growth' and the importance of implementation (2009–now). To delimit the first four phases, we use the same milestones identified in existing overviews of the history of European environmental policy (Hildebrand 1993; Knill and Liefferink 2007; McCormick 2001; Zito 1999): the combination of the rise of societal and political environmental groups, the UN Stockholm Conference and the first Environmental Action Programme (EAP) (the beginning of the 1970s), the entry into force of the Single European Act (SEA) (1987), and the Maastricht Treaty (1992). Expanding on the existing historical overviews, we distinguish a fifth stage of EU environmental politics. This stage starts in 2009 with the entry into force of the Lisbon Treaty, the outbreak of the financial–economic crisis and the EU's decreasing international weight on environmental politics. Besides delineating the basic characteristics of the five phases and discussing the evolution of European environmental policy, this chapter also discusses its principles and legal bases (see respectively Boxes 1.1 and 1.2).

Environment-related measures serving the common market (1957–1972)

At the beginning of the European integration project the member states did not transfer any environmental competence to the European level. Consequently, an explicit legal basis for European action in the field of the environment was lacking in the Treaties. However, this first phase was not characterized by a complete absence of measures relating to the protection of the environment. A limited set of environmental measures was adopted, albeit without a clear environmental objective, but rather serving the main aim of the initial years of European integration: the establishment of the common market.

In 1957, the Treaty of Rome – formally the 'Treaty establishing the European Economic Community' (TEEC) – constituted the definite starting point for the European integration process, which was already initiated by the European Coal and Steel Community in 1952. The basic rationale behind the start of the European integration process was that economic cooperation between European countries would result in such a high degree of interdependence that a new war between European nations would become extremely unlikely. Hence, the main focus of the European Economic Community (EEC) in its first years was economic integration in the form of the common market.

The early environmental policies of the first stage served economic purposes, especially the creation of the common market. The objective was not protecting the environment or fighting against environmental pollution as such, but diminishing trade impediments among the EEC member states in the newly created common market. If member states had continued to adopt their own (environmental) product norms, the free nature of the trade and the essence of the common market would have been undermined. Indeed, the first steps in the development of a European environmental policy concerned the harmonization of product standards, such as limitations on the lead content of petrol, at the European level in order to provide free market competition (Knill and Liefferink 2012; Weale et al. 2000). This is why the first environmental measures in the EEC are known as 'by-products of economic integration' or 'flanking policies of the common market' (Knill and Liefferink 2007: 2 and 4). Moreover, the member states at their domestic level hardly had a coherent environmental policy framework. As a consequence, there was very little need to harmonize existing national environmental policies or to undo their inconsistencies with the common market objectives.

As mentioned, the Treaty of Rome lacked any reference to the environment. In the first days of European integration, the member states did not attribute specific environmental competences to the EEC as they did, in contrast, for agriculture, transport or trade policy. However, the Treaty of Rome included three provisions that could be interpreted as a legitimization for adopting legislative measures to protect the environment. The first steps in the development of a European environmental policy were thus made possible as a result of a 'generous' – or even creative or environmentalist – reading of three provisions in the Treaty implicitly referring to environmental protection (Hildebrand 1993: 19; Weale et al. 2000: 40).

A first provision was the preamble of the Treaty of Rome, which included a reference to 'the essential purpose of constantly improving the living and working conditions of [the] peoples'.

Here, the improvement of the living and working conditions of Europeans was understood as a justification for taking measures that were intended to fight the pollution of the environment (Rehbinder and Steward 1985). Second, Article 2 TEEC, which set out the objectives of the EEC, stated that the EEC aimed to achieve 'an accelerated raising of the standard of living'. In both the preamble and Article 2 TEEC, the founding member states thus stated their objective to improve the circumstances of living in the EEC. The European institutions understood these provisions broadly, encompassing environmental objectives. Third, Article 36 TEEC allowed for exceptions to the general abolition of intra-European trade restrictions, which is the cornerstone of the common market. Such exceptions were possible if they were based on concerns about, among other matters, 'the protection of human or animal life or health [and] the preservation of plant life'. Hence, the Treaty of Rome authorized European measures that allowed for trade impediments if they contributed to the protection of health and life of humans, animals and plants (Knill and Liefferink 2007).

Notwithstanding the absence of formal legal competences, at the end of the 1960s and the beginning of the 1970s a couple of pieces of environmental legislation were adopted, mainly dealing with the limitation of vehicle emissions, permissible sound levels and exhaust systems of motor vehicles, or the classification, packaging and labelling of hazardous chemical substances. The fact that the first pieces of environmental legislation in the EEC were adopted as a contribution to the development of the common market objective is also illustrated by their legal basis. In the absence of an environmental legal basis, these first environmental measures were based upon Article 100 TEEC (Zito 1999), which authorizes the Council, on the basis of a proposal by the Commission, to unanimously 'issue directives for the approximation of such legislative and administrative provisions of the Member States as have a direct incidence on the establishment or functioning of the Common Market'. In other words, the first environmental legislation was legally based on the EEC's common market competences, but due to the broad interpretation of the TEEC's preamble, Articles 2 and 36 TEEC (see above), this common market Article 100 TEEC could also be used to adopt legislation intended to harmonize product-related environmental regulations (Knill and Liefferink 2007).

Expansion of environmental legislation (1972–1987)

The second phase of the development of European environmental policy was characterized, on the one hand, by the continuing lack of an explicit legal basis of environmental protection action at the European level, but, on the other hand, also by a considerable growth in the number of pieces of European environmental legislation and an expansion of the scope of environmental measures. The first component, namely the continuing lack of a legal basis, was basically due to the fact that policy-making in the EU was *de iure* still governed under the rules of the Treaty of Rome and no significant Treaty changes had taken place during this phase.

The second component of this period, namely the *de facto* expansion of environmental policies (see Figure 1.1), can be explained by four driving forces and dynamics. First, during the 1970s, civil society began to get organized on environmental issues. The consequence of this phenomenon, which started in the United States and then also occurred in Europe, was that environmental issues increasingly became societally debated and that this debate became progressively organized and institutionalized. The establishment and rapid growth of environmental NGOs is the most obvious illustration of this dynamic. This rising environmental awareness in society spilled over to the political sphere, where environmental concerns became more and more important. The establishment of the first green parties and the emerging environmental awareness among politicians led to an increased attention to environmental concerns in the political sphere. Second, developments at the international level, such as the UN Conference on the Human Environment (UNCHE, or the 'Stockholm Conference') of 1972 and the resulting Stockholm Declaration, reinforced the place of environmental concerns on the political agenda, not only globally but also in Europe (see Chapter 2). Third, several environmental catastrophes in Europe and beyond, such as the accident at the chemical plant in Seveso or with the oil tanker Amoco Cadiz, triggered policy initiatives to prevent recurrences of such accidents. Fourth, the inherent transnational character of environmental issues prompted the insight that solutions had to be found at the supranational level (see Introduction). Indeed, many environmental problems are more effectively handled at a higher level of authority than in single countries separately. The analysis of various driving forces and dynamics behind the development of European environmental policy will be further developed in Chapter 2, where the societal and political dynamics at the global level will also be taken into account.

The expansion of European environmental policy from 1972 onwards took place in the context of the launch of the first Environmental Action Programme (EAP). EAPs outline the priority goals for environmental action in the EU and give direction to the work of the European institutions that actually produce environmental policies (see Chapter 6). The first EAP originated in the Paris Summit of October 1972, which was a kind of European Council *avant la lettre* (see Chapter 3). It gathered together the heads of state and government of the six EEC member states of that time and those of the three countries that would join the EEC in the following years (UK, Ireland and Denmark). While the main aim of the meeting was to discuss further political cooperation, it also constituted a milestone in the history of European environmental policy. In Article 8 of the 'Statement from the Paris Summit', the heads of state and government 'emphasized the importance of a Community environmental policy' and they 'invited the Community Institutions to establish, before 31 July 1973, a programme of action accompanied by a precise timetable' (European Communities 1972). In the absence of formal Treaty provisions on the environment, this Statement can thus be considered as the first authorization by the member states to the European institutions to undertake more comprehensive policy action in the field of the environment, without it necessarily being linked to the realization of the common market. This is why the Paris Summit is often considered the starting point of a new phase in the evolution of the European environmental policy. The approach that characterized the first stage, resulting in a set of incoherent measures on environmental protection serving the common market, *de facto* shifted to an approach that made a more comprehensive environmental policy possible.

To carry out the assignment of the heads of state and government, a task force – the 'Environment and Consumer Protection Service' – was established within the Directorate-General (DG) Industry of the European Commission. This small unit was initially seen as being composed of 'green fundamentalists' (Schön-Quinlivan 2012: 104) where British officials occupied most of the key positions (Van de Velde 2014). It would later function as the core from which, in 1981, the Directorate General for the Environment (then DG XI, currently DG Environment) would originate (see Chapter 3) (Zito 1999). In April 1973, the Commission issued its proposal for a first 'Programme of Environmental Action of the European Communities', which was then adopted by the Council in October. This first EAP included an overview of proposed actions and projects to reduce pollution and nuisances, to improve the environment and to streamline the action of the member states in international organizations. Throughout the 126-page document, a number of environmental principles were introduced for the first time, such as the preventive action and the polluter pays principles. This unstructured list of principles can be considered as the foundation on which the current set of principles of EU environmental policy is based (see Box 1.1). The second and third EAPs, dating respectively from 1977 and 1983, followed the approaches outlined in the first EAP, while at the same time gradually expanding the scope of the principles, objectives and areas for prioritized action. For instance, the third EAP introduced the environmental integration principle (see Chapter 6). It is important to note that the EAPs cannot be thought of as – and were not meant to be – all-encompassing policy frameworks. Neither do they provide the legally binding basis for environmental policies. They should rather be seen as a first political step towards a common European environmental policy (McCormick 2001).

Following the Paris Summit of 1972, in the 1980s two other gatherings of the heads of state and government of the member states – which had by then assumed the format of a European Council meeting – gave additional impetus to the development of European environmental policy-making. These stimuli were given at the level of the highest political authority (see Chapter 3). The European Council of Stuttgart (June 1983) called for the acceleration and reinforcement of 'action at the national, Community and international level, aimed at combatting the pollution of the environment'. Less than two years later, the European Council of Brussels (March 1985) upgraded European environmental policy, insisting it should be treated as an essential element of the European economic, industrial, agricultural and social policies.

Box 1.1   Principles of European environmental policy

The European environmental policy is nowadays based on a number of principles. Six of them are in the current Treaty, the Treaty of Lisbon.

1. Precaution (Art. 191§2 TFEU)

The precautionary principle allows for taking measures that protect the environment and/or the health of humans, animals or plants in a situation of scientific uncertainty. The introduction of precaution was one of the innovations of the Maastricht Treaty as far as environmental policy is concerned (Wilkinson 1992). Since this principle is not clearly defined in the Treaty, the Court of Justice of the EU has developed 'complex and often subtle' case law on the precautionary principle (Lee 2014: 11). In this case law, the Court has also developed its own definition, which is now considered the genuine interpretation in the EU (de Sadeleer 2009): 'where there is uncertainty as to the existence or extent of risks to human health, protective measures may be taken without having to wait until the reality and seriousness of those risks become fully apparent'. The EU thus opts for an environmental policy regime that is much more cautious and restrained than most of its international economic competitors, notably the United States (see Chapter 8 on the case of genetically modified organisms).

2. Preventive action (Art. 191§2 TFEU)

The principle of preventive action implies that EU environmental policy should be more focused on preventing environmental damage than on restoring it. The rationale behind this principle is that preventive action is often both environmentally and economically less costly. Consequently, following this principle, European environmental policy should be proactive rather than reactive in nature.

3. Rectification at the source (Art. 191§2 TFEU)

Closely related to the preventive action principle and a part of the Treaty framework since the Single European Act (SEA), the rectification at the source principle stipulates that preference should be given to tackling environmental damage where and when it originates (i.e. at the source) rather than to taking measures combating the consequences of that damage elsewhere.

4. Polluter pays (Art. 191§2 TFEU)

Finding its origins in the first Environmental Action Programme (EAP) and included in the Treaties as early as the SEA, the polluter pays principle implies that the cost of possible pollution or compensation measures should be borne in the first place by the actor or organization that has directly or indirectly caused the environmental damage. The underlying rationale of this principle is that imposing the costs of preventing, eliminating or compensating environmental damage onto those who cause it creates incentives for environmentally friendly behaviour (Knill and Liefferink 2007).

5. Environmental integration (Art. 11 TFEU)

Mentioned under the environment title of the Treaties since the SEA but significantly broadened in scope only by the Amsterdam Treaty (Jordan 1998), the environmental integration principle has now taken an important place in European environmental policy. Nowadays, this principle is no longer part of the environment title of the Treaty, but is a part of the overall objectives of the EU. Although disagreement on a clear definition of this principle is lacking (for a discussion, see Jordan and Lenschow 2010), it starts from the observations that environmental policy *sensu stricto* is not sufficient to achieve environmental objectives and that decisions in other policy domains (such as transport, agriculture, industry or energy policy) often have important consequences for the environment. Therefore, environmental considerations need to be taken into account in other areas of public policy as well. The Treaty of Lisbon even introduced a particular integration principle for animal welfare (Art. 13 TFEU) (Vedder 2010). Although a number of initiatives have been taken to implement the environmental integration principle, it remains difficult to overcome fundamental conflicts between environmental objectives and other interests in society (see Chapter 7).

Continued

6. Sustainable development (Arts. 3 TEU and 11 TFEU)
Interwoven with the integration principle, the sustainable development principle was introduced into European primary law by the Treaty of Amsterdam. Although there are many definitions of this concept, the most widely accepted is the one formulated by the World Commission on Environment and Development in 1987 in the so-called Brundtland Report: 'Sustainable development is development that meets the needs of the present without compromising the ability of future generations to meet their own needs' (World Commission on Environment and Development 1987: 43) (see Chapter 2). In 2001, the Gothenburg European Council adopted the EU Sustainable Development Strategy, which was renewed in 2006 (see Chapter 7). It is important to note here that sustainable development is not only a principle of internal European policy, but that the Treaty also mentions it as one of the objectives of the external action of the EU (Arts. 3§5 and 21§2 TEU).

The developments outlined above made it possible for the 1972–1987 stage to be characterized by a remarkable expansion of environmental legislation during which more than 100 legislative pieces on the environment were adopted. This increase was remarkable for two reasons. A first reason is that environmental policy-making in the EU still occurred without an explicit legal basis in the Treaty. The interpretation of the existing Treaty provisions – mainly the common market Article 100 TEEC in combination with the articles outlying the EEC's objectives – allowed legislative action on the environment to be taken at the European level, although they did not explicitly refer to environmental protection. In the 1970s and 1980s, a second TEEC article was used as the legal basis for environmental measures: Article 235 TEEC, which authorized the EEC to take legislative action 'if any action by the Community appears necessary to achieve, in the functioning of the Common Market, one of the aims of the Community in cases where this Treaty has not provided for the requisite powers of action'. In other words, this article allowed legislation to be adopted in a field that is necessary for realizing the common market objectives of the EEC, even in the absence of a concrete legal basis. For this reason, although it is limited to the common market objectives, this article is often called the 'catch-all' provision (Hartley 1998; Weale et al. 2000).

In this period, the Court of Justice played an important role in further legitimizing the development of European environmental policy (see Chapter 3). The Court has regularly supported the development of environmental policies at the European level and with it a broad interpretation of the scope of the legislative competence, although this was not foreseen in the Treaty of Rome. Since it has legitimized environmental legislative measures at the EU level, the Court can be considered as a driving force behind more European integration in the environmental domain. Two sets of Court cases during the 1972–1987 stage particularly fulfilled that driving force function because they legitimized the use of Articles 100 and 235 TEEC, respectively, as the appropriate legal basis on which to take environmental measures (Koppen 1993). First, in cases 91/79 and 92/79, the Court stated that the common market Article 100 TEEC could be used as a basis for environmental legislation, but only to the extent that the harmonization of environmental measures at the European level was necessary to eliminate intra-EU trade barriers and thus to realize the common market. Second, in cases 68/81 to 73/81, it also legitimized the use of the catch-all Article 235 TEEC, which means that environmental policy can be seen as a so-called 'implied power' of the EEC, which was not foreseen in the Treaties but has nevertheless been established by the Court (Koppen 1993).

A second reason why the increase in the number of pieces of environmental legislation was remarkable is that the legal bases that could be used – the common market Article 100 TEEC and the catch-all Article 235 TEEC – contained two constraints on the conduct of environmental policy. Both articles stipulated that legislation had to be adopted unanimously in the Council, making lowest common denominator outcomes more likely than strong environmentally friendly ones (see Chapter 3). Moreover, both articles limited the scope of the environmental action they could underpin: Article 100 TEEC could only be used to take measures related to the common market, and the use of Article 235 TEEC was limited to measures that had primarily economic objectives (Knill and Liefferink 2007).

Notwithstanding these constraints, European environmental policy developed quite substantively in this phase with legislation principally focusing on water, air, noise, waste and nature protection measures (see Chapter 7) (Hildebrand 1993). This was mainly driven by member states that already had a considerable level of environmental legislation (the Netherlands and Germany are obvious examples). These existing national policies were essentially harmonized at the European level. The legislation adopted at the European level thus often took the form of a compromise between the various existing legal provisions of the member states (Zito 1999). Moreover, these environmental measures were spread to those member states that did not yet possess such legislation, particularly the southern member states, Greece, Spain and Portugal, that joined the EEC in the 1980s.

Because the areas covered by European environmental legislation had increased significantly by the mid-1980s, a more comprehensive approach began to characterize the environmental action of the EEC (McCormick 2001). However, these environmental policies were still conceived as responses to social, political and economic events and developments, making the environmental measures adopted in this period 'responsive' (Hildebrand 1993: 20). The shift from a reactive towards a proactive environmental policy at the European level became possible in the second half of the 1980s, when for the first time environmental competences were explicitly attributed to the European level in the SEA. This is where the third phase in the evolution of European environmental policy starts.

Legal basis, supranational decision-making and the '1992' impetus (1987–1992)

The SEA was the first substantial Treaty change since the Treaty of Rome. Having entered into force in 1987, the SEA did not only codify a number of existing practices in European decision-making, it principally set the objective of establishing a single market by the end of 1992, comprising the four essential freedoms: free movement of goods, services, persons and capital. This objective was not only embodied in the Treaty, but it was also driven by the determination of the European Commission led by Jacques Delors, which had come into office in January 1985. Only six months after its entry into office, the Delors Commission issued a white paper on the completion of the internal market, which proposed the abolition of all kinds of internal barriers. In order to realize the '1992' objective, new basic rules – and thus a Treaty revision – were needed: the SEA.

The SEA provisions had a twofold relevance for European environmental policy and policy-making. First, the SEA attributed new competences to the EEC, including environmental competences. It created an explicit legal basis for European environmental policy by adding a 'Title VII - Environment' to the SEA. The separate environment title in the SEA also made it possible to adopt environmental measures at the European level that are not primarily instrumental for the realization of the common market. The EEC could now also adopt environmental policies from merely an environmental protection logic. As a consequence, the SEA allowed for the transformation of the responsive or reactive nature of the European environmental policy of the second stage into a proactive and *sensu stricto* environmental type of policy. The rationale behind this broadening of the EEC's scope of action in the SEA was that to upgrade the common market to a genuine single market the EEC not only needed economic competences (as was essentially the case under the Treaty of Rome), but also competences in more regulatory areas, such as the environment. Indeed, in order to have a free market, an organized market had to be established, and for such an organization, regulatory policy areas need to be regulated.

Under Title VII of the SEA, three articles were created, then numbered Articles 130r, 130s and 130t. The basic structure of the environment title in the SEA is still the same today under the Treaty of Lisbon, where these (amended) articles are now numbered Articles 191, 192 and 193 TFEU. These three articles lay down the objectives and principles of European environmental policy; the legislative procedure for environmental policy-making; and the possibility of member states taking stricter environmental measures at their domestic levels than the harmonized ones at the European level (see Box 1.2).

Second, more effective decision-making rules and procedures were introduced by the SEA because they were needed to achieve the '1992' objective. These consisted of a bigger role for the European Parliament (EP) and a less stringent voting rule for the member states in the Council. Whereas the basic policy-making characteristic under the Treaty of Rome provisions was a dominant legislative role for the Council, making its decisions on the basis of the unanimity rule, the SEA strengthened the role of the

Box 1.2   Competences and legal bases of European environmental policy

Environmental policies are a shared competence between the EU and the member states (Art. 4 TFEU), meaning that both the EU and the member states can adopt environmental legislation, but that the member states can only do so 'to the extent that the Union has not exercised its competence' (Art. 2§2 TFEU).

Articles 191–193 TFEU are the current environmental articles under the Treaty of Lisbon. As argued above, the basic structure of these three articles is already in place since the SEA and has been considerably modified by the Maastricht Treaty and only slightly by the Amsterdam, Nice and Lisbon Treaties.

Article 191 TFEU: objectives, principles, restrictions, external action
- The first paragraph of Article 191 TFEU presents the *objectives* of EU environmental policy:
  - preserving, protecting and improving the quality of the environment;
  - protecting human health;
  - prudent and rational utilization of natural resources;
  - promoting measures at international level to deal with regional or worldwide environmental problems, and in particular combating climate change.
- The second paragraph depicts the *principles* that should guide EU environmental policy-making (see Box 1.1).
- The third paragraph stipulates the *restrictions* that need to be taken into account when making environmental policy in the EU:
  - available scientific and technical data;
  - environmental conditions in the various regions of the Union (which suggests the possible need for different approaches to environmental problems in different parts of the EU [Lee 2014]);
  - the potential benefits and costs of action or lack of action;
  - the economic and social development of the Union as a whole and the balanced development of its regions.
- The fourth paragraph deals with the division of competences for the EU's *external action* in the environmental area (see Chapter 10).

Article 192 TFEU: legislative process
Article 192 TFEU prescribes the legislative process to be followed to adopt environmental legislation in the EU.

- Paragraph 1 specifies the *basic rule*: the ordinary legislative procedure (OLP), in which the Council and the EP co-decide on the basis of a proposal by the European Commission (see Chapter 4).
- Paragraph 2 provides the *exceptions* to the general rule of paragraph 1. For the following issues, the special legislative procedure is applied, meaning that the EP's role is limited to being consulted and that unanimity – instead of qualified majority voting under the OLP – is required in the Council:
  a. provisions primarily of a fiscal nature;
  b. measures affecting:
     – town and country planning,
     – quantitative management of water resources or affecting, directly or indirectly, the availability of those resources,
     – land use, with the exception of waste management;
  c. measures significantly affecting a member state's choice between different energy sources and the general structure of its energy supply.
- Paragraph 3 stipulates that *Environment Action Programmes* (EAPs) (see Chapter 6) need to be adopted through the OLP.
- Paragraphs 4 and 5 require that member states will *finance and implement* the EU's environmental policy, but that in certain cases temporary derogations or financial support from the Cohesion Fund can also be used.

Article 193 TFEU: more stringent protective measures at the domestic level
Article 193 TFEU allows member states to maintain or to adopt environmental measures that are more stringent than those of the EU ('gold plating', see Chapter 6). Indeed, EU environmental policies provide 'for only a minimum level of environmental protection common to the member states and "shall not prevent any member state from maintaining or introducing more

Continued

> stringent protective measures"' (Lee 2014: 17). However, there is one important limitation to the member states' freedom in this regard: those stricter national measures need to be compatible with the (objectives of the) Treaty, which in practice means that they cannot impede the (completion of the) internal market.

EP in the legislative process by introducing the 'cooperation procedure' (see Chapter 3). The SEA also introduced qualified majority voting (QMV) for a (still rather limited) number of environmental issues. The introduction of the cooperation procedure and QMV for certain issues considerably changed the way environmental policy was made at the European level. It basically meant that the unanimity hurdle could be overcome on some issues and that environmental policies could be decided upon more easily than before.

The third stage was thus mainly characterized by the creation of a legal basis for European environmental policy, new decision-making rules and the impetus that was given by the '1992' goal of completing the single market. Other dynamics were also emerging in this period, but they are discussed in more detail elsewhere in this book. First, the EEC's international actorness, referring to its capacity to act in global environmental politics, became less and less contested in this phase. As will be explained in detail in Chapter 10, the struggle to be recognized as a full negotiation partner at the international level was won by the EEC in this phase. This, for instance, allowed the EEC to play a significant role at the United Nations Conference on Environment and Development (UNCED) in Rio in 1992, where the UN Framework Convention on Climate Change (UNFCCC) and the Convention on Biological Diversity (CBD) were signed.

Second, in this period, the first steps towards the creation of the European Environmental Agency (EEA) were taken (see Chapter 3). The EEA's main function is to collect information on the state of the environment in Europe, and to make this information publicly available so that it can be used by the European Commission to base its proposals for environmental legislation upon.

Third, because the environmental policy-making became increasingly Europeanized (due to more competences and more supranational dynamics), it continued to attract ever more attention from non-state actors, including environmental NGOs and business lobby groups (see Chapter 5). Not only did interest groups increasingly begin to focus their activities at the European level, they also intensified their organizational capacities there by creating European umbrella organizations, such as the European Environmental Bureau (EEB), or by expanding their Brussels-based activities.

Fourth, the 1987–1992 period was not only characterized by an increase in the legislative policy instruments, but also other types of policy instruments originated here (see Chapter 6). For example, a couple of financial instruments for environmental policy were launched in the 1980s. Then in 1992 these different instruments were rationalized and pooled into the LIFE Programme, which financially supports environmental and nature conservation projects in the EU, as well as in its eastern and Mediterranean neighbouring countries (see Chapter 6).

Legal, institutional and legislative consolidation (1992–2009)

Since 1993, with the entry into force of the Maastricht Treaty (signed in 1992), a shift in the overall development of EU environmental policy took place. In the fourth phase, the legal and institutional framework was consolidated and even strengthened through the provisions in the various Treaty changes that were adopted in this phase: the Maastricht, Amsterdam (signed in 1997, entered into force in 1999), Nice (signed in 2001, entered into force in 2003) and even the Lisbon (signed in 2007, entered into force in 2009) Treaties. These Treaties further developed the legal bases and institutional frameworks for environmental policy-making which led to a steady increase in the number of pieces of EU environmental legislation adopted in this period (see Figure 1.1). This stage is also characterized by the creation and growth of environmental policies in an area that was until then virgin territory, namely climate change. The main starting point for the fourth phase is the entry into force of the Maastricht Treaty, which formally consisted of the Treaty on European Union (TEU) and the Treaty Establishing the European Community (TEC). Three components of the new legal and institutional framework deserve particular attention here.

First, since the Treaty of Maastricht, 'a high level of protection and improvement of the quality of the environment' is now a general objective of the EU (Art. 3 of the current TEU), although the Maastricht Treaty only stated that the EU's economic activities had to 'respect the environment'. What is important here is the fact that the references to environmental protection in the Treaties are no longer limited to the environment title, but that environment now also has a place among the general objectives of the EU. This has – at least legally – 'strengthened the European Community's (EC's) commitment to environmental protection' (Wilkinson 1992).

Second, and probably most importantly, the Maastricht Treaty introduced the codecision procedure for a large range of policy domains, including the environment. This policy-making procedure significantly updates the role of the EP as co-legislator. Under this procedure, a legislative proposal of the Commission needs the approval of both the Council and the EP before it can be adopted (see Chapter 4). Consequently, under this procedure, the EP can act as a veto-player. With the abolition of the cooperation procedure, the Amsterdam Treaty even expanded the range of environmental issues covered by the codecision procedure, and subsequently the Nice and Lisbon Treaties confirmed this trend.

Third, the 1999 Treaty of Amsterdam also inserted the concept of 'sustainable development' in the Treaty framework of the EU (Jordan 1998). The then Article 2 TEU mentioned that one of the objectives of the EU was 'to achieve balanced and sustainable development'. This wording was later changed by the Lisbon Treaty, which broadened the scope of sustainable development and extended it to the external relations of the EU as well (Benson and Adelle 2012). Today, Article 3 TEU states the objective that the EU 'shall work for the sustainable development of Europe based on balanced economic growth and price stability, a highly competitive social market economy, aiming at full employment and social progress, and a high level of protection and improvement of the quality of the environment'.

The fourth phase in the history of EU environmental politics is characterized by the establishment and the steady growth of climate change policies in the EU. After having signed the Kyoto Protocol in 1997, the EU aimed to implement the Protocol's provisions and to make sure it achieved its 8 per cent emission reduction target. Moreover, the EU wanted to complement the global leadership it had shown in the Kyoto Protocol negotiations with strong internal climate change policies (Oberthür and Pallemaerts 2010). In the early 2000s, a substantial amount of climate legislation was therefore adopted, focusing on the reduction of greenhouse gases (for instance from passenger cars), as well as on complementary issues such as energy efficiency or biofuels. Importantly, the cornerstone of the EU's climate policy was established in 2003 with the adoption of the directive on the EU Emission Trading Scheme, which created a market for emissions trading in the EU (see Chapter 9). These developments resulted, at the end of the 2000s, in a situation where climate change had evolved towards the most salient and most important issue on the EU's environmental agenda.

Besides the dynamics of deepening (the various Treaty changes), the 1992–2009 stage was also characterized by a widening process in the EU (two enlargement waves), since the number of EU member states increased considerably through the enlargement waves of 1995 (with Sweden, Finland and Austria joining) and 2004/2007 (with ten Central and Eastern European countries joining, as well as Cyprus and Malta). On the one hand, these enlargements meant that the existing European environmental policy became applicable to an additional 1.2 hundred million European citizens. Moreover, the new Central and Eastern European member states that had to implement the environmental *acquis* as a precondition for acceding the EU were mainly countries with relatively highly polluting industries. This means that in terms of the impact of the environmental legislation on people and economies, the enlargement wave was significant.

On the other hand, the impact of the enlargement on environmental policy-making does not seem to be as big as many analysts presumed. Before the EU enlarged in the 2000s, opinion about the consequences that enlargement was expected to have on the making of European environmental policy was highly pessimistic, in the sense that it was anticipated that it would have 'an adverse effect on progressive EU environmental policy' (Jehliaka and Tickle 2004: 77), mainly because most of the applicant countries were still facing the consequences of 'communist misrule where political indifference left massive degradation of the environment' (Kramer 2004: 291) (see Chapter 2). However, assessing the impact of the biggest enlargement in EU history on its environmental policy, Lenschow concludes that it did not result in a 'retrenchment of the policy' (Lenschow 2010: 310). Likewise, Braun argues that 'new member states, at least so far, have not had the negative impact on EU environmental policy that had often been predicted' (Braun 2014: 1).

Nevertheless, this is not to say that enlargement towards Central and Eastern European countries had no impact at all on environmental policy-making. Even today these countries have more difficulties than the 'old' member states in taking up ambitious environmental targets. During their accession process to the EU around the turn of the century, they had to make up their arrears and to take on the burden of implementing existing EU environmental policies. Given these efforts, they usually seem to be somewhat reluctant to adopt stronger environmental policies (Wurzel 2012). This dynamic is well illustrated in the area of climate change, where a number of Central and Eastern European member states, with Poland in the front, have repeatedly jammed on the brakes for more ambitious policies (see Chapter 9).

The consolidation of the legal, institutional and legislative framework was in this fourth phase counterbalanced by a decreasing political ambition of the member states to further strengthen environmental regulatory framework at the EU level (Knill and Liefferink 2007). Member states seemed to prefer less strict environmental regulations since they feared that yet more environmental measures would undermine their international competitiveness. The economic rationale that strict environmental rules in Europe weaken the position of the EU in the global market vis-à-vis emerging economies where environmental standards are less stringent seemed to prevail. Moreover, member states preferred a flexible approach that gave them more room for manoeuvre in the national implementation of European legislation above the essentially harmonizing approach of the first stages.

'Green economy' and better implementation of a mature policy area (since 2009)

At the end of the 2000s, a number of developments prompted the start of a new stage in the evolution of EU environmental policy. The Lisbon Treaty entered into force in 2009, which determined the rules of the game of EU policy-making that are currently still in force. This happened at a moment when the financial-economic crisis in the EU was reaching its height. The resulting austerity policies of the EU and the member states had a decisive impact on EU policy-making in general. In the environmental field, the crisis mainly meant that, on the one hand, environmental issues received less political attention since the political agenda was mainly dominated by economic, budgetary and fiscal policies (Burns 2014). On the other hand, environmental policy became increasingly framed in economic terms, with 'green growth' being the new overarching baseline for EU environmental policy initiatives.

In the meantime, the EU had developed outspoken environmental leadership ambitions on the international scene but these ambitions were severely impaired at the 2009 Copenhagen climate change conference. Although tackling the climate change issue at this conference was a high priority for the EU, it was completely sidelined during the endgame of the negotiations and the outcome of the conference, the so-called Copenhagen Accord, did not at all reflect the EU's position (see Chapter 10). In Copenhagen, the EU was forced to face the fact that power relations at the international level were changing, that the EU's relative power in the world was falling with the rise of the emerging powers and that the EU's self-proclaimed 'leading by example' strategy had reached its limits (Bäckstrand and Elgström 2013; van Schaik 2013). In other words, it became clear that the context of the twenty-first century, with the Copenhagen experience and later also the EU's unsuccessful attempts to reach an ambitious outcome at the Rio+20 Summit on sustainable development, had become less favourable for the EU than the context of the end of the twentieth century with the Kyoto conference and the Earth Summit in Rio (see Chapter 2). It is against this backdrop that EU environmental politics and policy have evolved since 2009. These evolutions are still ongoing, as a result of which their ultimate impact and relevance is difficult to assess today. Notwithstanding this qualification, the remainder of this section discusses the current trends, many of them being further elaborated in the next chapters.

Lisbon Treaty

The impact of the Lisbon Treaty – which is formally made up of the Treaty on European Union (TEU) and the Treaty on the Functioning of the European Union (TFEU) – on EU environmental policy-making 'is most likely to be minimal' (Benson and Adelle 2012; Vedder 2010: 299). Because environmental policy is already a relatively mature area of EU competences, there was very little scope for radical changes in the Lisbon Treaty (Benson and Jordan 2010). Besides the new wording of the sustainable development objective (see above), the Lisbon Treaty also gives animal welfare a prominent place as an EU objective. No new competences on the environment were attributed to the EU in this Treaty, although the addition of a new sentence to Article 191 TFEU – with the objectives of European environmental policy mentioning the fight against climate change at the international level – may be used in the future by the European Commission to claim more external competences in this field, for example to represent the EU in international climate change negotiations (see Chapter 10). This is the first time that climate change is mentioned in an EU Treaty. The Lisbon Treaty also changed the name for the codecision procedure, which had, since the Maastricht Treaty, put the Council and the EP on equal footing in the legislative policy-making procedure. Under the Lisbon Treaty, this procedure is now called the 'ordinary legislative procedure' but the procedure as such has not changed: the Commission proposes environmental legislation and the Council and the EP adopt it (see Chapter 4).

Two other innovations of the Lisbon Treaty, which were transversal in nature and thus not specifically related to the environmental area, have had an impact on policy-making in the environmental field. They have led to conflicts over procedural issues, thereby interfering with substantive discussions. First, the Commission and the Council interpreted the impact of the Lisbon Treaty on the external representation of the EU differently, with the Commission considering it as a pathway to a bigger role for the Commission and the member states in the Council opposing this view (see Chapter 10). This discussion was intermingled with the post-Copenhagen debate and particularly with the observation of some actors in the EU that the EU's failure in Copenhagen was at least partly due to its inability to 'speak with a single voice' and thus to its system of external representation (Corthaut and Van Eeckhoutte 2012; Delreux 2012a). These discussions dominated the EU debate in the context of a number of international environmental negotiations in the early 2010s and prevented the EU from considering the (probably more important) questions about content and strategy. Second, the Lisbon Treaty also reformed the so-called 'comitology system', used to implement environmental policies at the EU level after their adoption (see Chapter 4). It created two types of implementation instruments (implementing acts and delegated acts), which give different powers to the Council and the EP depending on which instrument is chosen. The debate on the choice between implementing and delegated acts has in some cases created a hidden power struggle between the Council and the EP that has risked troubling the substantive debate.

At the same time as the entry into force of the Lisbon Treaty, though not an immediate consequence of it, climate change policies became more and more institutionalized in the EU. This institutional strengthening mainly took place in the European Commission, where the function of Climate Action Commissioner and a DG Climate Action (CLIMA) were created when the Barroso II Commission took office. Since the beginning of 2010, environmental policy-making is no longer the responsibility of one Commissioner and a single DG, but they were spread over an Environment and a Climate Action Commissioner, each with their respective administrative support in DG Environment and DG Climate Action. The new DG CLIMA was created out of an existing directorate of DG Environment. It started off with 60 staff members and quickly grew to about 150 officials. Five years later, at the start of the Juncker Commission, the responsibility for environmental issues was spread out over a further two additional Commissioners, with not only the Environment and Climate Action Commissioner having environmental issues in their portfolio, but also the vice-president responsible for the Energy Union and the first vice-president overseeing sustainability issues being responsible for environmental policy (see Chapter 3).

'Green economy' as a response to the crisis

EU environmental policy was not as directly affected as other policy areas by the financial-economic crisis and the Eurozone crisis that has had the EU firmly in its grasp since 2009. Indeed, the austerity policies in Europe and the resulting budgetary stringency did not immediately affect a regulatory policy area such as the environment to the same extent as it affected (re)distributive policy areas (such as social policies). Environmental policy is indeed regulatory in nature, which means that it mainly stipulates rules that limit the discretion of societal actors. It is not a policy area that primarily distributes or redistributes money between societal groups. However, although

EU environmental policy did not feel a direct effect of the crisis, it was indirectly influenced by the crisis in a twofold way.

First, the political attention and political importance attached to environmental policy steadily declined as the fight against the financial-economic crisis became the number one priority for EU and national policy-makers alike. The momentum for developing ambitious environmental policies disappeared and environmental issues were pushed into the background. This happened not only in the EU and in the member states, but rather was a worldwide trend that also affected global environmental governance (see Chapter 2).

Second, the framing and discourse of EU environmental policy changed. Environmental issues are no longer primarily approached from the perspective of environmental protection, but they are framed as a contribution to economic growth or competitiveness. In that sense, they are seen to be a part of the recipe for recovery from the financial-economic crisis (see Chapter 6). Catchphrases such as 'green economy', 'green jobs', 'green growth', 'sustainable growth' or 'low carbon economy' nowadays dominate the environmental debate and determine the way environmental problems are conceived in the EU. Positioning environmental policy under this 'green growth' umbrella is a key characteristic of the current stage of EU environmental policy. This fits within the 'ecological modernization' policy paradigm, which basically argues that ambitious environmental policies do not undermine economic growth, but contribute to growth and can even be a driver of it, for instance through technological innovation in the area of renewable energy (see Mol and Spaargaren 2000). Moreover, one could argue that the 'green economy' turn again puts EU environmental policy at the service of a broader economic objective, as was the case in the first decades of EU environmental policy (see the discussion of the first two stages above).

The 'green growth' approach is part of the 'Europe 2020' strategy, which is the overall growth strategy in the EU that is based on the EU's ambition to achieve 'smart, sustainable and inclusive growth' for the 2010–2020 period. Europe 2020 includes the 'resource efficiency' flagship initiative, which was the European Commission's new grand strategy in the environmental field in the 2009–2014 period under the then Environment Commissioner Potočnik. Under the resource efficiency framework, the aim is to achieve a more efficient use of natural resources. The issue is, however, not presented from the perspective of the impact of raw natural resources on the environment, but as a strategy to promote growth, jobs and competitiveness (see Chapter 6). Next to the resource efficiency flagship, other strategies with long-term targets were also adopted by the Commission in this period, which all have in common that they intend to pave the way for an evolution towards a low carbon economy in Europe. Examples include the 'Roadmap for moving to a low-carbon economy in 2050' and the 'Energy Roadmap 2050' (see Chapters 6 and 9). Importantly, the shift towards the green economy paradigm in EU environmental policy is particularly evident in the broader strategies and in the policy documents with long-term visions adopted by the European Commission (such as the Roadmaps mentioned above). By contrast, the impact of the green economy framing on specific environmental legislation adopted since 2009 is less obvious (Burns 2014).

Better regulation and enhanced implementation

Periods of economic crisis are often characterized by calls for less regulation as, from this perspective, too much regulation is considered to hamper economic growth (Jordan et al. 2013). However, looking at EU environmental legislation, neither the financial-economic crisis nor such calls for deregulation have actually led to a significant abolition of environmental legislation in the EU. In other words, serious environmental 'policy dismantling' – that is, the 'cutting, diminution or removal of existing policy' (Bauer et al. 2012: 203) – has not taken place as such and stringent cuts in both the quantity and the level of ambition in the EU's environmental *acquis* have, at the time of writing, so far failed to materialize.

The possibility of policy dismantling has, however, been the subject of recent controversy. For instance, when the Juncker Commission adopted its first work programme (for the year 2015), it announced the amendment or withdrawal of around 80 pending legislative proposals in various policy domains. One of the most contested withdrawals was the so-called 'circular economy package', which aimed at eliminating waste in the economic system. It had been proposed by the previous Commission as the culmination of the resource efficiency flagship promoted by former Commissioner Potočnik (see above). This legislative package was indeed withdrawn in early 2015 despite complaints from environmental groups, members of the EP and Environment Ministers from the member states. The Commission emphasized, however, that it remained strongly committed to the objectives of the package and that it would table an even more ambitious proposal on the circular economy by the end of 2015. Whether the withdrawal of the circular economy package can be considered as a case of policy dismantling will thus depend on the content of that new proposal.

The crisis and the call to soften the burden of environmental policy on Europe's industries forced the EU institutions and the national governments to think about more flexible and softer approaches to regulation. The increasing use of market-based environmental policy instruments illustrates this development (see Chapter 6). The evolution towards more flexibility is though not completely new in the EU. As early as the early 2000s, the Commission launched a 'Better Regulation' programme, which aimed to make European legislation more efficient. Since 2010, this effort has continued under the umbrella of 'smart regulation'. This focus on the quality of legislation – much more than on its quantity, which deregulation targets – has characterized EU environmental policy since the end of the 2000s. The fact that the first Vice-President of the Juncker Commission, Frans Timmermans, is in charge of better regulation again confirms the importance of this dynamic.

Part of this better or smart regulation effort is the Commission's Regulatory Fitness and Performance (REFIT) programme, which aims to simplify the European regulatory framework and to reduce so-called 'red tape' (that is, excessive regulation and administrative burdens). Although a couple of pieces of environmental legislation were explicitly targeted in the REFIT programme as having the potential for being simplified (Gravey 2014), its impact on environmental policy has in general remained relatively limited. The major impact of REFIT in the environmental field was probably the withdrawal by the Commission of its proposal for a Framework Directive on Soil (see Chapter 7), although it seems unlikely that a Soil Framework Directive would have been adopted, even in the absence of REFIT, given the major opposition in the Council to such a legislative instrument.

Environmental policy-making, particularly in the Commission and in the Council, is affected by these calls for better and smarter regulation. More than during previous stages, policy-makers tend to pay more attention to the avoidance of red tape and excessive bureaucracy. They also emphasize the necessity of having 'realistic' targets and objectives, as a result of which the level of ambition of newly adopted policies seems to be lower than in the past. However, the idea is also that it should be feasible to actually implement and realize these targets now, which was often not the case with the 'ambitious' targets from the past.

Furthermore, current environmental policy-making processes increasingly focus on subsidiarity and more particularly on the question whether the European level is the most appropriate level to deal with a particular environmental issue or not. Critical initiatives by countries like the UK and the Netherlands on the balance of competences between the EU and the member states have pushed the subsidiarity question to the forefront. Simultaneously, the rising level of Euroscepticism and the electoral successes of anti-EU political parties in many member states have made governments more reluctant to support a further Europeanization of regulatory policies. These developments make it no longer sensible to adopt environmental policies at the EU level on questions for which the added value of supranational action is less evident (or where it is less easy to convince national public opinion about their necessity).

Making EU legislation 'better' or 'smarter' has also led to the trend of bringing together multiple separate and already existing pieces of legislation into one single – and simplified – legislative instrument. For instance, the Industrial Emissions Directive (2010/75) compiles seven existing directives into one more integrated piece of legislation. Also, the Directive on Environmental Impact Assessment (2011/92, amended by 2014/52) brings together four separate pieces of legislation and aims to streamline the regulatory framework into one text. This also explains why the number of legislative pieces that are in force has decreased, for instance in 2010 or 2014 (see Figure 1.1). However, such a reduction in quantity does not necessarily lead to a narrowing of the scope of the existing EU environmental policies and does not necessarily reflect considerable environmental policy dismantling in the EU.

Simultaneously with the call for making better regulation, much attention is paid to enhancing the implementation of existing environmental policies. At the end of the 2000s, almost all subareas of environmental policy were covered by European policies. The establishment of major Framework Directives (for instance on air, water and waste policy, see Chapter 7) and the adoption of a number of more specific pieces of environmental legislation mean that there is almost no virgin territory for environmental regulation anymore in the EU (with perhaps the notable exception of soil policy). However, the main problem is that the existing environmental objectives, for instance in the areas of water or biodiversity policy, are not – or not adequately – achieved. The actual implementation record of environmental policy is among the weakest and most problematic ones of all EU policy areas (see Chapter 4). Hence, the rationale behind environmental policy developments in this stage was that progress in environmental protection should be achieved not through the adoption of more legislation, but through the improvement of the execution and the implementation of the existing rules.

Enhanced implementation is also part of the revision of existing legislation. A great deal of legislative activity today focuses on reviewing. Indeed, EU environmental politics is characterized by a 'continual process of amendment and revision' (Axelrod et al. 2011: 224). In these review exercises, special attention is paid to the implementation question, for instance by including so-called 'early warning systems' that require member states to submit a mid-term report about the progress they make in achieving their targets. When those mid-term reports indicate that realizing the targets is likely to be difficult, compliance plans can be adopted in order to help that member state to adjust its implementation so that the targets are actually achieved in the future and so that infringement proceedings can be avoided (see Chapter 4).

Conclusions

This chapter's discussion of the five phases in the evolution of the European environmental policy has shown that this policy domain has witnessed a remarkable growth in quantity, scope and impact. Characterized by a lack of legal competences in its first three decades, but expanding thanks to political will and judicial support, the EU's environmental policy is currently one of the most Europeanized policy areas. Summarizing the developments in each of the five stages, Table 1.1 presents an overview of the evolution of the European environmental policy.

In this chapter, we have mainly emphasized the legal and institutional developments as well as the various ways in which the making of European environmental policy was legitimized. The question remains, however, *why* these developments took place and which forces and dynamics were driving them. These driving forces will be dealt with in the next chapter, where we argue that the historical development and the current state of European environmental policy and politics can only be fully understood if one takes into

Table 1.1 *Overview of the evolution of the European environmental policy in five stages*

	1957–1972	*1972–1987*	*1987–1992*	*1992–2009*	*Since 2009*
start	Treaty of Rome	- societal and political organization - Stockholm Conf. - first EAP	Single European Act	Maastricht Treaty	- Lisbon Treaty - Copenhagen Conf. - financial-economic crisis
basic characteristics	- no legal basis - environment-related measures serving economic integration purposes (common market)	- no legal basis - origin of more coherent policies - increase in quantity, scope and political status of environmental policy	- explicit legal basis (environmental competences at European level) + introduction of more supranational decision-making - impetus of 1992 objective - environmental protection logic	- expansion of competences and supranational decision-making - establishment and growth of climate change policies - decrease of political ambition	- reduced political attention for the environment - framing of environmental policy as contribution to 'green economy' - more flexible forms of regulation - emphasis on better implementation
main institutions	mainly Council	mainly Council and Commission, also Court of Justice	mainly Council and Commission, limited role for EP	Commission, Council and EP	Commission, Council and EP
decision-making procedure	consultation procedure (incl. unanimity)	consultation procedure (incl. unanimity)	introduction of co-operation procedure (incl. QMV)	introduction of codecision procedure (incl. QMV)	quasi-generalization of ordinary legislative procedure (incl. QMV)

account the global context in which the EU is embedded. Therefore, the driving forces and dynamics behind the progress of the EU's environmental activities are linked to the processes of globalization and the formation of a global environmental governance architecture. The current state of play of this policy area can be fully understood only by taking them into account, and by acknowledging that the EU is not creating environmental policies in splendid isolation.

Chapter 2

The Global Context

In order to fully understand the environmental policies and politics of the EU, the global context in which European environmental policies emerged and are still embedded today needs to be taken into account. Situating the evolution of EU environmental policies and politics in the global context, this chapter makes it clear that the EU has been influenced by global dynamics and is not developing policies in a bubble. Fundamental processes of economic, political and environmental globalization considerably affect the EU's environmental challenges as well as its policy responses. The aim of this chapter is to provide the essential contextual elements that help to explain the emergence of environmental policy as a domain in which the EU is very active.

The first section elucidates the ascent of environmental issues on the political agenda, first at the national level and then at the international level. Understanding how environmental issues reached the political agenda is important, as many of the old debates remain relevant today. The second section discusses the formation of the global environmental governance architecture. The institutional choices made at the global level since the 1970s as well as the positions taken by the key actors in this process are crucial elements of the current governance architecture and the present role of the EU therein. In the final section, the interaction between the EU and other actors in global environmental politics – mainly the United States and the emerging powers – is discussed as well as the new challenges that recent changes in global governance pose to the EU.

The rise of the environment on the political agenda

After World War II, the industrialized world faced enormous social and economic challenges. Entire societies were recovering from the horrors of a five-year war. Much basic infrastructure was destroyed and restoring minimal living conditions for large groups of the population became the key policy priority in the European countries (Mak 2004). Economic recovery plans stimulated the building of housing, the reconstruction of roads and railways, and the restoration of basic industries (Van der Wee 1986).

This was the period in which the socio-economic model of the United States, based on the large-scale production of consumer goods, was adopted by the rest of the Western world. Also, in Europe an era of unprecedented growth of household consumption started. Increased purchasing power and a process of urbanization went hand in hand with the spreading of an urban middle class lifestyle. A swiftly growing number of people moved beyond the level of basic consumption, and by the 1960s the Western world was experiencing a period of continued growth labelled the Golden Sixties. Yet, a number of side effects of this model's almost exclusive emphasis on economic and industrial performance and on consumption became prominently visible (Kassiola 1990). One of the major side effects was the harmful impact on the environment, which resulted in environmental issues starting to make it onto the political agenda. Two factors triggered the emergence of the environment on the political agenda: a number of accidents with major environmental consequences and scientific developments demonstrating the harmful impact of environmental pollution.

First, a number of industrial accidents and incidents illustrated the lack of attention to environmental aspects of the system of industrial production and more in particular the pollution of the environment it caused. The dioxin accident in the chemical manufacturing plant in the Italian town of Seveso (Italy) in 1976 started a debate on the safety of industrial installations in the chemical sector and ultimately resulted in the adoption of the EU's Seveso Directive (82/501). The major oil spill of the Amoco Cadiz in 1978, along the coast of Brittany (France), caused weeks of public debate and eventually led to policies on the safety of vessels, namely provisions on the use of double-hulled tankers. Such accidents were obviously not limited to Europe. In Japan, in the bay of Minamata, mercury pollution made it into the food chain, causing very serious health consequences for the local population. This case is considered to be the starting point for the development of environmental policies in Japan. Likewise, in the United States, the consequences of a large-scale use of pesticides in industrial agriculture, where the introduction of DDT had a detrimental impact on biodiversity and human health, caused a big societal stir (Carson 1962). These incidents stimulated civic activism and the founding of environmental movements in most Western countries. Reinforced by an increasing media attention to the hazardous consequences of such industrial incidents, they contributed to the first societal and political debates about the need for serious environmental policies (Elliott 2004; Soroos 2011).

Second, at about the same time, biologists, ecologists and other natural scientists started to systematically study the link between industrial pollution, ecological quality and human health. This health factor was very important in the politicization of environmental issues in those early years. Citizens are indeed more worried, and can be more easily mobilized in environmental movements and in the political debate, when a clear link is demonstrated between sources of pollution and their own health or that of their children. Scientists played a crucial role in demonstrating the seriousness of environmental problems (for example acid rain) and the urgency to act to mitigate their effects (for example on ozone layer depletion) (Elliott 2004). To the extent that scientists started to influence the political process, they were defined as an epistemic community, which is a knowledge-based group of actors playing a role in processes of social change (Haas 1992). The most important early research groups dealing with environmental issues were situated in the United States and in a couple of European member states such as Germany and the Netherlands (Jänicke 1992). They influenced the political agenda by defining or framing problems and by providing a rational or objective basis for policy-making.

The political response to those developments consisted of several elements. First of all, industrialized countries made first attempts to adopt sectorial environmental policies. The pace was set in the United States, where the Clean Air Act (1963), the Water Quality Act (1965) and the Fauna Conservation Act (1974) were early examples of legislation aimed at tackling pollution and guaranteeing a minimum environmental quality (Vig and Faure 2004). Many of these policies served as examples for European countries which were adopting a leading role in national environmental policies, such as Germany, the Netherlands and Sweden.

Building on these early policy initiatives, a comprehensive environmental legislative framework was established during the 1980s and 1990s in all industrialized countries. Not only were environmental policies developed, the institutional structure to do so was established too. The creation of environment ministries and related agencies demonstrated that there was both a political choice and societal demand to treat environmental issues in the same way as other more traditional policy themes such as education and health care (Weidner and Jänicke 2002). The policy and institutional developments at the national level also formed a basis of expertise to assist the creation of similar dynamics at the international level. The fact that countries gained experience in how to design environmental legislation and their development of policy tools and of the necessary institutional framework were essential contributions to the creation of a global environmental governance architecture.

In Europe, the rise of environmental issues on the political agenda initially affected the member states rather than the EEC. In those early years of the development of environmental policy initiatives, the member states were undoubtedly the centre of gravity. The EEC did not yet have the formal competences or the institutional capacity to play a more coordinating role (see Chapter 1). The growing importance of the environment on national political agendas and the creation of an institutional, bureaucratic and legislative infrastructure were the necessary stepping stones for wider environmental policy initiatives at the supranational level. The issue had to reach a certain point of political salience and importance in a number of member states before any serious political action was possible at the higher level. Germany and the Netherlands, together with Denmark, played a key role in this early period, with the UK following suit.

The formation of a global environmental governance architecture

The Stockholm Conference

At the end of the 1960s, Sweden took the initiative in the UN General Assembly to call for a global meeting on environmental problems, leading to the organization of the United Nations Conference on the Human Environment (UNCHE) in Stockholm in 1972. This so-called Stockholm Conference is considered the starting point for global environmental politics (Andresen 2007; Birnie et al. 2009; Momtaz 1996; Soroos 2011).

With the exception of the communist countries, most countries of the world were present in Stockholm. They adopted the

Stockholm Declaration in which a number of fundamental principles that would guide the environmental policy area for the following decades were laid down (United Nations Conference on the Human Environment 1972). This Declaration outlines, among others, the common responsibility for the global environment and recognizes the undeniable necessity of protecting the environment, particularly through international cooperation. On the other hand, Principle 21 of the Declaration also highlights the principle of sovereignty and underlines the fundamental organizing principle of non-intervention in domestic affairs. The apparent paradox between the need for international cooperation and the sovereignty principle has characterized almost every international environmental regime from then on. States have a common responsibility for protecting the global environment, yet are frequently unwilling to surrender any fundamental right associated with traditional state sovereignty. The EU, as a multilateral environmental regime, is obviously the big exception when it comes to fundamentally reconciling these two principles. Indeed, the political system of the EU holds the middle ground between traditional intergovernmental policy-making emphasizing state sovereignty on the one hand, and an intricate system of supranational responsibility for the European environment on the other hand.

The six founding member states of the EEC (Belgium, the Netherlands, Luxembourg, West Germany, France and Italy) actively supported the process of internationalizing environmental concerns and policy responses in Stockholm. They participated at the Conference as independent states and outside the EEC framework, each defending national positions. Being in the process of developing their own basic environmental policies and at the early stages of institutionalization at the national level, they approached the international dimension in essence as an extension of emerging national policies and of traditional foreign policy. There was neither a common European position nor a system for joint representation at that time. The situation was thus fundamentally different from that of today (see Chapter 10).

However, the Stockholm Conference triggered the Europeanization of environmental politics in important ways. It certainly played a role in speeding up domestic processes in member states, as a result of which the political weight of environmental issues increased. It also put pressure on those member states that were slower to engage in environmental policy-making, as they had to prepare for serious debate in Stockholm by developing solid national positions. At the level of the EEC, the preparation of the first Environmental Action Programme, that was adopted in 1973 (see Chapter 1 and Box 6.2), coincided with the Stockholm process. The European environmental policies of the EEC member states of that time (Denmark, Ireland and the UK joined the EEC in 1973) became an important driver of emerging international environmental politics.

The European member states also initiated a process of deliberation among themselves in preparation for further international environmental policy initiatives. The need was increasingly felt to be able to act in a coordinated European way at the international level. It is obvious that this had no formal treaty basis at that time. However, the development of internal policies in an inherently transboundary issue area such as the environment required joint attention at the international level.

A first wave of international environmental agreements

During the 1970s and the early 1980s a first wave of multilateral environmental agreements (MEAs) was negotiated. The most important ones include the Convention on International Trade in Endangered Species (CITES, 1973), the Convention on Long-Range Transboundary Air Pollution (CLRTAP, 1979), the Convention on the Law of the Sea (1982) and the Vienna Convention for the Protection of the Ozone Layer (1985). The European member states were involved in the negotiations on these MEAs as sovereign states, but together they represented an important weight in all of them. This shows that the need for common positions increased as the EEC developed a more encompassing set of internal environmental legislation (see Chapter 1). Moreover, the EEC became an important actor for the translation of the international treaty obligations into actual policy measures. Significant parts of the European environmental policies indeed find their origins in international environmental policy-making dynamics.

Importantly, during this first wave of internationalization of environmental politics, the United States played a dominant role (DeSombre 2011). As a single state and an early starter in developing domestic environmental policies, it was better positioned to lead multilateral negotiations than the EEC, which still lacked formal competences, was hindered by large differences between the member states in terms of institutional capacity and was primarily occupied by the development of its internal regulatory framework. It was only in the mid-1980s that the EU took over the leadership role from the United States in global environmental politics (see Chapter 10). This shift in leadership positions between the United States and the EU still characterizes global environmental politics today.

The road to Rio: sustainable development as a framing concept

By the mid-1980s, more and more questions were raised on the functioning of the existing system of international environmental politics (Chasek and Wagner 2012). Although environmental regimes and institutional structures were set up in most sub-domains of environment policy, little fundamental progress was made in adequately addressing the environmental problems at stake. The state of the environment at the global level was not improving, economic growth and further industrialization had created serious pollution problems in developing countries, and development issues increasingly intersected with environmental degradation. This last point is important, as developing countries felt increasingly alienated from debates about the environment, which tended to focus on industrialized concerns, technological issues and scientific and market approaches. Developing countries, by contrast, wanted more attention for poverty reduction, basic economic development, transfer of technology and financing mechanisms that would allow them to be full participants in global environmental politics (Najam 2011).

In the light of this situation, the UN created the temporary World Commission on Environment and Development (WCED, 1983–1987) to formulate proposals on the linkages between environment and development. The WCED – which is also called the Brundtland Commission after its president, Norwegian former Prime Minister Gro Harlem Brundtland – concluded its discussions in 1987 with the report 'Our Common Future', also referred to as the 'Brundtland Report' (World Commission on Environment and Development 1987). The main concept put forward by the Report was sustainable development, which refers to the integration of economic, social and environmental concerns in a long-term global perspective (see Box 1.1). The WCED concluded that sustainable development ought to form the basis for the further development of policies in nearly all domains. The artificial separation of the economic, social and ecological spheres would lead to further environmental degradation and inability to make progress on development issues (Happaerts and Bruyninckx 2014).

Based on these conclusions, the UN General Assembly decided to organize a global conference in Rio de Janeiro. The United Nations Conference on Environment and Development (UNCED) – also known as the 'Rio Conference', 'Rio Summit' or the 'Earth Summit' – took place in 1992, twenty years after the Stockholm Conference. It was the largest global conference ever organized on any theme. With the notable exception of US President Bush Sr., all the world's important political leaders were present, which demonstrated the importance of the theme and the recognition of the inherent global nature of both the problem and the possible solutions (Andresen 2007; Elliott 2004).

The result of the Rio Summit was captured in Agenda 21 and in the creation of three multilateral environmental regimes (Chasek et al. 2012). Agenda 21 summarized the necessary actions to be taken, the stakeholders to be involved and the instruments to be used to strive for global sustainable development. The impact of the concept of sustainable development, as embedded in Agenda 21, on the EU was profound (see Chapter 7). It is a clear example of how the international context has played a fundamental role in shaping European (environmental) policies.

Three major multilateral environmental agreements – the so-called Rio Conventions – also find their origins at the Rio Summit. The United Nations Framework Convention on Climate Change (UNFCCC) and the Convention on Biological Diversity (CBD) were signed in Rio, and the United Nations Convention to Combat Desertification (UNCCD) was negotiated there before it was signed in 1994 in Paris. The EU and its member states are a party to these conventions (see Chapter 10). The member states generally managed to participate in these negotiations in a fairly unified way, albeit to a lesser extent in the case of the UNCCD negotiations (Delreux 2011). Moreover, the EU took a serious leap forward as a global actor in the environmental field in the run-up to Rio and even more so in the years immediately after the Summit. Preparations for the Conference itself were based on national processes, but to an increasing extent also on the creation of common EU positions. Although criticism was voiced on the weak bargaining position of the EU and its fragile 'actorness'

(Jupille and Caporaso 1998), the Rio Conference stimulated further institutionalization of internal coordination.

The end of the Cold War and East–West relations

In the Cold War era, cooperation between Eastern and Western European countries on environmental issues was limited to a number of negotiations on trans-boundary air pollution. It was apparent that the problems of acid rain were so serious for countries in both East and West that joint action was necessary, even in a Cold War context. In the low profile and rather apolitical context of the United Nations Economic Commission for Europe (UNECE), Eastern and Western European countries, together with the United States and Canada, found a space to negotiate the Convention on Long-Range Transboundary Air Pollution (1979). Its main goal was to limit sulphur dioxide emissions (SO_2) in order to prevent acid rain and thus the eutrophication of lakes and the so-called *Waldsterben* (that is, the dying of forests) (Lidskog and Sundqvist 2002; Wettestad 2002). During the height of the Cold War, it was no small feat to establish this type of pan-European cooperation. In addition, it contributed to the institutionalization of at least some basic aspects of environmental policy-making in the future member states (for instance monitoring systems and basic scientific research).

The dominant Cold War meta-paradigm of a bi-polar world, dominated by security concerns, was a major hindrance to the conclusion of international environmental agreements between East and West in the 1970s and 1980s. The communist countries initially ignored any international responsibility for pollution and other environmental problems. They were not present in Stockholm and in general were apprehensive of strong MEAs. In addition, communist regimes were notoriously neglectful of domestic environmental problems. After the fall of the Berlin Wall, an abominable record of heavy industrial and nuclear pollution, horrible urban air quality, ecologically dead rivers and serious health consequences became visible. The new political reality in Europe and the rapid political realization that EU membership for the post-communist countries was possible and desirable increased the expectations placed on the latter that they should become more constructive partners in global environmental governance.

The Chernobyl nuclear accident of April 1986 had a major impact on post-Cold War environmental developments in Europe. The meltdown of the nuclear power plant of Chernobyl, in present Ukraine, led to serious political controversy between the Soviet Union and the member states of the EU. Although the leader of the Soviet Union Michail Gorbachov based his reform policies on the concept of *glasnost* – meaning 'openness' –, the Chernobyl accident was reported to the rest of Europe very late. Radioactive fallout in Scandinavia and Western Europe led to strong accusations of irresponsibility and the questioning of the trustworthiness of the communist leaders. The fact that citizens in Eastern European countries could count on even less solid information further delegitimized those political regimes. The accident also had an impact on energy policy in the EU and the member states. In particular it stirred up a debate about the place of nuclear energy in Europe's energy system.

In the early 1990s East–West relations were fundamentally changed by the end of the Cold War. Since the end of the Cold War, environmental issues have become more prominent in international politics. This is not only illustrated by the steady rise of the number of MEAs, but also by the growing practice of including environmental provisions in numerous international agreements, such as trade and development agreements. Moreover, the end of the Cold War marked the beginning of essentially different relations, which would ultimately lead to EU membership for all but a few Central and Eastern European countries (see Chapter 1) (Darst 2001; Wettestad 2002). Indeed, the most important consequence of the end of the Cold War for EU environmental politics is beyond any doubt that a large number of the ex-communist countries have joined the EU since 2004 (see Chapter 1). They have all had to adopt the *acquis communautaire* on the environment, as a result of which about 500 million people in highly industrialized countries now fall under the same stringent and legally binding environmental legislation. This spread of environmental policies to countries with a relatively low level of environmental protection is probably one of the largest steps forward in the history of EU environmental politics. In terms of the dynamics of global environmental politics, it means that a large portion of the industrialized world is coming to international negotiations as a single negotiating bloc. This certainly simplifies international negotiations and, to the extent the EU manages to act in a united way, it creates a larger potential political weight for the EU (see Chapter 10).

Globalization as a driving force

The multi-dimensional process of globalization, which the world has witnessed since the 1980s, has had a profound impact on Europe's environment and on the EU's role in global environmental politics. Understood as the spreading of a Western model of production and a consumerist lifestyle, globalization has large environmental consequences. Indeed, this model of production and consumption is based on intensive energy use, on increased material inputs and on the creation of environmental externalities. The diffusion of this model results in pollution, natural resources depletion, pressure on renewable resources, etc. (Bruyninckx 2013; Mol et al. 2005).

The spreading of industrialization to Asia and Latin America has caused notable pollution, issues of waste management and degradation of natural resources. Countries like China, India, Brazil, Mexico and others are by now major contributors to global environmental problems such as loss of biodiversity, global warming, deforestation and trade in hazardous waste (Bruyninckx 2013). In a very short time period they have become important and necessary actors in the formation of global environmental regimes. The impact on the EU's international environmental diplomacy is obvious (see Chapter 10). Whereas focusing on a limited number of key Western countries was sufficient to reach a functional consensus in the past, much more complex negotiations, with demands from new major players on the international scene, are nowadays the rule (Happaerts 2015). In other words, in processes of environmental regime formation, globalization requires institutional adaptation on the part of the EU.

Globalization also puts increasing pressure on the international competitiveness of EU member states and their industries. The argument that the stringent European environmental policies create an unequal playing field for European companies is a standard line in industry lobbying activities and it has become increasingly important with the globalization of production. The competitive advantage of countries like China with lower labour costs and more limited social protection compared to the situation in Europe causes enough difficulties, so the reasoning goes. Laying strict environmental policies on top of that is threatening employment and investment in European production capacity.

However, this reasoning is countered by the so-called Porter hypothesis. Here, the argument goes that countries with strong environmental policies and stringent implementation and compliance contexts are more competitive because environmental regulation drives innovation based on research and development, which creates first mover advantages for the frontrunners. As the general tendency in international environmental norm-setting goes in the direction of progressively higher stringency, this means that those who run ahead are not only setting the benchmarks for norms and standards, but are also more prepared to provide the necessary knowhow for others who will follow (Porter and van der Linde 1995). Many of the EU's environmental policy initiatives are taken in the spirit of the Porter hypothesis. However, at the same time, the conflicts between environmental protection and other (economic) priorities are a constant tension in the EU's environmental policies (see Chapter 7). The debate on 'carbon leakage' in the EU's climate change policies is a prominent example of this area of tension (see Chapter 9).

The EU and other global actors in international environmental politics

In many global environmental regimes, the EU has clear leadership ambitions (see Chapter 10). The EU's acclaimed position of environmental leadership relates to a large extent to the role of the United States in environmental politics, both domestically and internationally. In the mid-1980s, the United States evolved from being a first-mover on environmental issues to a laggard's position in international environmental politics (DeSombre 2011). Since the mid-1980s the United States has signed very few MEAs and hardly ratified any. Moreover, it lost a considerable amount of capacity in international environmental diplomacy. For example, during the Bush Jr. administration, it became increasingly difficult for bureaucrats in the Environmental Protection Agency to attend foreign conferences or to work on international issues. This all led to serious loss of credibility for the United States in international environmental politics and left a considerable void in terms of leadership at the global level.

The shift in the American position since the mid-1980s can be explained by domestic shifts in the position of the majority in the American Congress. From the late 1980s onwards, the conservative wing of the Republican Party acquired a fairly dominant position, which resulted in opposition to further environmental legislation, both domestically and internationally. In addition, a renewed emphasis on strong sovereignty coloured American foreign policy. Multilateralism, especially under the umbrella of the UN, was largely mistrusted, and any suggestion of transfer of domestic power in favour of collective decision making opposed. This stands in stark contrast to the EU's commitment to multilateralism, in the environmental field and beyond (Keukeleire and Delreux 2014). President Bush Sr. announced during his 1992 State of the Union Address that he would not take any environmental policy initiatives. During the Clinton and Bush Jr. years (respectively 1993–2000 and 2001–2008), Congress remained under the control of a majority that determined the basic US position in global environmental governance, namely disengagement (Schreurs 2004). Even though the Obama administration (2009-2016) showed more goodwill on environmental multilateralism, for instance by ratifying the Minamata Convention on mercury by executive order, the US position has not fundamentally changed.

Since the turn of the century, the EU's role in global environmental governance has also been influenced by the shifting power balances in the world, particularly towards Asia. China and increasingly also India have become crucial countries in the global system of production. As a result, they have gradually brought significant bargaining power to the table in global negotiations (Mol 2006). This is the case for economic, trade or security issues, but also for environmental ones. Concerns over the expanding externalities of especially China's, and to a lesser extent India's, growth have influenced the external environmental policy of the EU. It is by now just as much part of the standard operating procedure to contact China and India in preparation of international negotiations, as it is to talk to the United States.

One of the difficulties is that these emerging powers bring positions and demands to the table that do not fit easily with European world views or that require specific attention and action. An example of the former is the Chinese understanding of, and adherence to, sovereignty (as opposed to the EU's adherence to multilateralism), which has consequences for the way MEAs can be designed and for the extent to which they can impact on future domestic policies (Keukeleire and Delreux 2014). An example of a specific demand relates to the problem of financial mechanisms in environmental governance. China and India are two of the most prominent voices in the 'historic responsibilities' discourse (Gupta 2010).

This discourse states that industrialized countries are the largest contributors to global environmental problems and have a historic responsibility, because of the development process, which they have experienced since the industrial revolution. The necessity of keeping these countries on board means that the creation of financial mechanisms and technology transfer schemes has become an essential part of the puzzle.

Changing economic and political power relations at the global level have also caused significant movement in the institutional architecture of global governance. Global governance is increasingly conducted in informal systems of 'club governance'. Environmental governance is not an exception to this general trend, as it is progressively taking place in a number of fora where the major structural powers meet in a rather informal way (Happaerts 2015). This is, for instance, the case in the G7/8, which has been supplemented by the G20. The EU is a full participant is these meetings, alongside four of its member states (France, Germany, Italy and the UK). Environment, and particularly climate, policies have been a recurrent theme in the G7/8/20. The EU is also active in other more recent informal arenas where global environmental politics is a theme, such as the Major Economies Forum. The attention paid to the environment in the increasingly informal global governance architecture is illustrative of the importance of environmental issues and particularly their possible economic and security consequences in global politics.

Conclusions

This chapter has illustrated that the development of environmental politics in the EU cannot be fully understood if it is disconnected from the broader international evolutions in the field of environmental politics. Indeed, environmental politics – be it in the EU or elsewhere – takes place in an ever-changing macro-political context. The end of the Cold War and the process of rapid economic and political globalization are key illustrations of this point. The rise of a global dimension to environmental politics has also had a profound impact on the institutional organization of the EU. Internal coordination mechanisms have had to be developed, new competences added to the existing treaties and an environmental diplomacy established.

The external dimension of EU environmental policy and the role of the EU in global environmental negotiations and regimes will be explored in Chapter 10. Before that the internal side of EU environmental policy and politics will be examined. Indeed, since the EU's external environmental policy is also a reflection of its internal policies, the latter needs to be looked at first. This discussion begins with the next chapter, which sketches the main institutional architecture within which EU environmental policy is developed.

Chapter 3

Actors and Institutions

Who are the main actors in the EU that develop environmental policy? How do they function internally and what political dynamics determine their role in the formulation of EU environmental policy? This chapter addresses these questions by focusing on the five main institutions that develop European environmental policy, as well as on the agencies that play a particular role in the EU's institutional architecture. The European Commission, the European Parliament, the Council of the EU, the European Council, the Court of Justice and the agencies (European Environment Agency and the European Chemicals Agency) are successively discussed. The interactions between these institutions determine the shape, scope and impact of the resulting environmental policy. These policy-making processes will be discussed in Chapter 4.

Figure 3.1 presents the basic institutional structure for the EU environmental policy-making process. The Commission, the Council and the Parliament form the so-called institutional triangle. They are the central players in the traditional policy-making process, linked together in an interdependent relationship. The Commission proposes legislation, which is then mostly amended and adopted by the two co-legislators: the Council and the European Parliament. The European Council and the Court of Justice are situated outside the institutional triangle, but they are equally important for understanding EU environmental policy-making. Determining the broad strategies of the EU, the European Council comes into the picture before the actual policy-making process in the institutional triangle starts. The Court of Justice plays its main role after the policy has been adopted as it judges questions related to implementation (see Chapter 4). This institutional structure is not specific for environmental policy-making in the EU, as most European policies – with the major exception of EU foreign policy – are developed in this way and by these institutions.

FIGURE 3.1   *The institutional structure for EU environmental policy-making*

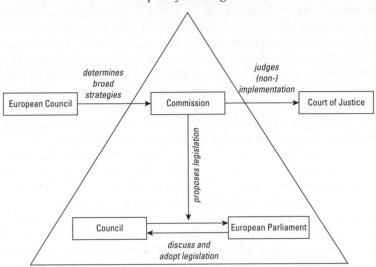

European Commission

A hybrid institution with a political and a bureaucratic branch

As the EU's main executive body, the European Commission is a hybrid institution insofar as it is partly political (the College of Commissioners) and partly bureaucratic (the administrative services and Directorate-Generals).

First of all, the Commission plays a political role. It consists of twenty-eight Commissioners, one per member state. Formally speaking, the Commission must be independent and it represents the interests of the EU as a whole. Individual Commissioners are not supposed to represent the interests or positions of their own member state in the policy-making process. However, as they often experience pressure from their home country to act in a particular way, and as they rely on their national government for a possible renewal of their mandate, Commissioners do not achieve full impartiality and independence from national instructions in practice (Nugent 2010). Each Commissioner, supported by a small cabinet of personal advisers, holds a particular portfolio. One portfolio includes environmental policy and another one includes climate action. Only since 2010 and the Barroso II Commission have climate policies no longer been part of the environment portfolio but administered by a separate Climate Action Commissioner (see Table 3.1 for an overview of the Environment and Climate Action Commissioners in the history of the European Commission). The creation of a separate Climate Action portfolio in the Commission in 2010 was not only the result of the EU's growing priorities on climate change policies, but also of the enlargement of the EU and the ongoing rule that every member state sends one Commissioner to Brussels, which required the creation of new portfolios.

In November 2014, the Commission team under the presidency of Jean-Claude Juncker took office. In this Commission, the Environment portfolio is held by the Maltese social-democrat Karmenu Vella, who is also competent for maritime affairs and fisheries. Climate action is administered by Miguel Arias Cañete from Spain, who also has energy policy in his portfolio. The choice of these commissioners, the mandates they received from Commission President Juncker and the new structure of the European Commission raised concerns among environmental NGOs and members of the European Parliament about a downgrading of environmental issues in the Juncker Commission. The withdrawal of the circular economy package was seen as an indication of the lowered environmental ambitions of the new Commission (see Chapters 1 and 7). The Green 10, which is a group of ten major European environmental NGOs, even suggested that this set-up would lead to a '*de facto* shut down of EU environmental policy making' (Green 10 2014: 2).

The initial concerns about the environmental portfolios of the Juncker Commission were threefold. First, questions were raised about the environmental commitment and the independence of the Environment and Climate Action Commissioners. Second, Juncker's mission letter for Commissioner Vella was considered to be too strongly based on a deregulation agenda. Third, merging the climate action and environment portfolios with energy and fisheries and maritime affairs respectively was interpreted as a move away from sustainability and a devaluation of environmental and climate policies in the Commission. Indeed, not having a Commissioner exclusively responsible for Climate Action was even seen as conveying a mistaken and unambitious message to the EU's international partners in the run-up to the 2015 Paris climate change conference. As a response to these criticisms, President Juncker argued that

Table 3.1 *Environment and Climate Action Commissioners*

period	Commission President	Environment Commissioner	nationality	political colour
1973–1977	Ortoli	Carlo Scarascia-Mugnozza	Italy	centre-right
1977–1981	Jenkins	Lorenzo Natali	Italy	centre-right
1981–1984	Thorn	Karl-Heinz Narjes	Germany	centre-right
1985–1988	Delors	Stanley Clinton Davis	UK	social-democrat
1989–1992	Delors	Carlo Ripa di Meana	Italy	social-democrat
1992–1993	Delors	Karel Van Miert	Belgium	social-democrat
1993–1995	Delors	Ioannis Paleokrassas	Greece	centre-right
1995–1999	Santer	Ritt Bjerregaard	Denmark	social-democrat
1999–2004	Prodi	Margot Wallström	Sweden	social-democrat
2004–2009	Barroso	Stavros Dimas	Greece	centre-right
2009–2014	Barroso	Janez Potočnik (Environment)	Slovenia	liberal
		Connie Hedegaard (Climate Action)	Denmark	centre-right
2014–2019	Juncker	Karmenu Vella (Environment)	Malta	social-democrat
		Miguel Arias Cañete (Climate Action)	Spain	centre-right

Vella's portfolio reflected the interlinkages between 'green growth' (see Chapters 1 and 6) and 'blue growth' (referring to the claim that maritime sectors have a large potential to contribute to economic growth) and that the construction of Cañete's climate-energy portfolio reflected the important role of renewable energy in the EU's climate policy.

The two Commissioners cannot run their portfolios completely autonomously. In the Juncker Commission, they both work under Vice-President of the Commission responsible for the Energy Union, the Slovak social-democrat Maroš Šefčovič, whose task it is to coordinate the work of Commissioners with related portfolios, but whose approval is also needed before an issue can be placed on the agenda of the College of Commissioners. Moreover, the first Vice-President of the Commission, the Dutch social-democrat Frans Timmermans, has been given responsibility for sustainable development (which was considered to be a concession by Juncker so as to receive the necessary support of the European Parliament for his Commission, after the social-democrats had raised questions about the candidature of Climate Action Commissioner Cañete). Another reason why the autonomy of individual Commissioners is limited is that all Commission decisions need to be taken in the College, which is the meeting of the twenty-eight Commissioners. Although the College can formally take decisions on the basis of majority voting, the norm is to strive for consensus. Moreover, the collegiality principle applies in the College, meaning that, once a decision is taken, every Commissioner is supposed to defend and implement it.

Besides its political element, the Commission also has a bureaucratic element. The Commission's bureaucracy consists of services (such as the Publications Office and the Legal Service) and thirty-three Directorates-General (DGs). Each DG is responsible for one or more policy area(s). The two DGs that play a major role in the EU's environmental policy-making are DG Environment (DG ENV, previously known as 'DG XI') and DG Climate Action (DG CLIMA). DG Environment is currently internally organized into six substantive Directorates: Green economy; Natural capital; Quality of Life, Water & Air; Implementation, Governance and Semester; Global & Regional Challenges, LIFE; and Strategy. Since 2010, DG Climate Action has been a separate Directorate-General for climate change policies, consisting of three substantive Directorates: International & Climate Strategy; European & International Carbon Markets; and Mainstreaming Adaptation &

Low Carbon Technology (on the establishment of DG CLIMA in 2010, see Schoenefeld 2014a). Importantly, in contrast to the mergers in the portfolios of the Commissioners, there are still separate DGs for Climate Action (CLIMA), Energy (ENER), Environment (ENV) and Maritime Affairs and Fisheries (MARE).

Like the other DGs, the DGs Environment and Climate Action are made up of a combination of EU officials and national experts who are temporarily seconded to the EU administration. In 2014, 500 officials were employed in DG Environment and 154 in DG Climate Action, counting for 1.5 and 0.5 per cent, respectively, of the overall Commission staff. Other DGs in closely related, yet also frequently competing, policy areas (see below), can count on a larger staff (for example almost 900 in DG Enterprise and Industry, or more than 1000 in DG Agriculture and Rural Development) (European Commission 2014a). Compared to the amount of European environmental policies and the legislative output in this domain, the staff numbers of DGs Environment and Climate Action are very limited. Consequently, their administrative capacity is restricted. These figures also sharply contrast with the emphasis that is sometimes put on the EU's international environmental leadership (see Chapter 10) and with the way in which environmental – and especially climate – policies are prioritized in the Commission's political guidelines. For example, leading on climate change was announced as one of the five priorities in the 2009–2014 political guidelines of the Barroso II Commission (Barroso 2009).

Agenda-setting

The main function of the European Commission in the environmental policy-making process is drafting policy proposals. The Commission is indeed the first mover in the policy-making process and enjoys the exclusive right of initiative. This means that every environmental policy-making process starts with an initiative of the European Commission and that environmental policies cannot be adopted without a Commission proposal. Nevertheless, the agenda-setting power of the Commission is not that exclusive in practice, since other actors and institutions habitually pressurize the Commission to take the first formal step in the policy-making process. The Commission's formal agenda-setting powers are challenged by four dynamics.

First, since the heads of state and government in the European Council determine the strategic lines of the EU's policies, agenda-setting on highly politicized environmental issues, such as overall climate targets, is in practice often the result of a ping-pong game between the Commission and the European Council. In recent years, the European Council's powers as *de facto* agenda-setter have increased in practice (see below).

Second, individual member states (see Bailer 2014) as well as interest groups (see Chapter 5) also pressurize the Commission. They can do so in both informal and more institutionalized contacts with the Commission. Moreover, member states can also urge the Commission to take a certain initiative by tabling a policy initiative at the national level in the hope that the Commission takes it up at the EU level.

Third, since EU environmental policy does not originate and develop in a global vacuum (see Chapter 2), the international context can force the Commission to become active on a particular environmental issue. After the EU has become a party to a multilateral environmental agreement, the Commission for instance often needs to initiate legislation in order to implement the international commitments of the EU (see Chapter 10).

Fourth, the Treaties allow the European Parliament, the Council and a group of at least one million citizens (the latter through the so-called European Citizens Initiative, ECI) to request the Commission to initiate legislation. Although the Commission is not obliged to follow such requests and to table a policy proposal accordingly, they have an important signalling function. After the creation of the ECI by the Lisbon Treaty, the first initiative that was accepted by the European Commission had an important environmental dimension. It asked the Commission to propose legislation to ensure the provision of water and sanitation as a fundamental human right. The Commission responded that it would enhance its efforts on this matter within the implementation of existing legislation (see Chapter 4) and it launched a public consultation (see below) on the quality of drinking water, but it refrained from proposing any new or additional legislation (European Commission 2014b).

Internal coordination

When drafting new environmental policy initiatives, DG Environment or DG Climate Action are usually the 'lead service', which is the

DG that is responsible for drafting the policy proposal. Being the lead service can enable a DG to promote its own interests in a dossier and in consequence the appointment of the lead service can sometimes be heavily disputed (Hartlapp et al. 2013). For example, the decision whether DG Climate Action or DG Enterprise and Industry is to be responsible for drafting the 'proposal for a regulation to reduce CO_2 emissions from new passenger cars' is likely to have an impact on the compromise that is made between the environmental and economic issues at stake.

In general, DGs Environment and Climate Action do indeed take the lead in the Commission for the preparation of environmental policy, but given the integrative and cross-sectorial nature of environmental policy, other DGs need to be involved as well. The Commission's fragmented institutional structure, with each policy area covered by a separate DG, neither favours coordination between policy areas nor does it allow for strong horizontal policies (Kassim et al. 2013; Smith 2014). As for environmental policy, this institutional fragmentation often contradicts the environmental integration principle (see Chapters 1 and 7), and, more fundamentally, the cross-sectorial nature of environmental policy. Indeed, in order to achieve effective environmental policy, linkages with other policy areas, such as agriculture, transport or industry, are often needed. The sectorial fragmentation in the Commission can hinder this inclusive environmental policy approach. Combined with the environmental integration principle, it also implies that DG Environment and DG Climate Action cannot draft policy proposals in isolation and only within the boundaries of their DG. As a result, intra-Commission coordination for environmental policy is a prerequisite for fulfilling the environmental integration principle. This coordination has two components: DGs Environment and Climate Action need to present their own proposals to other DGs concerned, and they have to contribute the environmental or climate perspective in the work of the other DGs. Intra-Commission coordination is organized both at the administrative and at the political level (for an in-depth case study of the development within the Commission of the Emissions Trading Scheme and the 2020 climate and energy package, see Dreger 2014).

In the administrative branch, coordination is arranged through a couple of mechanisms. DGs Environment and Climate Action usually send their draft proposals to a selection of other DGs in order to get feedback from the perspective of different policy areas (Spence

2006). The Commission's Secretariat-General is supposed to coordinate the activities of the different DGs. Furthermore, informal contacts between the responsible officials for a particular dossier in various DGs and meetings between the Directors-General are meant to strengthen administrative coordination. In the past, the effectiveness of inter-DG coordination has often been questioned since DGs regularly tried to circumvent internal coordination rather than to look cooperatively for common solutions, particularly in the case of environmental policy (Knill and Liefferink 2007; McCormick 2001). Rivalries between DGs and the interests related to their policy domain often characterize the internal decision-making process in the Commission. However, since the Barroso Commission, a couple of new initiatives have been introduced to improve internal coordination between DGs, which seem to be quite effective (Kassim et al. 2013). One of the major and most effective initiatives was the strengthening of the role of the Secretariat-General, as the latter oversees the so-called Interservice Consultations in order to make sure that an initiative is consistent with the overall political programme of the Commission and with initiatives prepared by other DGs. The role of the Secretariat-General has become even more important since the Juncker Commission due to the new Commission structure, where the Vice-Presidents do not steer 'their' own DGs but rely on the administrative resources of the Secretariat-General. Next to the Interservice Consultations, an Interservice Coordination Group with officials from multiple DGs can be established for policy initiatives that require repeated and long-term inter-DG coordination. For instance, the 'Interservice Group on Forests' brings together officials from, among others, DG Environment, DG Agriculture and Rural Development, DG Trade and DG Climate Action.

Another relatively recent procedure that can trigger cooperation rather than conflict between DGs is the impact assessment procedure. Here, the Commission is supposed to assess the expected social, economic and environmental consequences of every legislative and non-legislative policy initiative of significant importance. This indeed implies that the environmental consequences of the Commission's policy initiatives are calculated and quantified from the very beginning of the policy-making process. The impact assessment procedure is said to have 'reduced the habit of thinking about proposals in departmental silos, and increased the control of the Secretariat-General on the overall process of policy formulation'

(Radaelli and Meuwese 2010: 148). Although conducting impact assessments has become an established practice in the Commission and the quality of the Commission's impact assessment reports has now become satisfactory, their findings are still insufficiently integrated in the policy-making process (Adelle et al. 2012) and they are said to involve little added value (Krämer 2012a).

Next to intra-Commission coordination between the DGs at the administrative level, internal coordination also takes place in the Commission's political branch. Here, the Vice-President for the Energy Union can play an important role in steering and coordinating the work of the Environment and Climate Action Commissioners. Moreover, the cabinets of the other Commissioners, including the Vice-Presidents, play a crucial role. Their activity intensifies in the end game of the drafting at the administrative level. Any earlier involvement of the cabinets in drafting is relatively exceptional and, when it happens, it indicates the importance of a dossier for a particular Commissioner. All cabinets receive the draft proposals from DG Environment or DG Climate Action. Before this text is submitted to the College of Commissioners, the *chefs de cabinet* and the staff members of each cabinet who follow environmental dossiers meet weekly in their so-called hebdo meetings to discuss the draft proposal in order to incorporate the interests of the various Commissioners. Hence, environmental policy is not exclusively administered by the Environment and Climate Action Commissioners and their cabinets, but by a large number of various cabinets, depending on their interest in the issue (Christiansen 2006a). Finally, since the College needs to officially approve the Commission proposal, every Commissioner has a final chance to influence the proposal in that setting.

Consultation

DG Environment and Climate Action not only coordinate with their fellow DGs in the drafting process of new environmental policies, but they also engage in frequent exchanges with stakeholders and other political actors. Due to the limited administrative capacity of DG Environment and DG Climate Action, they seek expertise outside the Commission. Moreover, by consulting stakeholders and experts from member states, the Commission not only gathers expertise and information, but it also aims to acquire legitimacy and political support for its initiatives (Poppelaars 2009).

Alongside informal contacts between Commission officials and bureaucrats from the member states' administrations (Haverland and Liefferink 2012; Martens 2008), the Commission has established a broad range of more institutionalized consultation instruments that are employed when new policy initiatives are prepared and drafted. Obviously, these instruments do not only serve consultation purposes for the Commission, but they also serve as lobby venues for interest groups (see Chapter 5) (Quittkat and Kotzian 2011).

One way of consulting interested parties is through public or online consultations, where stakeholders and citizens have the opportunity to respond to a Commission survey on a future policy initiative. DG Environment is one of the most active users of the online consultation tool in the Commission (Quittkat 2011) with more than 150 organized consultations since 2000 (European Commission 2014c). Some consultations have led to broad mobilization, as witnessed by the almost 6400 contributions to the consultation prior to the REACH Regulation on chemicals (see Chapter 7). However, the same example also shows that broad participation does not necessarily imply equal participation, as industry and national actors from the biggest member states were overrepresented compared to, respectively, environmental NGOs and transnational actors (Persson 2007).

Next to public consultations, expert groups play an especially important role in the drafting process of environmental policy. Expert groups are consultative bodies, composed of experts from the member states and/or interest groups who advise the Commission on the policy initiatives the latter is preparing. Although scientists and interest group representatives play an important role in the expert groups, government officials from the member states are the principal actors and the Commission seems to rely primarily on the input of member state officials (Gornitzka and Sverdrup 2011; Haverland and Liefferink 2012). This is particularly true for the expert groups that are consulted by DG Environment, where one third of the expert groups are exclusively composed of officials coming from national administrations. As neither the existence nor the employment of expert groups is regulated in the Treaties, the Commission can autonomously create and dismantle them (Larsson and Murk 2007). The system of expert groups therefore resembles a patchwork and it is hard to draw general conclusions about their composition, impact and actual functioning. While the number of expert groups organized by DG Environment increased considerably in the period 2000–2007 to 127 expert groups (Gornitzka and Sverdrup 2008), the number of expert groups consulted by DG Environment and DG Climate Action then decreased to 64 expert groups more recently and is now relatively stable (European Commission 2014d).

Expert groups perform two main functions. On the one hand, they provide the Commission with valuable comments and suggestions about the topic of the policy proposal. This information function is particularly relevant for DG Environment, since it has a relatively limited capacity compared to other DGs in terms of staff members (see above). The Commission can also use this information later on in the policy-making process in order to reach a deal between the Council and the Parliament in an attempt to rationalize the debate (see Chapter 4). On the other hand, involving non-Commission actors in the early stages of the policy-making process allows the Commission to anticipate the formers' likely reactions later on in the policy-making process. This rationale is based on the fact that both the support of the member states (in the adoption phase in the Council) and the backing of interest groups (in the implementation phase) are required for an effective environmental policy. It does not mean, however, that expert groups are intended to function as the forum for national interest representation in the policy-making process. The officials from national administrations are not bound to national instructions, as they mostly participate in the expert groups in their capacity of (independent) 'expert', although their national background is rarely fully ignored. Moreover, in this drafting stage, member state positions often still need to be developed (Spence 2006).

European Parliament

Composition and function

The European Parliament (EP) is the institution where 751 directly elected representatives (MEPs, Members of the European Parliament) gather. The EP meets both in Brussels and in Strasbourg. It is internally organized along ideological – and not territorial – lines. Indeed, MEPs do not form national delegations with their compatriots, but transnational political groups with colleagues from fellow political families. The eight political groups in the current EP

(2014–2019) are the Group of the European People's Party (EPP Group), the Group of the Progressive Alliance of Socialists & Democrats (S&D), the Alliance of Liberals and Democrats for Europe (ALDE), the Greens/European Free Alliance (Greens/EFA), the European Conservatives and Reformists Group (ECR), the Confederal Group of the European United Left/Nordic Green Left (GUE/NGL), the Europe of Freedom and Direct Democracy Group (EFDD), and Europe of Nations and Freedom (ENF). The Green/EFA political group has always occupied between 5 per cent and 8 per cent of the seats since a green group was formed in 1989. Together with S&D and GUE/NGL, this group is traditionally the strongest defender of far-reaching environmental policy in the Parliament.

The EP's internal organization by political groups does not mean that nationality – and thus national interests – does not matter in the EP. Since MEPs are elected in national electoral districts and since they are dependent on their national constituencies for possible re-election, nationally inspired concerns are likely to affect their parliamentary behaviour. However, MEPs in general overwhelmingly vote along the lines of their political groups and not according to the interest of their member state (Hix et al. 2007). In the 2009–2014 parliamentary term, 91 per cent of the MEPs voted along the lines of their political group in the 138 plenary votes on environmental issues, suggesting a considerable level of group cohesion on environmental votes (our own calculations on the basis of Votewatch 2014).

The EP has both unique and traditional institutional characteristics. On the one hand, the EP has unique intra-parliamentary dynamics and it does not work like a typical national parliament because the Commission is not based on permanent majority in the EP. Consequently, the functioning of the EP is not characterized by a government-versus-opposition game. Instead, environmental policy-making in the EU is characterized by case-by-case majority building, making the parliamentary working less predictable – yet more intriguing – than in many national parliaments. Hence, environmental policies adopted in the same parliamentary term do not necessarily reflect the same majority. On the other hand, the EP has a couple of features similar to those of traditional national parliaments. First, it has the power to control the institution that performs executive functions, namely the Commission, although this power is not as far-reaching as in certain national political systems. Second, the EP has become an increasingly important actor in the legislative (and budgetary) processes in the EU. Today, the EP is a fully-fledged co-legislator on environmental policy, together with the Council.

The EP has not always been a co-legislator on environmental affairs. The EP's legislative powers have grown in recent decades since successive Treaty revisions have introduced new procedures granting more powers to the EP, and they have extended the range of issues subject to those procedures. Until the mid-1980s and the entry into force of the Single European Act (1987, see Chapter 1), parliamentary involvement in EU environmental policy-making was limited to the consultation procedure, meaning that the EP could only give non-binding opinions to the Council, which then had full decision-making powers on EU legislation. EP involvement increased with the introduction of the cooperation procedure in the SEA, as this procedure grants the EP the right of a second reading of the proposed legislation, although it still leaves the final decision with the Council. While the cooperation procedure does not at first sight grant a high degree of influence to the EP, this may be a misleading view, since this procedure allowed the EP to act as a 'conditional agenda-setter' (Tsebelis 1994). The codecision procedure, introduced by the Maastricht Treaty (1993) and expanded to most environmental issues under the Amsterdam (1999), Nice (2003) and Lisbon Treaties (2009), gives the EP the status of veto-player in the legislative process. While retaining the basic rationale and the steps of the codecision procedure, the Lisbon Treaty changed the name of this procedure into 'ordinary legislative procedure'. Under this procedure (see Chapter 4), the EP and the Council are on an equal footing in the policy-making process, with the agreement of both institutions needed to adopt EU environmental legislation. Importantly, the EP also has veto power in the EU's ratification decision on international environmental agreements. In other words, the EP must give its consent before the EU can become a party to such an international treaty (see Chapter 10).

Although the EP's major function in the environmental policy field is its role as co-legislator, its activities are not limited to that. First, it also issues non-legislative reports and resolutions dealing with environmental issues. These reports and resolutions deal with a wide range of issues related to EU environmental policy, ranging from the EP's position on an upcoming international environmental or climate change conference, the EP's views on non-legislative policy initiatives by the European Commission (such as communications, see

Chapter 6), or implementation problems with environmental policy in a particular area. Second, the EP organizes hearings and votes on the appointment of new Commissioners. In 2014, the EP was able to reject the Slovenian Commissioner-designate Alenka Bratušek who would have become the Vice-President for Energy Union in the Juncker Commission, where she would have coordinated the work of the Environment and Climate Commissioners. After her poor performance when she was challenged in the hearing, the EP resisted her candidacy and the Slovak Maroš Šefčovič was given the Vice-Presidency (see above). Third, once Commissioners are in office, the responsible parliamentary committee invites them each year for a so-called structured dialogue. Fourth, the Environment and Climate Action Commissioners engage from time to time in an *ad hoc* exchange of views with the environment committee (ENVI Committee, see below). Similarly, the Committee also organizes occasional meetings with other actors, such as representatives of the European Environment Agency (see below) or the Environment minister of the rotating Presidency, who presents the Presidency programme in the beginning of its term. Fifth, MEPs can also table questions to the Commission, which are either answered in writing or during question time sessions in the ENVI Committee. During the 2009–2014 term, question time sessions were organized on around forty environmental issues and topics (European Parliament 2014a). Finally, the EP also reaches out to non-EU actors in the environmental field. The ENVI Committee therefore organizes joint meetings with representatives of national parliaments to discuss environmental or climate issues. It also sends delegations to member states, accession countries and agencies, as well as occasionally to international environmental negotiations (mainly to the annual climate change conferences) (see Chapter 10). Next to its veto power when ratifying international agreements, the EP thus also has a number of more indirect ways of being involved in global environmental governance (Biedenkopf 2015).

ENVI Committee

Intra-EP decision-making is relatively decentralized, since the main work is largely done within the committee structure and since the committees enjoy quite a high level of autonomy in the EP's structure (Shackleton 2006). One of the twenty standing committees is the one on 'Environment, Public Health and Food Safety' ('ENVI

Committee'). In contrast to the situation in the Commission, where there is an institutional division between DG Environment and DG Climate Action (see above), climate change policies in the EP are still dealt with in the ENVI Committee and there is no separate committee for climate change. The ENVI Committee is not only one of the largest (sixty-nine members), but also one of the most important committees in the EP. The latter is due to the large number of environmental issues governed by the ordinary legislative procedure, which causes the ENVI Committee to incur a heavy workload. In the 2009–2014 term, the ENVI Committee was responsible for the highest number of legislative proposals falling under the ordinary legislative procedure of all EP committees (European Parliament 2014a). It is usually composed of MEPs with a special interest and/or expertise in environmental issues (McElroy 2006; Yordanova 2009). The European Parliament can also establish temporary committees to deal with a specific issue. In 2007, the Temporary Committee on Climate Change (CLIM) was set up to prepare the legislation needed to implement the climate and energy package (see Chapter 9) and to formulate the EP position for the upcoming international climate change negotiations in Copenhagen (see Chapter 10) (Burns 2012a).

When a legislative proposal of the European Commission arrives at the Parliament, the ENVI Committee is usually appointed as the 'responsible committee', that is, the one in charge of preparing a report with the EP's amendments for the plenary. Committees dealing with other policy areas that are also affected by the proposal can request to give an opinion (or indeed the ENVI Committee can ask the opinion of another committee). In most environmental policy-making processes in the EP there are a number of such 'committees for opinion'. For instance, on the F-gases Regulation (517/2004, see Chapter 9), ENVI was the responsible committee and the Industry, Research and Energy (ITRE), Internal Market and Consumer Protection (IMCO) and the Transport and Tourism (TRAN) Committees were able to give their opinion before the report was sent to plenary.

Given the horizontal nature of many environmental policy initiatives, it may also happen that a legislative file falls almost equally within the competence of the ENVI Committee and one or more other committees. In this case, the 'associated committee procedure' is followed and the responsibility for drafting a report is shared between multiple committees. Examples of an associated committee procedure include five of the six pieces of legislation that were negotiated in parallel on the so-called European Climate Change Package in 2008 and for which both the ENVI Committee and the ITRE Committee were responsible (Burns 2013). Although the associated committee procedure is likely to produce a weaker environmental position of the EP (Smith 2008), it is also plausible that such a procedure makes the committee report more easily acceptable to the plenary. Moreover, the associated committees normally seek a consensus in a cooperative way, although there are sometimes exceptions to this consensus-seeking rule. During the parliamentary debates on the Passenger Car Regulation (443/2009), for example, the leading ENVI Committee supported the Commission proposal, whereas the associated ITRE Committee aligned with the industry, leading to disputes between the two committees (Burns 2013).

After substantive discussions of the proposed environmental legislation, the ENVI Committee adopts a report with the amendments it wants to see included in the legislative proposal and sends it to the plenary for final adoption. The three political groups that are considered to be the most environmentally friendly ones (S&D, Greens/EFA and GUE/NGL) are the most successful groups in terms of getting their amendments adopted by the ENVI Committee. Hence, MEPs who are responsive to the concerns of environmental NGOs (see Chapter 5), are more likely to be successful in the ENVI Committee, causing Hurka to conclude that 'the lower an MEP's commitment for environmental protection, the lower her chance to get amendments fully adopted' (Hurka 2013: 289).

Key actors: committee chair and rapporteurs

Two members of the ENVI Committee play a key role in every policy-making process: the chair and the rapporteur. Whereas the former is appointed for two and a half years, the latter varies from legislative proposal to legislative proposal. The chair guides the discussion and guarantees the overall credibility, influence and political weight of the Committee. It is often said that the political leadership of the British ENVI Committee chairman Ken Collins from the social-democrats (1979–1984 and 1989–1999) enhanced the reputation of the ENVI Committee as a strong defender of the environmental interest (Weale et al. 2007). Under the leadership of this Labour politician, the ENVI Committee was transformed from a rather weak to an influential actor in EU environmental policy-making. His successors, respectively, the British and German centre-right MEPs Caroline Jackson (1999–2004) and Karl-Heinz Florenz (2004–2007), continued on this track (Burns 2012a). The ENVI Committee's reputation of environmental entrepreneurship plummeted in the following years under the chairmanship of the conservative Czech Miroslav Ouzky, who was an 'inexperienced east European MEP [...] with no record of interest in environmental issues' (Burns et al. 2012: 66). In the 2009–2014 term, the German social-democrats Jo Leinen (2009–2012) and Matthias Groote (2012–2014), who again had an environmental background, re-established the reputation of the ENVI Committee. In July 2014, the centre-right Italian Giovanni La Via was elected as the new ENVI Committee chair.

The rapporteur is the MEP who drafts the report with the EP amendments to the Commission proposal, making him/her the key actor in the development of the EP position on a legislative proposal. There is one rapporteur for each legislative file who becomes the central EP actor in the policy-making process. The rapporteur is also the key actor in conducting the negotiations with the Council on the legislative proposal for which he or she is responsible (see Chapter 4). Holding 'the most important leadership role on any given proposal', the rapporteur holds one of the most powerful positions in the policy-making process (Costello and Thomson 2010: 220). The rapporteur's main function is to build a consensus in the ENVI Committee (and later on also in the plenary) in order to maximize the cohesion of the EP in the negotiations with its fellow legislator – the Council – in so-called trilogues (see Chapter 4) (Finke 2012; Settembri and Neuhold 2009). The other political groups, those which are not providing the rapporteur for a specific legislative proposal, usually appoint their own 'shadow rapporteur' who closely follows the work of the rapporteur and who is the leading MEP for a particular dossier for his or her political group. Rapporteurships are allocated through a bidding system: each political group receives a certain number of points according to its size, which it can use to make bids on behalf of the group to 'win' a particular rapporteurship (Kaeding 2004). The allocation of the rapporteurship to a specific MEP is then undertaken within the political group. In the ENVI Committee, rapporteurships are proportionally spread among the various political groups (Yordanova 2009). In general, MEPs with parliamentary experience in the ENVI Committee and policy expertise on the environmental issue at hand are likely to get more (or more important) reports (Benedetto 2005; Yordanova 2013; Yoshinaka et al. 2010).

The EP as an environmental champion?

The EP generally has a considerable ability to find compromises on environmental issues. In the 2009–2014 term, 138 plenary votes took place on environmental matters and the average majority consisted of 82.7 per cent (our own calculations on the basis of Votewatch 2014). Also in the ENVI Committee, the average support for adopting reports takes a similar shape (Neuhold and Settembri 2007), which demonstrates both the consensus-building role of the rapporteur and the consensual nature of environmental policy-making in the EP. However, there have been some notable exceptions where the Parliament was completely divided and, consequently, majorities very tight. Most of these antagonistic votes dealt with climate change policies and more particularly with the EU Emissions Trading Scheme, the auctioning of greenhouse gas allowances and the risk of carbon leakage (see Chapter 9).

The EP has long been considered as the greenest institution in the EU institutional triangle and the EU's environmental champion (Weale et al. 2000), yet this picture needs to be nuanced for the period since the early 2000s (Burns et al. 2013). The EP has indeed become less environmentally radical since its 1999–2004 term. Not only have its amendments to the Commission proposals become less green over time, their number has decreased as well (Burns et al. 2012). This might reflect the shift of the political centre of gravity towards the centre-right in the EU institutions in this period. Other possible explanations for this declining greenness of the EP include, first, the increasing practice of adopting environmental legislation in first reading (see Chapter 4), which means that the EP's amendments nowadays already contain a compromise with the Council instead of an uncompromised EP position. Second, the EP has increasingly become a target for business lobby groups and no longer solely for environmental NGOs (see Chapter 5). Finally, the increased policy coordination between the Parliamentary committees, which has reduced the dominance of the ENVI Committee, has also diminished the EP's role as environmental champion (Rasmussen 2012).

Council

Functioning, member states' positions and voting rules

Whereas the European Commission ensures that the common European interest is incorporated in the environmental policy-making process and the directly elected European Parliament represents the interest of the European citizens, the interests of the member states are brought into the policy-making process through the Council of the EU (or briefly: the Council). This is the institution where the governments of the member states meet. The Council has been the main legislator in the EU environmental policy-making system, yet with the gradually increasing number of environmental subdomains governed by the ordinary legislative procedure, the Council nowadays shares this legislative power with the European Parliament (see above).

Formally, there is only one Council of the EU. In practice, however, there are various sectorial Council configurations, and the attendees differ according to the policy area at stake. One of the Council configurations is the Environment Council, which is composed of the Environment ministers from the member states. Besides Environment ministers, the Environment or Climate Action Commissioner and a representative of the Council Secretariat also attend these meetings. The fact that the Council meets in multiple sectorial configurations is a challenge to the EU's environmental policy integration principle, which urges the EU to treat environmental policy in connection with other policy areas that might have an impact on the environment (see Chapters 1 and 7) (Wurzel 2012). The structure of the Council impedes this, since environmental policy is discussed there in an 'environment only' configuration. This problem has been recognized, which has led to the so-called Cardiff process, requiring the other Council configurations to take environmental concerns into account in their activities (see Chapter 7).

The Environment Council's main institutional feature is thus to include member state interests in the environmental policy-making process. Although the distribution of preferences among the member states on environmental policy varies a good deal from issue to issue and from legislative proposal to legislative proposal, there are some trends in the positions they take in the Council. Member states such as Austria, Denmark, Finland, Germany, the Netherlands and Sweden are usually called 'environmental leaders' in the EU. However, not only does this characterization date from the EU15 era (e.g. Jordan and Liefferink 2004; McCormick 2001), which makes it difficult to extrapolate it to the current situation, but also more recently leaders such as Germany or the Netherlands have 'lost some of [their] appetite to lead' in EU environmental policy-making (Wurzel 2012: 90). On climate change policies in particular (see Chapter 9), Denmark, France, Austria, Germany, Portugal, Slovakia and Sweden are considered to be the leaders, whereas member states such as Estonia, Ireland, Poland or Romania usually have more conservative positions (European Council on Foreign Relations 2015).

The extent to which a member state generally supports or opposes strong environmental legislation in the EU depends to a large extent on its economic development, which in its turn affects both the preferences and the capacity for action of a particular member state in the environmental domain (Börzel 2002). This presumably explains why member states such as Spain, Portugal, Greece and some of the Central and Eastern European member states are mostly characterized as 'laggards' in the environmental area (Lenschow 2005). However, economic development is not the only criterion determining the extent of environmental leadership among the member states. Strong institutionalized traditions in environmental policy-making, as is the case in the Netherlands or Germany for example, make certain member states a leader to a greater extent than others with a similar level of economic development.

How are the twenty-eight national positions that are defended around the negotiation table of the Environment Council combined into a single position? Two formal voting rules to aggregate the member states' preferences and to come to a decision are used in the Environment Council: qualified majority voting (QMV) and unanimity. First, QMV is more than a simple majority of the members of the Environment Council. It is a *qualified* majority, which is defined by two necessary conditions. The first condition states that at least 55 per cent of the member states need to support the adoption of a decision. The second one implies that those member states need to represent at least 65 per cent of the EU's population. Moreover, to form a blocking minority in the Council, at least four member states are required. Second, unanimity implies that every member state has to agree and that, consequently, every member state has a veto power.

Which voting rule – QMV or unanimity – is applicable in a particular policy-making process depends on the issue at stake, and more in particular on the Treaty article on which the proposal for legislation on this issue is based. Legislation based on Article 192§1 TFEU is handled by the Environment Council on the basis of QMV (see Box 1.2). Today, the lion's share of EU environmental policy is adopted through QMV. Article 192§2 TFEU lists the only exceptions of legislation that still require unanimity: taxation; land management, quantitative management for water resources and land use (with the exception of waste management); and matters affecting the choice a member state makes between energy sources and the general structure of its energy supply. QMV has not always been the general rule for adopting environmental legislation. As mentioned in Chapter 1, the history of European environmental policy has been characterized by an increasing usage of QMV, since the successive Treaty amendments expanded the scope of QMV in the environmental area.

Council negotiations in practice: less intergovernmental than expected

The discussion on the voting rule is more than a merely institutional or legal one. It has a significant impact on the range of possible environmental policy outcomes, which is larger when QMV is applicable than when unanimity is the rule. Since unanimity implies veto power for each member state, the outcome of the preference aggregation is most likely to be the lowest common denominator. This is the environmental policy to which the most conservative member state (the member state with the preference that is located the closest to the status quo) can still agree. By contrast, QMV allows for more reformist (and usually more environmentally friendly) policy outcomes, since the most conservative member state is no longer able to veto a decision but needs to build a sufficiently broad blocking minority. Hence, as a general rule of thumb, QMV not only allows the Environment Council to reach decisions more easily, it is also likely to generate more reformist and 'green' policies than unanimity does.

Although the Environment Council is the institution for defending national preferences *par excellence*, it generally runs in a less intergovernmental way than one would expect on the basis of its composition (national governments) and its institutional function (aggregating national positions). Indeed, a couple of political dynamics mean that negotiations in the Environment Council go beyond mere hard bargaining between member states.

First, policy-making in the Council is characterized by a number of institutional yet unwritten norms that governments usually follow. One of the most important institutional norms is the fact that member states *de facto* avoid voting and strive to find a consensus that is acceptable to all of them (or that is at least not publicly rejected by one of them). This is the 'culture of consensus' that informally rules Council decision-making (Heisenberg 2005: 68), as a result of which it is still very common for the Council to take decisions by consensus, even since the enlargement rounds of the 2000s (Häge 2013a). Member states in the Environment Council usually strive to achieve a consensus instead of outvoting each other and suffering a loss of face when returning to their capital (Novak 2013). Moreover, they are aware that they will need to cooperate with each other in future meetings and that they do not want to get each other into trouble unnecessarily. Since the implementation of most environmental policies lies with the member states (see Chapter 4), it is also in the interest of the member states not to take decisions against those actors whose cooperation will be needed in the implementation stage (Christiansen 2006b). A policy-related consequence of this consensus reflex, which tries to include all the sensitivities of the member states in the final compromise, is that European environmental policy often includes 'exemptions, derogations, differentiated deadlines and vague phrases which allow for a wide interpretation of legal obligations during the implementation process' (Wurzel 2012: 82).

In the 2009–2014 period, thirty-eight votes took place on issues discussed in the Environment Council. Almost half of them (eighteen) resulted in all member states voting in favour. In another ten votes, none of the member states voted against but a limited number of them (numbers varying between one and four) abstained. As a result, about 75 per cent of the votes were taken without negative votes. Hence, in only ten votes one or more member states were outvoted (one single member state in seven votes, two member states in two votes, and three member states in one vote) (our own calculations on the basis of Votewatch 2014). Remarkably, in the least consensual vote – on the Ship Recycling Regulation (1257/2013) – the three member states that voted against did not do so because of substantive concerns about the regulation but because of their concerns about the comitology procedure that was foreseen for further implementation of the regulation (see Chapter 4).

Besides the effort to achieve consensus, other normative dynamics affect the functioning of the Environment Council: member states are aware that they will have to cooperate with each other in the future (the so-called shadow of the future), which affects their current behaviour; close interpersonal relationships are developed between member state representatives, which can lead to trust; and member states tend to justify the (background of their) positions and to explain their domestic difficulties, which leads to a better understanding of each other's negotiation behaviour (Lewis 2000). As a result of these norms and the 'esprit de corps' (Lempp and Altenschmidt 2008; Trondal and Veggeland 2003) they create among the member state representatives, policy-making in the Council can come more closely to resemble problem-solving than hard bargaining. This particularly holds in the Environment Council, where it is mostly regulatory policies that are relatively lowly politicized that are discussed (Elgström and Jönsson 2000). This does not mean that environmental policy-making in the Council is completely uncontroversial and non-conflictual. It only means that within the limits determined by national preferences, there is room for mutual understanding and common problem-solving.

Second, policy-making in the Environment Council is not merely intergovernmental since defending national interests is only one side of the picture. The other is that member states share a collective interest, namely reaching an agreement (Hayes-Renshaw and Wallace 2006). Indeed, member states have taken the view that the most effective way to tackle certain (transnational) environmental problems in Europe is to do it in a collective, cooperative manner at the EU level. Hence, the member states are constantly confronted with the tension between the pressure to reach a collective solution to a common environmental problem on the one hand and the defence of their own national interest on the other hand. This tension partly explains why policy-making in the Environmental Council is more than hard bargaining between member states that only aim to maximize their national interests: the member states also have an interest in reaching an agreement and in regulating that particular environmental issue at the European level.

Third, the relation between the environment ministries in the national capitals and the Environment Council in Brussels is not characterized by a one-way process in which ministers upload national interests from the national to the EU level. It is rather a two-way process in which the uploading and representation of national preferences is complemented by dynamics in the opposite direction. On the one hand, information about the policy-making process and about the positions of the other actors (other member states, the Commission, etc.) is transferred from the EU to the national level via the member state representative in the Council. This information is likely to lead to further development – and possibly adjustment – of national positions. Indeed, member states in the Environment Council do not always enter the policy-making process with fixed preferences that are, come what may, held until the end of the process. On the contrary, national preferences are initially quite unstable and still in development through an iterative process between Council meetings and internal national coordination processes. On the other hand, Environment ministers can transmit the pressure they have experienced in the Council to their national level, as a result of which they are sometimes able to strengthen their position within their own government. Because of the sectorial fragmentation of the Council configurations, Environment ministers meet with their counterparts at the EU level. Although the Environment ministers represent their member state – not just their own environment portfolio – the Environment Council has a tendency to be 'greener' than other Council configurations. This can be used by the Environment ministers in their own national governments, where they constantly have to fight for their own issues.

Internal organization of the Environment Council

The meeting of the Environment ministers is only the tip of the iceberg in the working of the Environment Council. Below the ministerial level, a complex institutional machinery of working parties and committees underpins the daily work of the Council, whose aim is to prepare the ministerial meetings. It consists of deliberation and negotiation between member states at different levels: ministerial, diplomatic and bureaucratic. The meetings at diplomatic and bureaucratic level are also attended by Commission officials from DG Environment or DG Climate Action.

At every level, the meetings are chaired by a representative from the member state holding the Presidency, which rotates six-monthly between the member states following a prearranged order. The Presidency is responsible for the following tasks: managing the day-to-day work of the Council, coordinating, chairing Council meetings, mediating and representing the Council inside and outside the EU (Schout and Vanhoonacker 2006). In short, the Presidency can be considered as a 'process manager' (Tallberg 2004) and is supposed to behave impartially and neutrally in order to effectively manage the debates in the Council (Smeets and Vennix 2014). However, a much debated question is whether the Presidency actually is a neutral broker and deal maker or whether it is able to influence policy-making in the Council in the direction of its own preferences (Niemann and Mak 2010). Studies show that this is particularly the case in the final stages of the legislative process (Schalk et al. 2007; Thomson 2008). If a certain piece of legislation is important for the member state holding the Presidency, the latter is in some cases able to shape the Council's agenda in order to achieve a breakthrough (Tallberg 2003). Although the agenda-setting power of the rotating Presidency is limited because it is the Commission that puts proposals into the legislative pipeline (Warntjen 2008), the Presidency is able to shape the agenda, for example, by not putting on the agenda a certain proposal for the Council meeting or by prioritizing certain dossiers above others. The main challenge for the Presidency thus consists in finding a balance between achieving an efficient policy-making process and defending its own interests. Achieving results is also important for a Presidency, since it contributes to the perception of a successful Presidency.

The basic rationale of the Environment Council's internal organization – with a bureaucratic, diplomatic and ministerial level – is that only the decisions on the most controversial and most politicized issues are left to those actors that have the political authority to decide on them, namely the Environment ministers. On the other issues, political decisions are taken as much as possible in the preparatory process of the ministers' meeting, with the aim of reaching an agreement that only needs to be rubberstamped at ministerial level. This preparatory process takes place in three steps. First, member state officials in the working party discuss the proposals at a technical level and they try to find consensus on as many issues as possible. Second, the issues that cannot be solved among officials are then transferred to the deputy permanent representatives of the member states, who meet in COREPER I (Committee of Permanent Representatives). Third, COREPER I then submits two kinds of agenda items to the Environment ministers: A-items are rubberstamped without substantive discussions since an agreement among the member states has been reached at a lower level of the Council, while B-items still need to be discussed at ministerial level.

This implies that a lot of decisions are taken by officials and diplomats in the Council (Hayes-Renshaw and Wallace 2006), but the ministers retain an important role in environmental legislative policy-making (Häge 2013b). However, because of the rising practice of concluding the environmental policy-making process in first reading (see Chapter 4), where the trilogue deal is adopted by COREPER I for the Council, nowadays a legislative file often does not reach the level of the Environment ministers. In any case, the logic behind the three-step process in the Council is a funnel system in which the less controversial issues are solved at the lower level and only the most controversial ones are left to the Environment ministers. These three steps are in theory consecutive, but this is seldom the case in reality. Dossiers often go back and forth between the various levels of the Council. They mount in the hierarchy when political guidance is needed and political knots need to be cut in order to be able to make progress and they descend when they are not yet sufficiently advanced for a final decision to be taken.

At the level of the officials, EU environmental policy is handled by two working parties in the Council: the Working Party on the Environment (WPE) and the Working Party on International Environmental Issues (WPIEI). The former discusses *internal* EU environmental policy, while the latter deals with the EU's *external* environmental policy and the preparation of EU positions for international environmental negotiations (see Chapter 10). Whereas there is only a single WPE handling internal EU environmental policy, multiple WPIEI constellations often meet to discuss subdomains of international environmental politics. Hence, there are separate WPIEIs for global issues, desertification, synergies, biodiversity, climate change, biosafety, chemicals, etc. Another difference between the WPE and the WPIEIs lies in their composition. While the WPE is made up of the environmental attachés serving in the Permanent Representation of their member state in Brussels, WPIEIs are usually attended by experts on international environmental issues coming from the national capitals. As the representatives in the WPE are Brussels-based, it is not unusual for this working party to convene approximately three times a week. These frequent contacts among member state representatives also facilitate the activation of the institutional norms of the Council (consensus striving, diffuse reciprocity, mutual responsiveness, etc.). Particularly in the working parties, this leads to a densely institutionalized and less intergovernmental policy-making style (Beyers 2005; Trondal 2001).

At ambassadorial level, environmental issues are dealt with in COREPER I, composed of the deputy permanent representatives at the Permanent Representations to the EU and meeting weekly. These Permanent Representations are a kind of embassy to the EU for each member state. Each Permanent Representation is led by a diplomat, the permanent representative, and staffed by attachés, who are each responsible for a particular policy domain. COREPER I not only prepares the meetings of the Environment ministers, but also of other Council configurations (Employment, social policy, health and consumer affairs; Competitiveness; Transport, telecommunications and energy; Education, youth, culture and sport). Hence, COREPER I not only serves as the intermediary in the funnel system from the WPE and WPIEI towards the Environment Council, but it also allows for horizontal coordination and trade-offs between the environmental and other policy domains such as transport, industry, internal market, etc.

At ministerial level, the Environment Council meets four times a year: in March and December in Brussels, in June and October in Luxembourg. In principle, each member state is represented here by its Environment minister, but practice shows that it is not exceptional for a minister to be replaced by a deputy or high-ranking diplomat (often the COREPER I ambassador). Environment ministers also meet twice a year at an informal Environment Council, organized by the rotating Presidency in its own country. Such informal Environment Councils do not have the authority to take binding decisions, but allow the twenty-eight Environment ministers to discuss a broader theme that is not immediately related to the issues that are in the legislative pipeline or to exchange views on new ideas in a less strict institutional framework compared to their formal Brussels and Luxembourg meetings. The member state holding the rotating Presidency can also use such informal Councils to put forward their own priorities in the environmental domain by organizing a special session that deals with that particular topic. For instance, during the May 2014 informal Environment Council in Greece, ministers debated the Greek 'Blue Growth' priority with a focus on the marine environment. Moreover Environment ministers from countries that are involved in accession negotiations with the EU (such as Turkey or Western Balkan countries) and/or countries of the European Free

---

Box 3.1   Agenda items of the June 2014 Environment Council

3320th Council meeting – Environment – Luxembourg, 12 June 2014

ITEMS DEBATED
– Cultivation of genetically modified organisms
– 2030 framework for climate and energy
– Clean Air Programme for Europe
– Convention on Biological Diversity

OTHER BUSINESS
– CO_2 emissions from maritime transport
– Doha amendment to the Kyoto Protocol
– Plastic carrier bags
– International meetings and events
– Endocrine disruptors
– Highly fluorinated substances
– Work programme of the incoming presidency

OTHER ITEMS APPROVED
GENERAL AFFAIRS
– Tax reductions for spirits produced locally in Madeira and the Azores

---

Trade Association (EFTA) (such as Switzerland or Norway) often attend these informal Environment Councils.

Box 3.1 presents, as an illustration, the agenda of the Environment Council of June 2014. A number of observations may clarify the functioning of the Environment Council. First, a clear distinction is made between 'items debated' and 'other items approved', which correspond to respectively the B- and the A-items. The A-items for the Environment Council also (even principally) contain issues from other policy areas and other Council configurations. Here, the Environment Council rubberstamps political deals from other Council configurations (or other Council configurations rubberstamp deals from the Environment Council) which still had to undergo translation and legal fine-tuning after the political

– Tax exemptions and reductions on products from French overseas departments
– Tax exemptions and reductions for local products of the Canary Islands

COMMON SECURITY AND DEFENCE POLICY
– EULEX Kosovo

JUSTICE AND HOME AFFAIRS
– Eurojust annual report – Conclusions

EUROPEAN ECONOMIC AREA
– Amendment to protocol 31 to the EEA agreement (civil protection mechanism)
– Amendment to protocol 30 to the EEA agreement

DEVELOPMENT COOPERATION
– Relations with ACP states

FISHERIES
– Position of the EU in several international fisheries management commissions
– Partnership between the EU and Mozambique
– Negotiations for a renewal of the protocol

agreement was reached. Second, the items that were actually substantively debated by the Environment ministers included, on the one hand, legislative proposals on which a political agreement was reached (here on GMOs) or on which an orientation debate was held to give political guidance to the discussions in the WPE and COREPER I (here on the Clean Air Programme). On the other hand, discussion of non-legislative items (here the 2030 climate and energy framework) was also part of the ministers' workload. These discussions can serve as input for the Commission when the latter, in a later stage, prepares legislative proposals on that topic.

Third, an important task of the Environment Council is also to establish the EU position to be defended in international environmental negotiations (see Chapter 10). For instance, the June 2014 agenda item 'Convention on Biological Diversity' (CBD) dealt with determining the EU's negotiation position for the 12th Conference of the Parties to the CBD in October 2014. Fourth, the Environment Council can also adopt 'Council Conclusions', which are political and non-legally binding statements by the Council that require consensus between the member states. For instance, the EU's position for international negotiations (such as the CBD meeting mentioned above) is usually adopted under the form of Council Conclusions. All the examples of the Environment Council's non-legislative activity mentioned above clearly indicate that it is not only the major law-making forum in EU environmental policy-making, but also increasingly a forum for policy coordination between member states (Puetter 2014).

Fifth, the 'other business' agenda items are usually topics on which the rotating Presidency and/or the European Commission informs the Environment Council on the state of play in ongoing issues, but on which no decisions are taken. Also individual member states can request the Presidency to include an issue under 'other business' on the agenda to brief their fellow member states or to bring an issue to the attention of the Council (the three last 'other business' items of the June 2014 meeting were put on the agenda by France, Sweden and Italy). Sixth, what does not appear on the agenda is important too: ministers also meet during lunchtime, where often the most sensitive and difficult issues are discussed. This implies that the most salient debates are often evacuated from the formal Council arena, where debates on legislative issues are transmitted via the EU's audiovisual services, to the informal lunch table, where only ministers attend and where there are no transparency rules. The outcome of the discussions over lunch is then usually formally approved by the Council in the afternoon session without a debate.

European Council

The European Council is the institution that brings together the heads of government (prime ministers) and the heads of state (presidents, as is the case for Cyprus, France, Lithuania and Romania) of the member states as well as the President of the European Commission and the Union's High Representative for foreign affairs and security policies. It is chaired by its own European Council President (since the end of 2014 the Polish centre-right Donald Tusk). Although it has only been a formal institution in the EU's institutional framework since 2009, the European Council has for a long time been regarded as the 'supreme political body in the EU' (Tallberg 2008). Since it gathers together the leaders of the member states at the highest political level, it has a vast political influence in the EU. Although the Commission President is a member as well, the European Council mainly performs the function of national interest representation. In this sense, the European Council resembles the Council, but its meetings attract much more media attention then the meetings of the Environment Council. Another difference is that the European Council's field of action is broader than that of the different sectorial Council configurations. Indeed, the European Council can discuss issues from all policy areas and is, in contrast to the Environment Council, not challenged by sectorial fragmentation.

The European Council's main task is to provide political direction and to determine the broad strategies for future EU policies. In the environmental field, this mainly occurs on climate change policies. On the major policy choices, the European Council indeed instructs the Commission and the Council to work towards specific objectives (Puetter 2014). Strategic decisions in both the EU's internal (such as the 2020 climate and energy package or the 2030 climate and energy framework, see Chapter 9) and external climate policies (such as the adoption of the EU's position for major international climate change negotiations, see Chapter 10) are currently made in the European Council. At its meeting of October 2014, where the EU's 2030 climate and energy framework was agreed, the European Council confirmed that it would 'continue to give strategic orientations' with respect to the main issues of the EU's current climate policies (European Council 2014).

Importantly, the European Council does not have legislative powers. The Treaty of Lisbon explicitly mentions that it 'shall not exercise legislative functions' (Art. 15 TEU). The European Council is supposed to give political impulses, which can then be transformed by the European Commission into concrete policy proposals or which can be refined and decided upon by the Council. However, since the 1990s, the European Council has increasingly been dealing with environmental – and mainly climate – policy and is *de facto* increasingly involved in the legislative policy-making processes. Three dynamics underlie the European Council's growing legislative role in environmental policy-making.

First, the European Council is increasingly active in the EU's legislative agenda-setting since its decisions serve more and more as the political basis for the Commission's legislative proposals. In that respect, the 'European Council may initiate legislative activity [...] by reaching non-legislative consensus' (Puetter 2014: 138). The development of the climate and energy package that established the 20-20-20 climate targets (see Chapter 9) between 2005 and 2008 illustrates the growing agenda-setting role of the European Council in environmental affairs quite nicely (Bocquillon and Dobbels 2014: 29–30). Following a preparatory stage of close coopera-tion between the European Commission President Barroso and the then European Council president Tony Blair (as the prime minis-ter of the British rotating Presidency), it was initially the European Council of October 2005 that kicked off this policy-making pro-cess by requesting the Commission to strengthen EU action on cli-mate and energy policy. The Commission then prepared a green paper, which was approved by the European Council, after which the Commission presented its first proposals on the 20-20-20 tar-gets. In March 2007, the heads of state and government sealed a deal on these targets and invited the Commission to table legislative proposals to incorporate these commitments into binding legisla-tion. In 2008, the Commission then presented its legislative pro-posals. This continuous interaction between the Commission and the European Council illustrates the influence of the latter in the legislative agenda-setting process.

Second, the European Council is becoming more and more the intergovernmental forum for cutting the knots on issues on which the Environment Council fails to do so. In other words, where Environment ministers fail to reach a deal because they do not have sufficient political authority to commit their member state on a cer-tain issue, the dossier can be raised to a higher political level where a deal can be achieved. The European Council becomes then the level for 'ultimate decision-making' (de Schoutheete 2006) or even a 'court of final appeal' (Hayes-Renshaw and Wallace 2006). This primarily applies to issues that are so politically sensitive that only the highest level enjoys the necessary ability and authority to take decisions.

Third, the European Council is, because of its non-sectorial nature, the principal forum for decisions on cross-sectorial issues on which multiple Council configurations that are competent on the issue have been unable to find an agreement (Nugent 2010). European climate change policy is a clear example where both dynamics – a high degree of politicization and a cross-sectorial policy nature – meet. For instance, the above-mentioned 2007 climate and energy package (with climate targets for 2020) and the 2014 climate and energy framework (with targets for 2030) (see Chapter 9) were politically negotiated and approved by the European Council. This work was not left only to the Environment ministers, since the ministers responsible for energy policy or industrial policy were also involved in this process. Likewise, the EU position for the 2009 Copenhagen climate change conference was prepared in the Environment Council and in the Economic and Financial Affairs Council (ECOFIN, where the ministers of finance meet), but finalized by the European Council (in October 2009) (see Chapter 10).

The emphasis on climate change politics in the European Council during the last decade does not imply that climate change was the first environmental topic discussed at this level. In fact a couple of essential environmental decisions were taken here in earlier years even though environmental issues are not usually the main dish on the European Council's menu. Most of these decisions entailed an incentive for the development of future EU environmental policy or principles. Examples are the Paris Summit of 1972, where the initiative for the first Environmental Action Programme was taken (see Chapter 1), or a number of European Council meetings between 1998 and 2001, which dealt with the implementation of the environmental policy integration principle (see Chapters 1 and 7) (Lenschow 2002). In the period 1992–2013, environmental policy appeared on the European Council agenda in 30 of the 118 European Council meetings (Puetter 2014), and most of these agenda items dealt with climate change. This indicates that the most salient issues of environmental policy-making in the EU are increasingly subject to policy coordination between member states in parallel with the classic Community method between the Commission, Council and Parliament (see Chapter 4).

Court of Justice

The Court of Justice of the EU, which is the EU's judicial branch, is not involved in the environmental policy-making process as such, in the sense that it does not play a role in the formulation and adoption of environmental policy. This does not imply, however, that the Court is not an important institution in EU environmental politics. It has influenced the state of play of EU environmental policy in three ways.

First, the Court is a central actor when the implementation of environmental policy by the member states is contested (the compliance mechanisms of EU environmental policy and the role of the Court will be extensively discussed in Chapter 4). More specifically, the Court comes into play in the final step of the infringement proceedings that the Commission can initiate against a member state in the context of no, partial or untimely transposition of EU environmental policy in national legislation. When a member state is taken to the Court and loses the case, the Court can impose sanctions if it comes to the conclusion that a member state has not or has only poorly fulfilled its compliance duties. Although most infringement proceedings against member states do not actually bring it before the Court, these procedures still matter, since they function as a stick for the Commission, which the member states will try to avoid.

Second, particularly in the pre-SEA era (that is, before 1987), the Court played a key role in the development of EU action on environmental matters (see Chapter 1). In this period, when environmental policy lacked a clear Treaty basis, the Court repeatedly argued that the Commission was legally allowed to propose policy measures related to the environment. According to the Court, for instance in Case 91/79 (Commission vs Italy), legislation covering environmental protection could be proposed on the basis of the internal market article (currently Art. 114 TFEU, then Art. 100a TEEC) or the so-called catch-all article (currently Art. 352 TFEU, then Art. 235 TEEC) (McCormick 2001).

Third, the Court of Justice has issued several important judgements on the relation between trade liberalization on goods and environmental protection, the most significant case being 302/86 (Commission vs Denmark) (Lenschow 2005). The Court basically concluded here that certain trade restrictions could be justified if they are considered necessary to realize the EU's environmental objectives (Knill and Liefferink 2007).

Taking together these three ways in which the Court affects EU environmental policy, its activities in this domain are not insignificant: between 1976 and 2010, the Court issued more than 700 judgments dealing with environmental affairs, accounting for 9 per cent of all Court cases (Krämer 2012b). Approximately three-quarters of these judgments were delivered in the framework of infringement proceedings against member states with regard to non- or incorrect implementation of environmental directives within their national legislation (see Chapter 4).

Agencies

Given the high level of expert knowledge and specific information needed to develop effective policies, the EU has established a couple of specialized bodies to support the EU institutions and the member states in the formulation of policies. These bodies are called 'agencies' and the EU currently has more than thirty of them. This process of 'agencification' (Wonka and Rittberger 2010), which is not a typical EU phenomenon but seen in many Western democracies, has contributed to the emergence of a 'European executive order' (Trondal 2010) where more and more executive decisions are taken by different types of bureaucratic processes. Most EU agencies are regulatory agencies, meaning that they have the power to make executive decisions on the existing policies. Examples include the European Medicines Agency (EMA) or the European Food Safety Authority (EFSA), which evaluate medicines and food before they come onto the European market. However, there is no overall regulatory environmental agency in the EU, such as the Environmental Protection Agency in the United States.

The main agency in the environmental domain is the European Environment Agency (EEA), based in Copenhagen and operational since 1994. Instead of being an agency with a regulatory function, the EEA is considered to be an 'observation centre' (Lelieveldt and Princen 2011: 269) or an 'information-gathering agency' (Martens 2010: 882). Indeed, the main task of the EEA is 'to provide the [EU] and the Member States with: (a) objective, reliable and comparable information at European level enabling them to take the requisite measures to protect the environment, to assess the results of such measures and to ensure that the public is properly informed about the state of the environment, and to that end; (b) the necessary technical and scientific support', as is stated in Article 1 of the most recent version of the Regulation on the EEA (401/2009). Besides the twenty-eight member states of the EU, also Turkey and the four EFTA member states (Iceland, Liechtenstein, Norway and Switzerland) are member countries of the EEA.

The rationale behind collecting information at the European level is to counteract the fragmented and *ad hoc* nature of existing information on the environment at the national levels. Many fields of environmental policy rely on a data gathering and monitoring process whereby a set of indicators is formulated by the EU, and data are centralized there by means of national reporting. The EEA plays a significant role in that process. The aim to dispose of centralized and uniform information on the environment across Europe compels member states and other actors to systematically provide information to the EU level (Halpern 2010).

In order to fulfil its data-gathering task, the EEA makes use of the data collection capacities of its members. What the EEA does is to aggregate and combine domestically generated data on the environment by coordinating a network of information suppliers, which are national research centres and institutions. That network is called 'EIONET' (European Environment Information and Observation Network), and it involves approximately 1000 experts and 350 national institutions (Martens 2010). It consists of so-called national focal points (i.e. experts or groups of experts in national environmental institutes acting as the EEA's main contact point and coordinating the work at the national level to provide the EEA with the necessary information) and 'European topic centres' (i.e. groups of institutes from EEA members with a specific expertise in a particular area that the EEA wants to work on). The EEA is thus dependent on the information put at its disposal by the various countries through EIONET. In this respect, the flow of information from the domestic level to the EEA is a voluntary process; in contrast, for example, to the obligation that member states have to provide information on the transposition of environmental directives to the Commission (see Chapter 4). By coordinating that network of national information providers, the EEA has played an important role in standardizing environmental methodologies in Europe, for instance on how the effectiveness of environmental policies can be evaluated.

On the basis of the information received from the members through the network, the EEA generates two kinds of output. On the one hand, every five years, a 'State of the Environment Report' is published, which includes an assessment of the current state of the environment in Europe (see Introduction). Since 1999, trends, prospects and suggestions for improving Europe's environment have also been included in that Report. Throughout the years, 'these high-profile reports have commanded a wide audience and served as major "flagships" for the EEA' (Martens 2010: 889). On the other hand, the EEA publishes more targeted reports on specific environmental topics. This type of report is produced because the Commission, and in particular DG Environment, started to request more policy relevant information that it could use as an information basis for developing its legislative proposals for EU environmental policy (Groenleer 2009). In 2008, a new information system was launched that aims to provide policy-makers with up-to-date environmental data. This 'Shared Environmental Information System' (SEIS), which is a collaborative initiative of the Commission and the EEA, is an online information exchange system on the environment.

Does the information generated by the EEA matter for EU environmental policy and can the EEA have an impact on the content of the policies? Stating that 'through the central position that the EEA has acquired in the network and the role it has developed in initiating and coordinating activities, the EEA is now having a substantial impact on environmental policy-making in the EU' (Groenleer 2009: 237), Groenleer concludes that the EEA does indeed seem to matter. This is also confirmed by an earlier EIPA/IIEP study, which argues that the EEA has 'an influence [...] on the environmental policy agenda that goes much beyond data gathering' (EIPA & IIEP 2003: 60).

The EEA's first years were characterized by frequent tensions with the Commission's DG Environment on whom exactly the EEA should serve, and on the extent to which it could extend its task beyond pure data gathering (Martens 2010). However, this tense relation between the EEA and the Commission, initially characterized by a desire for task expansion by the EEA and a fear of competition by DG Environment, has nowadays evolved into a more cooperative one. Both bodies seem to have found their place in the environmental governance architecture of the EU and their mutual relation is now one of complementarity (Groenleer 2009), in which the EEA considers DG Environment as one of its privileged partners (Martens 2010). The fact that the EEA receives an annual financial grant from DG Environment also contributes to this privileged position of the Commission.

Besides the information-gathering EEA, a number of regulatory agencies play an important role in European environmental politics. Two of them deserve particular attention here. First, the Helsinki-based European Chemicals Agency (ECHA), which started its activities in 2007, is responsible for – or even the 'chief administrator' (Martens 2012) of – the technical, scientific and administrative aspects of the REACH (Registration, Evaluation, Authorisation and Restriction of Chemicals) regime.

Under the REACH Regulation (1907/2006, see Chapter 7), producers and importers of chemical substances are required to register
these substances in the EU system before they can be brought to the
market. This registration must be submitted directly to ECHA. The
latter does not have the competences to take the final decision on
the authorization of chemicals, but it does provide scientific advice
to the Commission, on the basis of which the Commission then prepares a proposal to be discussed and adopted through a comitology
procedure (see Chapter 4) (Martens 2012). Moreover, ECHA also
has an advisory function, since it helps companies to comply with
EU chemicals legislation and it provides information on chemicals
to the public.

Second, the European Food Safety Authority (EFSA), operational since 2003 and based in Parma, provides scientific advice
with regard to food and feed safety. It plays an important role in
the authorization procedure for genetically modified organisms
(GMOs). EFSA conducts scientific risk assessments on the consequences on health and the environment of any GMO variety that a
producer wants to place on the European market. It is on the basis
of EFSA's risk assessment that the Commission drafts a recommendation on the authorization, which is subsequently subject to the
comitology procedure (see Chapters 4 and 8). Although the EFSA
opinion is not binding to the Commission, the latter must provide
an explanation when its recommendation differs from the outcome
of EFSA's risk assessment (Skogstad 2011).

Conclusions

The Commission, the EP and the Environment Council are engaged
in an interdependent relationship when developing environmental
policy. How this interdependence is translated in a policy-making
process is the topic of the next chapter. These institutions not only
need to cooperate with each other, but they have to work along the
broad lines set out by the European Council and within the limits of
the Treaties as clarified by the Court of Justice. Three conclusions
about the institutional framework for EU environmental policy-
making can be drawn.

First, the interdependency among the institutions is illustrated
by an anticipatory logic in their decision-making behaviour. The
rationale of certain institutional choices is often to avoid surprises
in future stages of the decision-making process by assessing in

advance the positions of other institutions and actors. The expert groups consulted by the Commission, and composed of – among others – member state officials, are an example of this, as well as the inter-DG coordination processes in the Commission, which reduces the likelihood that DG Environment will be recalled by the other DGs at the end of the decision-making process in the Commission.

Second, the formal institutional set-up of the EU is characterized by a high degree of sectorial fragmentation. DG Environment in the Commission, the ENVI Committee in the EP and the gathering of Environment ministers and the WPE in the Council deal exclusively with environmental policy-making. That environmental policy is usually prepared in an 'environment only' setting hinders the realization of the environmental policy integration principle, which can only be fully realized by opening the borders between EU policy areas. Moreover, it can impede the creation of package-deals and issue-linkages between various policy-making processes in different areas. The disadvantages of this sectorial fragmentation are institutionally counterbalanced to some extent by the interservice consultations within the Commission, the College of Commissioners, COREPER and the European Council, all of which provide a forum for a more horizontal and cross-sectorial approach to policy-making. Moreover, the rotating Council Presidency also has the opportunity to overview – and where necessary coordinate – the developments in various Council configurations. In that respect, some Presidencies have recently organized a joint informal Council meeting of Environment and Energy ministers (as was the case under the 2008 French Presidency to discuss the climate and energy package) or a joint informal Council of Environment and Employment Ministers (for example under the 2014 Italian Presidency, where 'green growth and employment' was debated).

Third, day-to-day EU politics and policy-making is characterized by committee governance. The expert groups, working parties and parliamentary committees conduct a significant part of the policy-making job. Moreover, the expert groups consulted by the Commission and the working parties preparing the Environment Council provide an excellent link between the national levels of governance and the European one, to such an extent that they can be considered as a 'melting pot' of national and supranational governance systems (Egeberg et al. 2003). In each of these committees, socialization processes and the emergence of an 'esprit de corps' is likely. This may well increase mutual understanding and lead to an effective problem-solving policy-making atmosphere, but it also entails the danger of yet more sectorial fragmentation and isolation. The same can be said for two other instances of committee governance in EU policy-making, namely trilogues and comitology committees, which are discussed in the next chapter.

In sum, these three dynamics will recur as the next chapter deals with the policy-making process. It discusses, on the one hand, how the institutions interact and cooperate to formulate and implement environmental policies. On the other hand, it analyses the ways in which environmental policy is implemented after it has been adopted by making a distinction between implementation at the EU level (through comitology) and at the level of the member states (through transposition of European environmental legislation into national law). The relevance of anticipatory behaviour during policy-making, intra- and inter-institutional coordination and committee governance should thus become fully clear.

Chapter 4

Policy-Making

This chapter explains how environmental policy is made in the EU. How do the EU's institutions cooperate in order to formulate policies? And once environmental policy is adopted, how is it then implemented? The chapter is divided into two main parts. First, it examines the policy-making process leading to environmental legislation. This process starts with a proposal by the Commission and ends when the Council and the European Parliament have agreed upon a joint text. It discusses both the formal procedure as well as the increasingly informal practices that lead to so-called early agreements and make the adoption of environmental policy more efficient (but also less transparent) than the formal procedures suggest. The current chapter thus analyses the *inter*-institutional relations in the policy-making process (i.e. how do the institutions cooperate and interact?), whereas the *intra*-institutional relations of the policy-making process (i.e. how do the institutions function internally in that process?) were discussed in the previous chapter.

Second, the implementation of EU environmental legislation is considered, focusing on implementation processes both at the EU level and at the member state level. In the EU, environmental legislation is implemented by the Commission through comitology procedures that allow the member states to be involved as well. At the national level, environmental policy needs to be implemented and particularly environmental directives need to be transposed into domestic law. EU environmental policy in particular suffers, however, from a considerable implementation deficit. This chapter also discusses the monitoring role of the Commission and the possibility of bringing badly performing member states before the Court of Justice. The main reasons for the poor implementation record of member states are examined too.

Policy formulation

The greater part of EU environmental legislation is adopted through the 'ordinary legislative procedure' (OLP). This procedure is sometimes also called 'codecision', referring to the requirement that the two legislators, the Council and the European Parliament, agree upon the same version of the legislation that is to be adopted. The environmental policy field is the policy area with the largest share of legislation conducted under the OLP (14 per cent of all OLP dossiers dealt with environmental policy in 2009–2014 and 20 per cent in 2004–2009) (European Parliament 2014b). As explained in Chapters 1 and 3, only a small number of environmental issues are not covered by the OLP. These are governed under the so-called consultation procedure, where the role of the EP is limited to merely being consulted by the Council instead of being a fully-fledged co-legislator. The exceptions that are not subject to the OLP are recorded in Article 192§2 TFEU and deal with taxation, land management, quantitative management for water resources and land use (with the exception of waste management) and those affecting the choice of a member state between energy sources and the general structure of its energy supply (see Box 1.2). This last point basically refers to the member states' authority in deciding on their own energy production system.

The ordinary legislative procedure: formal steps

Formally speaking, the OLP consists of three consecutive steps, which are also called 'readings'. The three readings are presented in Figure 4.1 and briefly discussed below. As will be explained below, environmental legislation is usually adopted in the early stages of the procedure. Indeed, in the lion's share of environmental policy-making processes, the third stage of the OLP is never reached because an agreement has already been found in the first or second reading.

The first formal step ('first reading') of the OLP consists of the Commission proposing environmental legislation to the EP and the Council. The formal proposal is developed within the Commission, usually led by DG Environment or Climate Action, after having consulted stakeholders and having internally coordinated among DGs and cabinets (see Chapter 3). This proposal is then examined by both the European Parliament and the Environment Council, each following its own institutional procedures. In the Parliament,

FIGURE 4.1 *The ordinary legislative procedure*

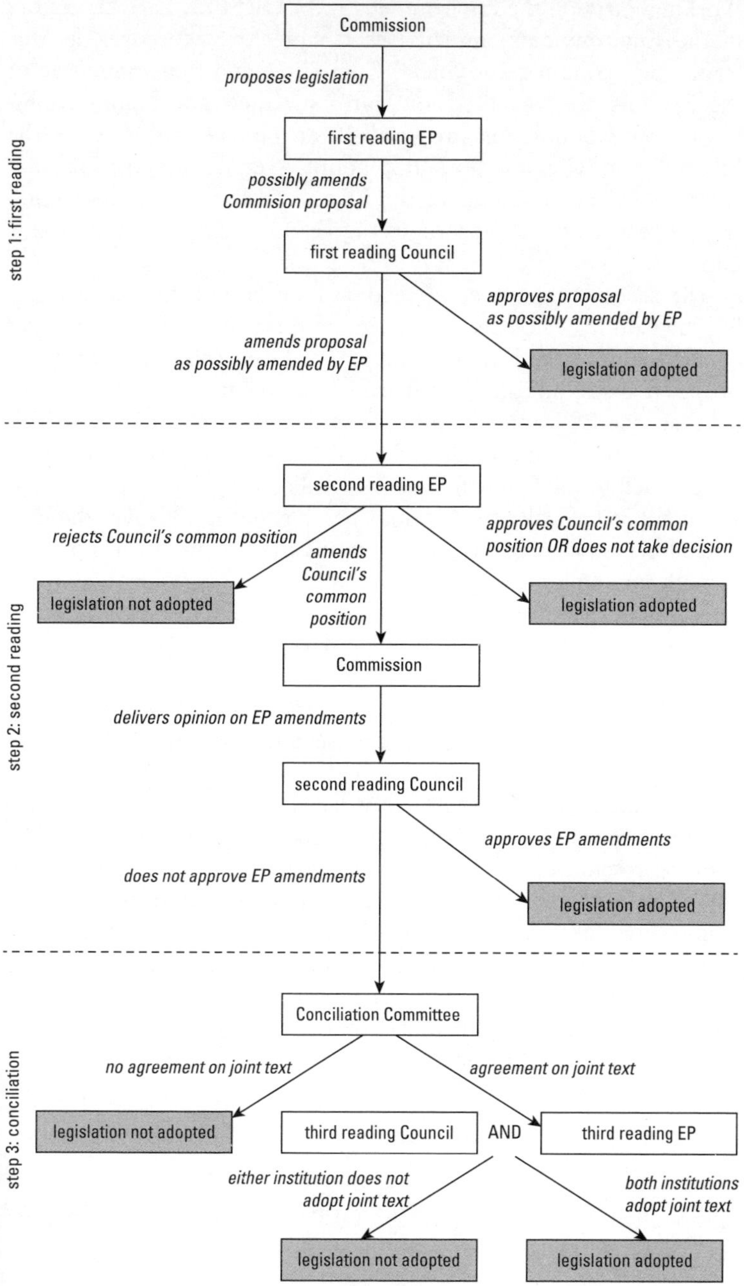

step 1: first reading

Commission

proposes legislation

first reading EP

possibly amends Commision proposal

first reading Council

amends proposal as possibly amended by EP

approves proposal as possibly amended by EP

legislation adopted

step 2: second reading

second reading EP

rejects Council's common position

amends Council's common position

approves Council's common position OR does not take decision

legislation not adopted

legislation adopted

Commission

delivers opinion on EP amendments

second reading Council

does not approve EP amendments

approves EP amendments

legislation adopted

step 3: conciliation

Conciliation Committee

no agreement on joint text

agreement on joint text

legislation not adopted

third reading Council

AND

third reading EP

either institution does not adopt joint text

both institutions adopt joint text

legislation not adopted

legislation adopted

the leading role is played by the ENVI Committee, whereas the Working Party on the Environment and COREPER I are key actors in the Environment Council (see Chapter 3). Moreover, at this stage, the Economic and Social Committee and the Committee of the Regions are consulted and can issue their non-binding opinion on the Commission proposal. If, at the end of this stage, the Environment Council does not adopt a common position that confirms the amendments of the EP, the OLP moves to its second step. Alternatively, if the Council agrees, the legislative proposal is adopted.

The second step ('second reading') starts with the EP discussing the Council's first reading common position. The EP can either decide to adopt the Environment Council's position, leading to the proposal being adopted, or it can reject or amend it. In the latter case, the EP's amendments are sent to the Commission, which issues its opinion about the EP position, and they are then transferred back to the Council for its second reading. The Environment Council has basically two options here. Either it approves the EP's amendments (with QMV if the Commission's opinion was positive, or with unanimity if the Commission's opinion was negative), or it rejects the Parliamentary amendments. If the Environment Council does not agree with the EP, the legislative procedure moves to its third step.

In this third step ('conciliation'), the logic of policy-making changes. Whereas in the first and second steps the EP and the Council separately and successively discuss the legislative proposal and the amendments of their fellow legislator, the conciliation stage implies a reversal towards a policy-making setting where twenty-eight representatives of the Council, twenty-eight representatives of the EP and representatives of the Commission meet around a single negotiation table in the so-called Conciliation Committee. Their aim is to reach an agreement on a joint text through direct interaction. However, that joint text of the Conciliation Committee always needs to be accepted afterwards by the EP and the Council separately in their third reading before the legislation can be adopted.

Fast-tracking environmental legislation: early agreements and trilogues

Although the gradual rise of the OLP as the main policy-making procedure in the environmental domain (see Chapter 1) increased the legitimacy of environmental policy-making by giving the directly elected EP a fully-fledged legislative role, it has also established a formal policy-making process that can take a long time before the legislation is actually adopted. When policies are adopted in three readings and through the Conciliation Committee, the policy-making process can easily take a couple of years. Moreover, because of the steady rise of environmental issues covered by the OLP, the legislative workload has grown, leading to efficiency problems. In order to make policy-making more efficient and faster, the EU has increasingly opted to reach an agreement in the early stages of the OLP, namely in first (or second) reading. Such 'early agreements' are nowadays part and parcel of EU environmental policy-making. Consequently, going as far as the Conciliation Committee in the policy-making process has become exceptional. This evolution of 'fast tracking' legislation (de Ruiter and Neuhold 2012) has become a general trend in the EU, and environmental policy-making is no exception. The first three bars in Figure 4.2 present this evolution towards early agreements in the EU in all policy areas. In the period 2009–2014, 85 per cent of the policy-making processes covered by the OLP were concluded in first reading, 13 per cent in second reading and only two per cent of them made it up to the Conciliation Committee (European Parliament 2014b; 2014c). This strongly

FIGURE 4.2   *The proportion of OLP files adopted at first, second or third reading*

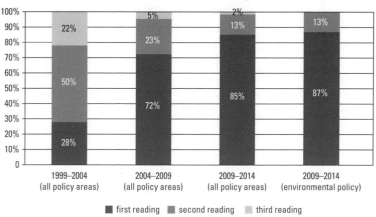

Source: based on European Parliament 2014a; 2014b; 2014c

contrasts with, for instance, the 1999–2004 period when only 28 per cent of the cases was concluded in first reading, 50 per cent in second reading and 22 per cent through conciliation (European Parliament 2012).

Environmental policy-making follows this general pattern. The numbers clearly indicate that environmental legislation is generally adopted today under the form of first reading agreements. The last bar in Figure 4.2 shows that in the parliamentary term 2009–2014, sixty-one pieces of environmental legislation handled by the ENVI Committee were adopted through the OLP. No less than 87 per cent of them (fifty-three cases) were already concluded in first reading and 13 per cent (eight cases) in second reading (European Parliament 2014a). No single environmental dossier reached the Conciliation Committee in this period.

The shift to early agreements has generated a radical shift in the practice of negotiating environmental policy in the EU. Early agreements are achieved by complementing the formal policy-making procedure with informal practices that allow for direct negotiations between the EP and the Council. Early agreements are made possible by a 'move from formal sequential to informal simultaneous interaction between the EP and the Council' (Häge and Kaeding 2007: 346). At first and second reading stages, where the Treaty stipulates that the institutions sequentially discuss each other's amendments, direct negotiations are now established between the two co-legislators. These negotiations take place in so-called trilogues. These are informal gatherings of representatives of the EP, the Council and the Commission who meet at first and second reading stages with the aim of finding a deal that can be presented to and adopted by the EP and the Council. Trilogues are indicative of the informalization of the policy-making process where a deal is pre-cooked in an informal way, after which it is formalized and rubberstamped according to the procedures that are foreseen in the Treaty (Reh et al. 2013). Indeed, it is still the EP and the Council, each according to their internal voting procedure, that have to approve the deal before it can be adopted as legislation.

In practice, a trilogue agreement is negotiated before the EP issues its opinion and before the Council adopts its common position. In the environmental domain, on average three trilogue meetings are needed to reach such an agreement, although five or more meetings are not exceptional for more complex dossiers (European Parliament 2014a). In the 2009–2014 Parliamentary term, no less than 172 trilogue meetings were conducted for proposals that were handled by the EP's ENVI Committee (European Parliament 2014b). Once an inter-institutional compromise is found in the trilogue, the EP includes that compromise in its own amendments, which are voted on in first reading. Then, it is sent to the Council, where COREPER I accepts it in its first reading. As mentioned in Chapter 3, the key role of COREPER I here means that early agreements can be adopted by the Council without a detailed discussion on its precise content by the Environment ministers.

Trilogues are attended by representatives of the EP, the Council and the Commission, which each functions as a 'relais' between the trilogue and their respective institution (Farrell and Héritier 2004). The delegation of the EP in the trilogues is led by the rapporteur of the legislative dossier, but the shadow rapporteurs from the other political groups and the chair of the ENVI Committee are also part of the EP negotiating team (see Chapter 3). For the Council, the situation is more clear-cut: it is the rotating Presidency that conducts the trilogue negotiations on behalf of the Environment Council, and the other member states are not able to participate in trilogues. In practice, it means that the environment attaché of the member state holding the Presidency (who chairs the Working Party on the Environment) and/or the deputy Permanent Representative of that same member state (who chairs COREPER I) participate in the trilogues. The Commission is represented by a leading official from DG Environment or DG Climate Action.

Since the practice of adopting early agreements has increased the interdependence of inter- and intra-institutional negotiations (Héritier and Reh 2012), the rapporteur and the Presidency face a subtle negotiation challenge. On the one hand, they are expected to reach an inter-institutional deal in order to speed up the legislative process and to adopt the policy in first reading. This implies that they are expected to compromise and to make concessions. On the other hand, they also have to ensure that they retain the support of their own institution – the EP and the Council, respectively – from whom they need backing in order to formalize the trilogue deal and from whom they have received a mandate for the trilogues. Consequently, the rapporteur and the Presidency are playing a delicate game in which they need to find the right balance between an inter-institutional deal and intra-institutional support for that deal.

The policy-making process on the Passenger Car Regulation (333/2014, see Chapter 9) illustrates the subtleties of such a negotiation process. In June 2013, the then Irish Council Presidency and the EP's negotiating team led by rapporteur Thomas Ulmer (EPP Group) agreed upon a deal after a number of trilogue rounds at the first reading stage. In that compromise, the Irish Presidency and the rapporteur had committed themselves to a CO_2 emission target for new cars of 95 g/km for all cars sold from 2020 onwards. However, three days after that trilogue meeting, when the Irish Presidency went back to COREPER I in order to obtain a formal approval, it had lost the support of the Council. Germany, with its important automobile sector, felt that that target was too ambitious. It pressured other member states to block the compromise, even threatening to scale back production plans in those countries. Although Germany could formally be outvoted by the other member states (the voting rule was QMV), the consensus culture of the Council (see Chapter 3) prevented the other member states from isolating the EU's most important car manufacturing country and they rejected the Presidency's formula. The trilogue deal was thus turned down by the Council, as a result of which the policy-making process was delayed. The deadlock was finally solved in November 2013 when a new round of trilogue meetings, now with the Lithuanian Presidency representing the Council, resulted in a deal that was closer to the German position. Although the target of 95 g/km was retained, two elements were added to gain German support: the target should be achieved by 2021 with a 'phase-in' from 2020 and 'super credits' were created for the least-polluting cars in each manufacturer's range. On 30 November 2013, Germany abandoned its resistance and COREPER I confirmed the trilogue deal. The ENVI Committee also approved the deal.

Adopting legislation through trilogues has generated two sets of concerns. First, accountability issues have been raised in relation to the secret and secluded nature of trilogue negotiations (Héritier 2007). Trilogues are indeed meetings taking place behind closed doors and transparency is mostly lacking. This means that the 'democratization of the political decision-making process by empowering the EP [through the generalization of the OLP] has paradoxically resulted in a closing down of the decision-making process in trilogues, which has weakened the EU's democratic legitimacy' (Héritier 2013: 1079–1080). Second, trilogues are said to favour some actors (the rapporteur and the Presidency) above others who have lost their grip on the policy-making process (the MEPs in the ENVI Committee and the member states in the Council) (Farrell and Héritier 2004). However, a number of studies have recently demonstrated that the trilogue practice is not as problematic as was previously assumed: in practice, the rapporteur and the Presidency have not gained much power vis-à-vis their respective institutions, as the outcomes of trilogues are not located significantly closer to the preferences of the rapporteur or the Presidency than is legislation adopted via three readings (Rasmussen 2010; Rasmussen and Reh 2013).

The trilogue meetings are not the only instances where representatives from the Commission, EP and Council meet and have the opportunity to informally discuss the legislation during the policy-making process. Three other venues are also important for inter-institutional interaction during the legislative process. First, each Environmental Council meeting, at the level of the working party, COREPER I or the ministerial meeting, is attended by a representative of the Commission, who is usually relatively active in those meetings. The Commission can even influence the Council's decision-making in the direction of its interests, for instance by playing a 'divide and rule' game vis-à-vis the member states (Schmidt 2000), by threatening to issue a negative opinion as a result of which the member states would need unanimity instead of a qualified majority to adopt the legislation, or by threatening to withdraw its proposal. Second, the EP's ENVI Committee meetings are public and often attended by representatives from the Commission and the member states. Third, member state representatives also have opportunities to participate in the expert groups convened by the Commission in the drafting process of the legislative proposal. Most expert groups are indeed attended by member state officials and many of them are in fact exclusively composed of national officials (see Chapter 3). Hence, the preparation of the drafting is *de facto* not an exclusive Commission business. Given this, it is rather remarkable that MEPs are rarely invited to the expert groups (Larsson and Murk 2007). These informal possibilities for involvement in each other's work mean that the policy-making process in practice consists of more direct interactions between the institutions than the formal OLP suggests and that institutions succeed relatively well in avoiding surprises and deadlocks.

Although the Commission, the Council and the EP are engaged in an interdependent relationship while developing environmental policy, the long-lasting debate about the relative power of these institutions is still ongoing. This is basically a debate between intergovernmentalists, arguing that it is essentially the Council and the member states that pull the strings in the EU, and the supranationalists, who attribute a high degree of power to the Commission and the EP. A comprehensive study of a relatively large number of legislative processes seems to support the Council-centric view (Thomson and Hosli 2006). Indeed, although the OLP has upgraded the EP to a fully-fledged co-legislator, it is still not on an equal footing with the Council, which still seems to dominate the legislative process under the OLP (Costello and Thomson 2013; Hagemann and Høyland 2010). However, the growing tendency to conclude the environmental policy-making process as early as the first reading and to adopt environmental legislation as early agreements has empowered the EP vis-à-vis the Council. The former does indeed have a higher impact on the content of the policy when an agreement is found in the early stages of the OLP compared to policies that are adopted through a deal in the Conciliation Committee (Costello and Thomson 2011; Franchino and Mariotto 2013). In other words, the EP succeeds in getting more concessions from the Council in the early than in the final stages of the OLP (Häge and Kaeding 2007).

Policy implementation

The adoption of environmental legislation does not close the policy-making cycle since policies still have to be implemented in order to be able to make a difference in the field. The implementation of EU environmental policy takes place at the level of the EU and at that of the member states. At the level of the EU, the technical details of the legislation are further specified by the Commission through the so-called comitology process, whereas, at the domestic level, environmental directives have to be transposed into national law by the member states. This section successively discusses policy implementation via comitology and transposition.

Implementation at the EU level: comitology

Although European environmental legislation is often rather long and detailed, not all operational details are included in the directives or regulations from the start. This is why the legislators in almost all pieces of environmental legislation include a provision by which they delegate the responsibility for determining these details to the

European Commission. In environmental legislation, such details typically refer to annexes with substances, products, species and so on. For instance, the Habitats Directive (92/43, see Chapter 7) stipulates that certain species and areas must be protected, but the exact list of which species and areas are concerned is determined at the policy implementation stage by the Commission.

A large part of the environmental *acquis* therefore consists of 'little rules' adopted by the Commission (called Commission regulations, Commission directives and Commission decisions), which refine the operational details that were not foreseen in the legislation itself (Brandsma 2013: 3). However, the technical nature of these details does not imply that they are by definition trivial or have limited importance. Since the devil is often in the detail, implementation measures are indeed highly important for the addressees of the environmental policy (citizens, companies, etc.)

The member states establish committees to monitor or to assist the Commission when the latter executes the legislation (Blom-Hansen 2011; Franchino 2000). As a result, the Commission is not completely autonomous in implementing environmental policies at the EU level, since member states also have a say through the so-called comitology committees in which they are represented. Comitology committees are composed of policy experts from national administrations or agencies. They are chaired by Commission officials, who also organize the meetings and prepare the documents. Comitology is thus essentially 'a permanent discussion between the Commission and member state representatives on technical details, annexes and values of new EU policies' (Versluis et al. 2011: 168).

The use of comitology is part and parcel of the day-to-day environmental decision-making process in the EU. Almost every environmental directive and regulation includes a comitology procedure. Together with agricultural, industrial, health, consumer and research policy, the environmental policy area is among the champions of comitology use in the EU (Blom-Hansen 2011). Of the more than 250 comitology committees in the EU, 37 are active in the area of environmental and climate policy (although the exact number may change, for instance when new legislation is adopted) (European Commission 2014e). Examples include the Ambient Air Quality Committee (on the Directives 2008/50, 2004/107 and 2001/81), the Committee on the conservation of natural habitats and of wild fauna and flora (on the Habitats Directive 92/43) or the LIFE Committee for Environment and Climate Action (on

Regulation 1293/2013). Those environmental and climate comitology committees met fifty-five times in the course of 2013 (European Commission 2014e).

Environmental legislation can be executed at the EU level by means of two types of legal acts: 'implementing acts' and 'delegated acts'. The main difference between the two is that implementing acts do not modify the legislation but are only intended to execute it in a uniform way, whereas delegated acts amend the legislative act or supplement it with new non-essential elements. Implementing acts determine, for instance, the format of the procedure that member states must use when reporting to the Commission on progress in a certain area. Delegated acts, on the other hand, amend or supplement existing legislation by, for instance, adding new species or products to annexes. However, in practice, it is not always clear-cut whether environmental legislation should be further dealt with by means of implementing or delegated acts and the choice between the two is often the subject of political debate during the policy-making process which leads to the legislation. Another difference is that, in contrast to implementing acts, delegated acts do not require the involvement of formal comitology committees (but only 'expert groups for delegated legislation'). Nonetheless, the term 'comitology' is in practice still used for describing the implementation procedures at EU level, encompassing both implementing and delegated acts (Brandsma 2013).

Implementing acts can be adopted through various procedures, which imply different levels of control powers to allow the member states to monitor the Commission in its implementation tasks. The 2011 Comitology Regulation (182/2011) prescribes the procedural details for adopting implementing acts and its Article 2(b) stipulates that the 'examination procedure applies, in particular, for the adoption of [...] implementing acts relating to [...] the environment'. In this examination procedure, the comitology committee is rather powerful, because the Commission needs the support of a qualified majority in the committee in order to adopt its draft implementing act. More particularly, the examination procedure provides for three scenarios.

First, if the committee adopts a *positive opinion* on the draft implementing act of the Commission with a qualified majority, the Commission is obliged to adopt the implementing act. Second, if a qualified majority in the committee adopts a *negative opinion*, the Commission cannot adopt the implementing act, but it can still lodge an appeal with an appeal committee, which is also composed of member state representatives, or it can amend its draft implementing act and resubmit it to the committee. In the appeal committee too, a qualified majority is required to adopt a positive opinion (in which case the Commission shall adopt the implementing act) or a negative opinion (in which case the Commission cannot adopt the implementing act). Third, if the committee *does not adopt an opinion* (mainly because it is too divided to reach a qualified majority either in favour or against the Commission proposal), the Commission *may* adopt the implementing act autonomously (unless the environmental legislation on which the implementing act is issued disallows this or if a simple majority in the committee voted against), it can resubmit an amended version to the committee or it can refer the case to the appeal committee. Importantly, in the pre-Lisbon era, the Commission was obliged to adopt the measure in this third scenario, but this obligation is no longer in place.

In practice, the first scenario accounts for the lion's share of the cases. Indeed, in the environmental field, the comitology committees mostly agree with the Commission, as a result of which the draft implementing act as proposed by the Commission is adopted (Lee 2014). However, the fact that the committees mostly agree with the Commission does not necessarily mean that there is no contestation or controversy among the member states in the committee about the Commission proposal. It only implies that, normally, a qualified majority can be found that supports the Commission (Dehousse et al. 2014). There are, however, some contentious areas in which neither the committee nor the appeal committee is able to find a sufficiently large majority to adopt either a positive or a negative opinion. Consequently, the Commission may adopt the implementing act without the backing of the member states (i.e. the third scenario). In the environmental field, two examples can be given of such contention, lack of qualified majority among the member states and autonomy for the Commission. First, the Regulation on the placing of plant protection products on the market (1107/2009) regulates the authorization of pesticides to protect plants and crops in agriculture. The list of substances that are approved is adopted through comitology. Since neither the comitology committee nor the appeal committee could adopt an opinion on the authorization of neonicotinoids pesticides, the Commission took a decision autonomously (Lee 2014). Second, certain genetically modified organisms (GMOs) have been authorized in the EU by the Commission following a stalemate in the comitology and the appeal committees (see Chapter 8). This implies that the Commission can indeed authorize GMOs in the EU even if a majority of the member states opposes it, but when that majority is not sufficiently broad to be a qualified majority. However, as mentioned, these examples are rather exceptional and the general rule seems to be that comitology is usually characterized by a 'seemingly harmonious relationship between the Commission and the committees' (Hix and Høyland 2011: 39).

The member states thus play a crucial role in the adoption of implementing acts in the environmental field. By contrast, the role of the European Parliament is much more limited here. The only way the EP can scrutinize the comitology process is by indicating to the Commission that it considers that the latter is exceeding the executive implementation powers it was granted in the basic act of legislation (Georgiev 2013). The other legislative institution, the Council, also enjoys this right of scrutiny. If the EP or the Council do consider that the Commission is overstepping its executive powers, the latter has to review its draft implementing act while taking into account the concerns of the EP or the Council.

The second type of acts, delegated acts, are meant to supplement or amend 'non-essential elements' of the legislation. The rationale is that only non-essential elements can be addressed by delegated acts, leaving the essential elements to be addressed by the legislation itself. Examples of EU environmental policies that are further implemented through delegated acts include the amendments of the annexes with lists of endangered species (Brandsma 2013) or the Industrial Emission Directive (2010/75), where the Commission can adjust some provisions of the directive in line with 'scientific and technical progress' (Lee 2014).

For the adoption of delegated acts, and in contrast to implementing acts, the Commission is not obliged to consult formal comitology committees, but only *ad hoc* expert groups for delegated legislation, which are composed of member state officials whose role is limited to giving a non-binding advice to the Commission. It also has to keep the European Parliament and the Council informed. However, even in the area of delegated acts, the Commission cannot implement legislation in a completely unbound manner. Here, the EP and the Council enjoy extensive scrutiny rights, since they have the right to object to the Commission's delegated acts during the two months (and possibly more) after their adoption. In other words, the EP and the Council enjoy *ex post* veto power on delegated acts, since their objection prevents the delegated act from entering into force. Moreover, the EP and the Council can revoke the delegation of executive powers to the Commission in a certain piece of legislation. However, the dynamics with regard to delegated acts differ insofar as the EP's position is thus clearly stronger here than in the case of implementing acts. This explains why the EP usually prefers to implement environmental legislation at the EU level by means of delegated acts. Combined with the fact that the defining notion of 'non-essential elements' of delegated acts leaves room for political interpretation, the precise implementation procedure for a piece of legislation has, since the entry into force of the Lisbon Treaty, been a source of conflict between the EP and the Council in the policy-making stage of most environmental legislation (see above).

Implementation at the national level: transposition

The implementation of EU environmental policies at the national level can refer to two types of implementation: the practical application of the policies on the field and the legal transposition of the policies into national legal frameworks. The first type of implementation refers to the practical effects of European environmental policy on the activities of the addressees of the policy and, consequently, on the state of the environment. The question here is whether the objectives of the environmental policy are actually achieved on the ground and whether legal policy instruments lead to societal change and environmental improvement. Although the availability of systematic data on the state of the environment in Europe has improved the last decade (for instance, through work by the European Environment Agency, see Chapter 3), assessing this kind of policy effectiveness is rather challenging. It is indeed difficult to isolate the effect of a particular European policy on the quality of the environment – although it is generally assumed that the state of the environment in Europe is largely influenced by EU environmental policy – and to disregard the effects of other context variables.

The second type of implementation refers to the transposition requirement of environmental directives. After environmental directives are adopted by the European institutions (see above), the member states are responsible for transposing these directives into their own national legislation within a certain time period and in compliance with the provisions of the directive in question. Member states are indeed obliged to adopt legal and administrative provisions in order to incorporate the directive into their national legal order. In some cases, member states opt to create new legislation, in others to modify existing law, to adopt ministerial decisions or even to do nothing (when the existing national regulatory framework is already coherent with the new EU environmental policy) (Lelieveldt and Princen 2011). The fact that directives need to be transposed gives the member states some flexibility with regard to the way in which the objectives stipulated in the directives will be met in a particular national context. This contrasts with regulations, which are another type of legislative act in frequent use and which are directly applicable in all member states without having to be transposed (see Box 6.1).

Compared to the other policy areas of the EU, environmental policy has been, and still is, the area with the least effective transposition and thus the highest implementation deficit in the EU (Knill 2006; European Commission 2013a). Environmental policy accounts for approximately one fifth of the transposition deficit of all legislation adopted at the European level. This proportion has been relatively stable in the last decade. Transposition is most problematic in the environmental subfields of waste and water policies (see Chapter 7), which jointly account for half of the compliance problems in EU environmental policy (European Commission 2014f). The fields of impact assessment (the Environmental Impact Assessment Directive, now 2014/52) and biodiversity (mainly the Birds and Habitats Directives, respectively 79/409 and 92/43) (see Chapters 6 and 7) also face considerable transposition challenges (European Commission 2013b).

The transposition deficit has two components. First, member states can fail to transpose the directive in time, that is, within the time limit that is determined by the directive in question (usually two years). Untimely transposition constitutes a large part of the transposition deficit (Kaeding 2006; Steunenberg and Rhinard 2010). In this respect, the environmental domain is the worst of all European policy domains (European Commission 2013a). This seems to be related to the length and complexity of environmental directives, to their saliency, to the involvement of national veto players in the transposition process, to the degree of freedom (flexibility) environmental directives give to the member states on how to achieve the predetermined environmental objectives, and to the degree of policy compatibility between the EU and the domestic level (that is, the extent to which the environmental legislation coming from the EU level diverges from the existing national legislation in that area) (Kaeding 2006; Spendzharova and Versluis 2013; Steunenberg and Rhinard 2010; Steunenberg and Toshkov 2009; Thomson 2009).

Second, directives not only have to be transposed on time, but also correctly. Incorrect transposition may have nothing to do with the formal factors mentioned above (such as complexity and flexibility of the directive, or the compatibility between the directive and existing national legislation), but with the member states' political priorities and preferences, which do not entirely correspond to the content of the adopted European policy.

The implementation responsibility of the member states, and more particularly the question whether the member states implement on time and correctly, is monitored by the European Commission. The Commission has the power to start a so-called infringement proceeding when a member state does not comply with EU legislation in a timely or correct manner. Such a proceeding can ultimately end up in the Commission bringing the non-compliant member state to the Court of Justice of the EU (see Chapter 3). Briefly, the division of labour is as follows in the EU: the member states are responsible for the implementation of environmental policy, the Commission for monitoring that implementation and the Court of Justice to judge whether the Commission or the member state are right when they disagree on an implementation question and ultimately to sanction the non-complying member state.

The Commission has three sources of information to identify implementation problems in the member states: non-communication, own initiative and complaints (Lelieveldt and Princen 2011). First, the Commission can relatively easily monitor whether the member states have communicated their transposition activities to the EU, since member states need to notify this through an online database. If a member state has not communicated with the Commission after the transposition deadline, the Commission is informed about the implementation problem. Second, policy officials working in the Commission's DG Environment and DG Climate Action constantly scrutinize whether national environmental legislation corresponds to the requirements of the European directives they aim to implement. Through this resource-intensive work, the Commission is able to detect shortcomings or inadequacies in the national legislations, although some of them may still escape from the Commission's eye.

Third, the Commission invites citizens and non-state actors to report the implementation problems they witness in the member states. Indeed, as far as the practical effectiveness of European environmental policy is concerned, it is not easy for the European Commission to perform its role of 'guardian of the Treaties'. The Commission has no direct enforcement competences, since it is not present on the ground where the actual environmental policy needs to be applied. It has for instance no inspection authorities that can be sent to the member states to examine whether European environmental rules are followed in practice. In this respect, the Commission is 'geographically and politically dissociated from what goes on on the ground level in the member states' (Jordan 1999: 71). One of the consequences is that the Commission is highly dependent on information from third parties in order to play its role as monitoring agent of the implementation. Therefore, the Commission has set up a system through which interest groups, NGOs, citizens and other actors can provide so-called complaints to the Commission on the difficulties with the application of European environmental policies they witness in the member states. In 2012, for instance, the Commission received 588 complaints about non-compliance in the environmental domain and six complaints on climate issues (European Commission 2013b).

One has to be prudent with drawing conclusions on the state of implementation in the member states on the basis of the number of non-communications, own initiatives and complaints. Lower numbers do not necessarily mean that implementation is going better on the ground, since it can also indicate the Commission pays less attention to the issue or that non-state actors are less interested in complaining (Jordan 1999; Knill 2006; Knill and Liefferink 2007; Mastenbroek 2005). It could indeed be that the non-implementation cases observed by the Commission may only be the tip of the non-compliance iceberg (Falkner et al. 2005).

In cases where the Commission, on the basis of these three sources of information, has reasons to believe that a member state has not implemented European environmental legislation adequately or on time, it can start infringement proceedings against that member state, which consist of three steps and can ultimately lead to bringing that member state before the Court (Knill 2006; Lelieveldt and Princen 2011). Recently, the Commission has established a 'pre-infringement stage', which is based on the 'EU

Pilot' system and which operates without a formal Treaty basis. An online communication tool between the Commission and the member states, EU Pilot is an online platform that aims to resolve implementation problems at an early stage without starting formal infringement proceedings (Andersen 2012). It is actively used by the Commission. In 2012, for instance, 403 environmental and climate cases were opened in EU Pilot (European Commission 2013b).

When a formal infringement proceeding is started, the first step consists of the Commission sending a so-called *letter of formal notice* to the member state in which it reports the non-compliance and asks the member state to explain within a certain time limit (usually two months) why the non-compliance with European environmental legislation has occurred. This step opens the formal infringement proceeding. The interaction between the Commission and the member state in question can lead to a consensual solution as early as this stage of the process, making subsequent steps unnecessary (Knill and Liefferink 2007).

As a second step, depending on the answer (or lack of an answer) from the member state to the letter of formal notice, the Commission can address a *reasoned opinion* to the member state. This step, just like the next one, is based on the procedure prescribed in Article 258 TFEU. Here, the Commission explains the reasons why it considers the case to be infringing EU legislation, it proposes how the implementation problem should be remedied and it prescribes the time limit in which this should be done by the member state. However, simultaneously with this formal procedure, informal bilateral negotiations usually take place between the Commission and the member state with the aim of finding a last minute deal that resolves the issue and prevents further steps being taken. As a result of these informal bargaining dynamics, a majority of the infringement cases are already resolved before the judicial power of the EU – the Court of Justice – needs to come into play.

This third – and final – step consists of the Commission deciding to *refer the member state to the Court of Justice of the EU* if that member state does not succeed in presenting an adequate strategy to meet the concerns of the Commission and to solve the implementation problem. This final step in the infringement proceedings is considered to be the option of last resort in European environmental politics (Jordan 1999). The Commission also prefers a more informal bargaining solution, because a Court case demands considerable resources and because it may increase tensions with the member states and undermine their political goodwill in other simultaneous environmental policy-making processes. On average it takes approximately two years before the Court adopts a ruling in which it judges whether there has been an infringement or not. In general, most Court cases – approximately 90 per cent – are won by the Commission (Lelieveldt and Princen 2011).

If a member state continues to not comply with European environmental policy after the ruling of the Court, the Commission can start a new infringement proceeding (this one being based on Article 260 TFEU), which again passes through the stages of a letter of formal notice, a reasoned opinion and possibly a referral to the Court. Under Article 260 TFEU, the Court has a 'real' sanctioning mechanism at its disposal: if the Court then rules that the member state is still not complying, it can impose financial penalties (Börzel et al. 2010). However, Article 260 TFEU proceedings – and thus financial penalties – are relatively rare in the EU. By 2014, only 21 cases had reached this second-round judgment. Eight of them were related to implementation problems in the environmental field: on waste (Greece), wastewater (Ireland, Belgium and Luxembourg), bathing water (Spain), fishing control (France), GMO control (France) and environmental impact assessment (Ireland). Financial penalties can also be imposed on member states the first time the Court considers an infringement case, but only if the infringement is about a failure by a member state to notify its transposition measures to the Commission.

Figure 4.3 shows the number of infringements on environmental policy per member state for the years 2011, 2012 and 2013. It is apparent that the implementation deficit varies greatly between member states. Member states on the right-hand side of the graph have the biggest implementation deficit. They include southern member states (Italy, Spain, Greece, Portugal, France and Bulgaria) but also Poland. In contrast, the left-hand side features the best implementation students in the European class: the Baltic States, the Netherlands, Luxembourg, Malta and Denmark belong to this group. Interestingly, the 'new' member states do not perform significantly better or worse than the 'old' member states (Steunenberg and Toshkov 2009). The data also demonstrate that each year every member state – even those on the left-hand side on the graph – has been confronted with an infringement proceeding against it in

FIGURE 4.3 *Infringement proceedings opened against member states in the environmental domain per member state in the period 2011–2013*

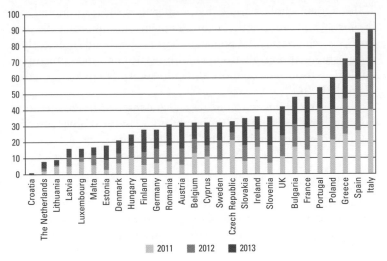

Source: based on European Commission 2014f

the environmental domain, again making it clear that the implementation deficit remains considerable in the entire EU. In other words, every member state is a non-complier, but some more so than others.

How can this variation between member states be explained? Basically, the main explanatory variable seems to be the degree of misfit (or the degree of incompatibility) between European environmental policy and the domestic context of the member states. In other words, the less the EU requirements fit with the existing situation in a member state, the higher the degree of implementation deficit is likely to be (Knill and Liefferink 2007). This means, for instance, that the instruments in the EU legislation are highly incompatible with those in the existing national law or that the environmental change that is envisioned in the European environmental policy is at variance with the one embodied in the national law. Some authors point to the importance of the degree of fit between the institutional structures in the member states (administrations, agencies, etc.) that are responsible for the domestic implementation on the one hand and the requirements of the EU environmental policy on the other hand (Knill and Lenschow 2000). In other words, implementation deficits are more likely in cases where European environmental policy requires a member state to change its national governance styles and structures substantially (Knill 2006). Other scholars argue that, rather than the institutional misfit, it is the policy misfit that causes implementation problems: if the European environmental policy does not correspond sufficiently to the existing national environmental legislation on the same topics, implementation will be more difficult due to 'adaptational costs' (Börzel 2000).

However, the misfit argument is also contested in the literature. Focusing on the realization of the objectives of the Biofuel Directive (2003/30) in the member states, Di Lucia and Kronsell argue that bad implementation records can be explained by the preferences of the member states (the 'unwilling' member states, which do not want the EU environmental policy to work on the ground) or by the administrative capacity of the member states (the 'unable' member states, which are not able to carry out effective implementation, even if the EU and the national institutions and policies fit) (Di Lucia and Kronsell 2010, see also Falkner et al. 2005; Falkner and Treib 2008).

Besides the (institutional and policy) misfit arguments, other explanations for the variation in the implementation deficit are also discussed in the literature. More effective implementation seems to be more likely if the national bureaucracies are more effective and have more administrative capability, better performing staff or higher budgets (Börzel et al. 2010; Toshkov 2008). Another reason for more effective implementation can be strong domestic mobilization by environmental interest groups or by the media in favour of effective implementation (Börzel 2000). A higher number of veto players in the transposition process, as in most federal states, has a negative impact on a member state's transposition record (Haverland 2000). Other studies emphasize that the causes of a bad implementation record are not necessarily located at the level of the member states, but they can also result from the ambiguities of European environmental legislation, which often contains vague formulations or exception clauses (Knill 2006), or from the complex or controversial nature of these policies (König and Luetgert 2009; Steunenberg and Kaeding 2009).

As a better implementation record has become one of the main priorities in the environmental domain, a couple of initiatives have been taken in order to address this problem. Those initiatives include, for example, the establishment of the 'European Union Network for the Implementation and Enforcement of Environmental Law' (IMPEL), which is a forum in which environmental officials from the Commission and from the member states meet in order to discuss the feasibility and the 'implementation-friendliness' (Martens 2008: 641) of a draft Commission proposal very early in the policy-making stage, namely when the Commission is still preparing the proposal (see Chapter 3) (Lenschow 2010). Moreover, IMPEL also offers a forum for exchanging best practices and other experiences with implementation among the member states, aiming to improve its consistency (Van Tatenhove et al. 2006). Another example of developments that aim to improve compliance with environmental legislation is the Commission initiative to provide a so-called implementation plan for each environmental directive. Since 2008, the Commission has indeed coupled a plan for the implementation of environmental legislation to the legislation itself. It prepares, for example, scoreboards and transposition checklists, which are informal and unenforceable documents aiming to help the member states in the implementation of the EU environmental policy concerned.

Conclusions

This chapter has set out how EU environmental legislation is adopted and implemented. As far as its adoption is concerned, this chapter has explained that the Treaty provisions (and in particular the ordinary legislative procedure) only tell one part of the story. Other informal dynamics are of crucial importance for understanding how EU environmental legislation is adopted. Early agreements are the rule rather than the exception and trilogues have become key policy-making forums. The increasingly important 'informalization' of the ordinary legislative procedure has led to a more efficient, yet also more secretive, environmental policy-making process. Another rather invisible, yet important, dynamic in EU environmental policy-making is the comitology system at the implementation stage. Finally, the chapter has made clear that European environmental policy suffers from a serious compliance problem in the member states. However, recent developments suggest that a better implementation record has become a political priority for European policy-makers.

The next chapter goes yet one step further, arguing that besides the EU institutions and the member states another type of actor needs to be taken into account when analysing environmental politics in the EU: non-state actors or interest groups, which attempt to lobby the European institutions in order to get their interests heard and represented as much as possible in the outcome of the policy-making process. In this way, both diffuse and specific societal interests are injected into the policy-making process. The first type of interests relates to the overall protection of the environment and the second one to the wishes and concerns of particular economic sectors and industries.

Chapter 5

Lobbying and Interest Representation

Formally speaking, European environmental policies are made within the institutional framework presented in Chapter 3 and through the procedures discussed in Chapter 4. We argued in Chapter 3 that from a theoretical point of view the different actors and institutions that formulate environmental policies each represent a particular type of interest in the policy-making process. To put it simply, the Commission initiates policy proposals from the perspective of a collective European interest; the Council offers the institutional platform for the member states to represent their national interests in the process; and by co-deciding, the European Parliament allows for the incorporation of citizens' interests. This does not, however, tell the entire story. Societal interests too are included in the policy-making process through lobbying activities of interest groups. Such interest groups are organizations that are politically active and that attempt to influence policies without having (or seeking) a political mandate (Beyers et al. 2008). They can present a broad scope of different interests, ranging from business to environmental ones.

The practice of lobbying is largely accepted in the EU, just as in other democratic political systems. Interest representation by NGOs, lobby groups and other private actors has become part and parcel of the day-to-day policy-making culture in Brussels. This is certainly the case for environmental policy-making, since the environmental policy area is one of the domains where lobbying is most prominently and intensively used (Bunea 2013; Coen 2007). DG Environment is considered to be the most intensely lobbied DG in the entire Commission (Coen and Katsaitis 2013). The level of interest group activity and the number of interest groups have considerably increased in recent decades at the EU level. In 2014, almost 7000 consultants, lobbyists, NGOs, think tanks, research institutions and organizations were registered in the EU's transparency register, which is a database of interest groups that have voluntarily registered, in return for which they get easier access to the European Parliament and the Commission (European Union 2014). Although it is not an easy task to determine exactly how many interest groups are lobbying the EU in the environmental field (Lelieveldt and Princen 2011), the growth in interest group activity in the EU is certainly evident insofar as environmental politics is concerned. As the scope of EU environmental competences has grown, as the field of action of environmental policy has expanded and as the volume of environmental legislation has steadily increased (see Chapter 1), it does not come as a surprise that interest groups active in this field have focused their attention more and more on environmental policy-making at the EU level. Of the 7000 registered interest groups, almost 3600 declared 'environment' to be one of their areas of interest, and more than 2000 did so for 'climate action'. Moreover, closely related fields such as 'enterprise' (approximately 2800), 'energy' (almost 2700) or 'transport' (almost 1900) are important self-declared areas of interest for these lobbyists (European Union 2014).

Two types of interest groups aim to be heard in EU environmental policy-making. On the one hand, environmental NGOs defend and represent the general environmental and ecological interests and concerns. They are usually considered to be the 'green' voices in environmental politics. On the other hand, business lobby groups defend and represent the particular interests of a certain economic sector, economic activity or single company affected by environmental norms and legislation. They typically include lobby groups representing the oil and gas, chemicals or steel industries or economic sectors such as the agricultural or pharmaceutical sector.

Before this chapter discusses how these two types of interest groups are organized at the EU level and how they are involved in European environmental policy-making, it examines the functions they fulfil. Assessing the question whether interest groups matter in EU environmental politics, the final section of the chapter discusses the influence of interest groups. The functions, strategies and resulting influence of environmental NGOs and business lobby groups in European environmental politics are summarized in Figure 5.1.

FIGURE 5.1   *Functions, strategies and influence of interest groups in EU environmental politics*

Functions	Strategies	Influence
• aggregating and representing interests • providing input-legitimacy • contributing expertise, know-how and information • increasing political awareness • monitoring implementation • relaying information between EU and national level • increasing national interest for EU environmental politics	• inside lobbying • outside lobbying • in multiple stages of the policy-making process • in a multi-level setting	no definite answer, but business lobby groups seem to be more influential than environmental NGOs due to: • more resources • longer tradition • type of interest (concentrated interests mobilize more easily than diffuse interests)

Functions and strategies of interest groups in EU environmental policy-making

Functions

The involvement of interest groups in politics and lobbying practices are often – for instance in the mass media – seen as something
negative, as a back stage practice that undermines the democratic
level of policy-making or as businesses and overpaid consultants taking over the tasks of elected politicians and government
officials. However, this image is far from adequate and complete,
since lobbying also allows for incorporating social interests in the
policy-making process and for voicing particular concerns that
would not necessarily be of prime importance to public policy-
makers, but which may nonetheless be of interest to society. In this
respect, interest groups that are active in environmental policy-
making in the EU perform seven types of functions.

First, environmental NGOs as well as business lobbies *represent
a particular interest*, aiming to have an impact on EU environmental legislation. Many interest groups do not only represent interests,
but they also first aggregate them. This is the case for umbrella
organizations (or member organizations) which act as the voice of
their constituents at the EU level. The constituencies of European
environmental NGOs are national NGOs and citizens who are
members of the organization. Those of business lobby groups
are national business organizations and individual companies.
Individual lobbyists, such as consultants of individual companies,

do not necessarily aggregate interests, but they directly represent their own interest in the policy-making process.

Second, by aggregating and representing societal interests and by uploading these interests towards a political system at the supranational level, interest groups also *provide input-legitimacy* to that system and the policy-making process that is taking place within it. Increasing the input-legitimacy of European environmental politics is considered a valuable side-effect of environmental lobbying. Moreover, this argument is also often used by the European institutions – and in particular by the European Commission – as a rhetorical tool to justify giving access to interest groups (Adelle and Anderson 2012).

Third, interest groups do not only offer legitimacy to the environmental policy-making, they also *contribute expertise, know-how and information*. Environmental policy-making in the EU deals with 'highly complex regulatory matters requiring niche expertise, such as industry information about the technical feasibility and cost-effectiveness of different policy options', which 'increases demand for technical information' (Rasmussen 2015: 377). In many cases interest groups that are active in the environmental policy area or that represent actors who face the consequences of EU environmental policy have information that would be too costly for the policy-makers to develop themselves. Business groups, for example, often prepare reports in which they quantify the costs and the benefits of (ideas for) forthcoming environmental legislation (Grant 2012). Or they provide technical expertise on, for example, the production processes that will be affected by the forthcoming policies. In a similar sense, environmental NGOs often attempt to present science-based evidence to advocate their argument. Information coming from interest groups is usually an important asset for policy-makers. Taking this information into account allows the European institutions to avoid strong opposition from these non-state actors in later stages of the process, for instance when the environmental policies need to be implemented on the field. In other words, it enables the policy-makers in Brussels to anticipate the future reactions of those actors they need later on to make their policies work. This is particularly true in regulatory policy areas, such as the environmental domain, where a lot of technical input is required in order to develop effective policies (Coen 2007).

Fourth, interest groups can play an important role in the agenda-setting stage of EU environmental policy-making. Environmental

NGOs can *increase political awareness* for particular environmental problems and put pressure on the Commission to take an initiative in that area. Environmental NGOs and industry lobby groups can be very active in their attempts to get an issue on the political agenda (or to make sure that it does not appear on the agenda) and to frame the issue according to their interests. They are therefore primarily active in the early stages of the policy-making process (see below).

Fifth, environmental NGOs also play an important role after the actual policy-making process, namely in the implementation stage. They can *monitor the application* of European environmental policies on the field in the member states and they raise the alarm when things go wrong in the implementation phase (Long and Lörinczi 2009). Introducing a complaint to the European Commission in order to bring an implementation problem to the attention of the Commission is a frequent method of doing so (see Chapter 4).

Sixth, Brussels-based interest groups act as an *information relay* between the European institutions and their member organizations at the domestic level. By having informal contacts or participating in Commission consultations or expert groups (see Chapter 3), they collect information about (future) developments in, and directions of, European environmental policy. This information is then transmitted to the nationally organized groups, which are in their turn enabled to anticipate what may be coming (Eising 2004).

Seventh, this link with the national interest groups also *increases the interest* and involvement in European environmental policy among interest groups in the member states. Indeed, by listening to their European federations, national interest groups – both from environmental NGOs and from business – are not only likely to be better informed about European environmental policy and politics, but they also become increasingly aware of the importance of environmental policy-making at the European level (Hallstrom 2004).

The role of interest groups in European (environmental) policy-making is often described as a trading exercise or an exchange game, in which the European institutions and the interest groups are interdependent (Bouwen 2004; Chalmers 2012). Environmental NGOs and business lobby groups trade their resources in exchange for influence with the European institutions. Interest groups provide the European policy-makers with resources such as legitimacy, political support, knowledge or information and they get access to the policy-making process and potential influence in return (Dür

2008). The policy-makers in the EU often lack the resources to be sufficiently informed, as a result of which they are a demanding party for the involvement of – and the resources offered by – interest groups.

In Chapter 3, we demonstrated that the relatively limited resources and capacities of the Commission's DG Environment and DG Climate Action *de facto* forces the Commission officials working in these DGs to look for policy-making resources outside their institution – and thus to consult interest groups. Therefore, the Commission has established consultation instruments through which it asks for the opinions and comments of interested citizens and interest groups. Such consultations take various forms in the environmental domain: online consultations, broad stakeholder fora or seminars in which the Commission asks for feedback on early ideas, or more restricted expert committees for specialized advice on the technical details of its proposals (see Chapter 3). These consultations serve as lobby venues, which are frequently targeted by interest groups since they allow the latter to be involved in the early stages of the policy-making process where they can be quite influential (see below).

Hence, interest representation in EU environmental policy-making can only be fully understood if the demand-side of lobbying is also taken into consideration. This counters a dominant image of lobbying and interest representation which suggests that lobbying is an aggressive practice that is unwanted by the public institutions (Coen 2007). European institutions should not automatically be seen as victims of hostile lobbying campaigns. They often encourage interest group involvement as well. Interest representation in EU environmental policy-making is a typical example of this dynamic (Broscheid and Coen 2007).

Strategies

In practice, environmental NGOs and business lobbies active on environmental issues do more in Brussels than merely offering resources to the institutions in order to get a grip and influence on the policy-making process. In order to get access to the institutions and to get their voice heard, the life of lobbyists encompasses various activities: 'The political activities of many interest groups are not limited to lobbying on specific issues, but include diffuse practices such as attending workshops, receptions, press conferences, monitoring newspaper and other media stories' (Beyers et al. 2008: 1115).

Interest groups basically have at their disposal two sets of strategies for influencing environmental policy in the direction of their preferences and interests (Lelieveldt and Princen 2011). On the one hand, both environmental NGOs and business lobbies attempt to have direct contacts with policy-makers in the European institutions ('inside lobbying'). This includes private meetings with the officials from DGs Environment and Climate Action, with MEPs from the ENVI Committee or with people from national ministries and Permanent Representations, but also participation in institutionalized lobby settings such as consultations, stakeholder fora or expert groups set up by the Commission (Quittkat and Finke 2008).

On the other hand, in contrast to lobbying inside the institutions, interest groups can also operate outside the institutions, aiming to mobilize public opinion by generating media attention for their demands (Kollman 1998). This strategy principally works when interests are at stake to which public opinion is sensitive. Therefore, such 'outside lobbying' is more likely to be used by environmental NGOs than by business lobby groups. This explains why, for example, outside lobbying is a more appropriate strategy for Greenpeace when it campaigns for whale protection than for BASF when it tries to get a special treatment for a particular chemical substance under a particular regulation or directive. However, many environmental NGOs, such as World Wide Fund for Nature (WWF) or Birdlife International (see below), also prefer inside lobbying to outside lobbying strategies, whereas others such as Friends of the Earth Europe or Greenpeace have a tendency to complement their inside lobbying activities with direct action campaigns and outside lobbying (Adelle and Anderson 2012).

Environmental NGOs and business lobby groups have multiple ways of influencing European environmental policy (Long and Lörinczi 2009). In every stage of the policy-making process, interest groups have the opportunity to be involved. This is the case in the formulation of policy proposals by the Commission (for example through expert groups), in the actual legislative work by the European Parliament and the Environment Council, in the comitology system (where technical details, which are often important for the interests of private actors, are decided upon), and in the implementation and enforcement stage (where interest groups can act as watchdogs).

Lobbying is not only possible at multiple stages of the policy-making process, but it also requires activities at different levels of governance. Hence, just like EU environmental policy-making, EU environmental lobbying is a multi-level activity. First, the interest groups themselves are organized at multiple levels. Individual companies or national NGOs can opt to approach policy-makers themselves, but they can also decide to lobby through national federations or through European umbrella federations. Second, the targets of interest groups are located at multiple levels as well. Lobbying activities are usually not focused on either domestic actors or on the EU institutions, but on a combination of both (for a case study on multi-level lobby strategies in the negotiations on the Renewable Energy Directive 2009/28, see Ydersbond 2014). The multi-level nature of European environmental policy-making may affect the role and the strategies of the interest groups, although there is no agreement in the literature about the direction in which this effect goes (Lelieveldt and Princen 2011). On the one hand, the multi-level architecture can increase the number of access points for the interest groups, as a result of which the number of channels available to them in order to influence environmental policy also grows. On the other hand, the multi-level nature of the political system can also lead to a situation in which interest groups are driven from pillar to post by the policy-makers.

Environmental NGOs

The boost in the development of EU environmental policy in the 1970s and the 1980s (see Chapter 1) went hand in hand with an increasing number and level of institutionalization of environmental NGOs in Europe. They started to pay more and more attention to environmental politics at the EU level and they became increasingly aware of the importance of the environmental policies adopted there.

The ten major environmental NGOs currently active in Brussels have gathered together institutionally in the so-called Green 10. Initially established as the 'G4' (with the four founding members the European Environmental Bureau, Friends of the Earth Europe, WWF and Greenpeace – nowadays still referred to as the 'Gang of Four' within the Green 10), it is now a 'loose but co-ordinated network of the ten leading environmental NGOs active at EU level who coordinate joint responses and recommendations to EU decision-makers' (Greenwood 2011: 150). The Green 10 is nowadays composed of the following ten organizations:

- The *European Environment Bureau (EEB)* was established in 1974 as the first environmental NGO working at the European level. It is active on a broad range of environmental issues and it represents more than 140 member organizations from 31 countries. Among the first members of the EBB were Friends of the Earth Europe (FoEE), Greenpeace and the WWF. Whereas it initially suffered from a reputation for poor leadership (McCormick 2001), it is now considered by the European Commission as a preferred partner in environmental policymaking, although it is often blamed for not being a very effective environmental lobbyist, likely to slip back into broad historical discussions instead of defending concrete environmental claims (Greenwood 2011). The EEB is responsible for managing the Green 10 organizationally on a day-to-day basis.
- *World Wide Fund for Nature European Policy Office (WWF-EPO)* is the European branch of WWF, striving for the conservation of endangered species, the protection of threatened habitats and keeping global environmental threats on the political agenda. WWF-EPO has played an important watchdog function in the past, e.g. by providing evidence of environmental harm that resulted from the use of EU structural funds in Spain (Greenwood 2011).
- *Friends of the Earth Europe (FoEE)* is the European pillar of Friends of the Earth International, which calls itself a grassroots environmental network. It is said to be – and seen as – a valuable contributor of information to European environmental policymaking (Greenwood 2011).
- *Greenpeace European Unit* is the Green 10 member that is likely to be the most inclined to direct-action campaigns and boycotts, although this organization has also increasingly learned to apply inside lobbying strategies. Dividing lobbying tasks among its different national offices, Greenpeace functions in a rather decentralized way, as a result of which the work not only of its Brussels office but also of the national ones needs to be taken into account in order to fully grasp its activities. In order to ensure its (perceived) independence (see below) Greenpeace is the only member of the Green 10 that does not accept financial resources from public and private actors, including the European Commission.
- *BirdLife International* is a partnership organization of NGOs from more than one hundred countries striving for the conservation of birds, their habitats and global biodiversity.

- *CEE Bankwatch Network*, with members primarily in Central and Eastern European countries, is an advocacy network that monitors the work of international financial institutions with particular relevance in that area, such as the European Bank for Reconstruction and Development (EBRD) or the European Investment Bank (EIB). It encourages those financial institutions not to finance environmentally and socially harmful investments.
- *Climate Action Network Europe (CAN-E)* is an umbrella group of more than 150 member organizations active on climate change issues. In its turn, it is a member of CAN-International.
- *Naturefriends International (NFI)* is an environmental NGO which emphasizes the social dimension of the environment and environmental policies. Aiming to make access to nature as easy as possible, it is, for example, active in lobbying activities on the promotion of eco-tourism.
- *Transport and Environment (T&E)* is the main NGO in Brussels that acts on the issues of sustainable and green transport policies in the EU. Its main areas of activity have been the various pieces of European climate legislation, for instance on CO_2 targets for cars and light utility vehicles, or on the inclusion of aviation in the EU ETS (see Chapter 9).
- The *Health and Environment Alliance (HEAL)* works on the relationship between the environment and public health, emphasizing in its lobbying activities the importance of the environment for peoples' health and quality of life.

The Green 10 makes use of the various opportunities this rich and varied membership offers. On the one hand, the ten organizations represent a mix of 'light green' NGOs that are rather establishment-friendly and put their money towards inside lobbying (like WWF or Birdlife International) and 'dark green' environmental groups that are more oriented towards outside lobbying activities (such as Greenpeace or FoEE) (Adelle and Anderson 2012; Greenwood 2011). On the other hand, it also has a mix of organizations with institutionalized power, which primarily contribute expertise and networks to the Green 10 (EEB, WWF or Birdlife International), and mass membership organizations, which contribute public mobilization opportunities to the Green 10 (FoEE or Greenpeace). The Green 10 claims to represent a combined membership of more than 20 million people.

Generally speaking, the Green 10 has succeeded rather well in establishing effective coordination and cooperation among its members through regular meetings and information exchanges (Greenwood 2011). Through the Green 10, the ten environmental NGOs maintain a dense network of informal contacts with Commission officials and manage to have frequent meetings with members of the cabinet of the Environment Commissioner and a yearly encounter with the President of the European Commission. The Green 10 as such is also a member of the EU Civil Society Contact Group, which is an even broader NGO umbrella organization assembling citizens' interests NGOs working on social, environmental, human rights, women's rights and development issues and maintaining close relations with the European institutions.

Besides its delicate inside lobbying undertakings, the most visible activities by the Green 10 include its 'Greening the Treaty' initiatives in which it has pushed at most Intergovernmental Conferences since the 1980s to try to strengthen the green character of the new European treaties. Likewise, through its 'Greening the EU budget' initiatives, the Green 10 strives for a reform of the annual EU budget away from environmentally harmful measures in, for example, agricultural policy or the structural funds. Moreover, for the 2014–2019 term of the European Parliament it produced a manifesto with key recommendations related to the environment and to sustainable development and it is active in monitoring the commitments the EU made in its Sustainable Development Strategy (see Chapter 7).

The activities of the Green 10 are not necessarily supported or conducted by all of the ten members. Indeed a common practice is to divide the work among the members by forming 'policy clusters' of individual NGOs for collective action on particular issues, which non-Green 10 members can also join. Such policy clusters have been established on the reform of the Common Agricultural Policy, the reform of the cohesion policy, the EU's climate and energy policy or the REACH Regulation (Long and Lörinczi 2009). These issue-specific coalitions are important for a full understanding of the role environmental NGOs play in European environmental policy-making.

Most of the environmental NGOs that are active at the EU level are financially supported by the European Commission. Except for Greenpeace, which does not accept financial support from governments, EU institutions or industry, all Green 10 members receive funding from the Commission. For some NGOs, more than half of their financial resources come from Commission funding, as is the case for Justice and Environment (a network of environmental law organizations offering legal expertise on EU environmental law) (70 per cent), CEE Bankwatch Network (64 per cent) or FoEE (55 per cent). EU contributions count for 41 per cent of the EEB budget and for 22 per cent of the WWF budget (European Commission 2013c).

In 2013, the Commission granted approximately 9 million euros to thirty-two environmental NGOs through the Financial Instrument for the Environment (LIFE+), which has currently (that is, for the period 2014–2020) been succeeded by the LIFE programme (see Chapter 6) (European Commission 2013c). The top three recipients consisted of the EEB (€830.700), FoEE (€751.064) and WWF European Policy Office (€573.647). The Commission, which is one of the most important public funders of NGOs in the world, justifies the fact that it financially supports environmental NGOs by arguing that this results in a more balanced interest representation at the EU level, where environmental concerns would otherwise be disadvantaged (Sanchez Salgado 2014). However, this rationale – which fits within a typical European political culture of organizing the relations between public and private actors – is not supported by everyone, as critics point out that such financing leads to a bias in interest representation in EU environmental policy-making. Moreover, it may raise questions about the independence and the credibility of the environmental NGOs and their ability to run counter to the preferences and political choices of the Commission (Van Deth and Maloney 2011; Warleigh 2000). This is the argument that made Greenpeace refuse that type of public financial support. On the other hand, other NGOs deny that there is a link between the source of their financial resources and the content of the message they convey.

Business lobby groups

Whereas the environmental concerns represented by NGOs in EU environmental policy-making are so-called diffuse interests, business lobbies usually defend particular, or 'concentrated', interests. Diffuse interests refer to 'collective interests held by large numbers of individuals, such as environmental protection' (Pollack 1997: 572–573). Concentrated interests, by contrast, are the interests of particular actors in a socio-economic system, such as companies or economic sectors (including the pharmaceutical, chemical or agricultural sector). EU environmental policy does indeed have a substantial effect on (the interests of) the production system employed by industry and businesses. Environmental policy is a typical example of regulatory policy, which controls or sometimes even prohibits the use of particular substances, products or processes (Grant 2012). Moreover, European industry has a particular interest in regulating environmental affairs at the EU level. Certainly those businesses that are to a large extent dependent on exports have an essential interest in a harmonized regulatory framework that is applied by all European companies in their sector. In other words, they prefer an environmental regulatory framework at the EU level, which creates a level playing field that does not upset competition. In that sense, it is clear that industry and business groups have interests in being involved in EU environmental policy-making.

There are many industrial federations in Brussels involved in environmental policy-making, although many of them do not exclusively focus on the environmental policy area, but also on, for instance, the internal market, competition, industry or trade domains. Examples of such federations include (Grant 2012: 177; McCormick 2001: 112–113):

- The *European Chemicals Industry Council (CEFIC)* represents the interests of approximately 29,000 companies from the chemicals industry in the EU.
- The *European Crop Protection Association (ECPA)* also represents the chemicals industry, but with a particular focus on companies producing substances that are used for agricultural technology (for example crops and pesticides).
- The *Committee of Professional Agricultural Organisations/ General Committee for Agricultural Cooperation in the European Union (COPA/COGECA)*, being the umbrella organization of the farmer lobby groups and organizations of agricultural cooperatives of the member states, is one of the oldest interest groups at the European level and is considered as well to be one of the most influential groups.
- The *European Petroleum Industry Association (EUROPIA)* is the federation of the oil refining industry in Europe.
- The *European Automobile Manufacturers Association (ACEA)* is the main interest group of eighteen car, truck and bus manufacturers in the EU.
- *BusinessEurope* does not focus solely on environmental affairs, although environment and climate change is one of the topics it is working on.

Influence of interest groups

The question remains whether interest groups really matter in European environmental policy-making and to what extent they are able to influence (the content of) European environmental policies. Measuring the influence of interest groups is, however, a difficult exercise due to the lack of counterfactuals (Beyers et al. 2008; Dür 2008; Lowery 2013). Until now, studies have not succeeded in giving definitive – or even non-contradictory – answers on questions dealing with the extent of influence of environmental NGOs and business lobbies in the making of environmental policies at the EU level. Moreover, environmental interest groups can be influential on some issues, while failing to see their preferences reflected in other cases.

Nonetheless, a couple of factors and conditions can be identified which shed light on the influence of interest groups in European environmental politics. Obviously, the specific context of the policy-making process, including the salience and the technicality of the issue and the size and the unity of the lobbying coalitions, substantially affect the likelihood of being influential (Klüver 2011; Rasmussen 2015). Alongside context-related factors, it is generally assumed that business lobby groups have a larger influence on European environmental policy than environmental NGOs (Bunea 2013; Greenwood 2011; Mazey and Richardson 2006; Rasmussen 2012). However, the opposite has been argued as well, namely that interest groups advocating environmental protection have, on average, been more successful in achieving their preferred policy outcomes in the EU than business interest groups (Dür et al. 2015). The general understanding of business lobby dominance over environmental NGOs in EU environmental politics can be explained by three factors.

First, political influence seems to be a function of the available *financial and informational resources*. The more resources an interest group has, the more influential it is likely to be. This reasoning is perfectly in line with the exchange game rationale outlined above. Since environmental NGOs, despite public funding from the European Commission, tend to have fewer financial resources than business lobby groups, their influence is more limited as they can rent less office space, hire fewer personnel and therefore develop less policy-relevant expertise. Business interest groups thus have a comparative advantage in terms of their organizational capacity, financial resources and expertise, which might give them a stronger 'insider status' in the European institutions than environmental NGOs (Coen 2007). In addition, the effect of this resources disadvantage is reinforced by the fact that environmental policy-making in the European Commission is increasingly dealt with by multiple DGs (see Chapter 3). Indeed, not only DGs Environment and Climate Action, but also other DGs like Enterprise and Industry or Internal Market and Services are often involved. The quasi-exclusive focus on DGs Environment and Climate Action in the lobby activities of the environmental NGOs – with some notable exceptions such as Transport and Environment – is seen as one of their main weaknesses compared to the broader lobbying activities by the business lobbies, which have more resources to target other DGs as well (Adelle and Anderson 2012).

Second, business lobby groups *have a longer history* of being organized and active at the EU level than environmental NGOs. Since the EU was initially conceived as a customs union, primarily focusing on economic integration in its early years, economic interests were rapidly organized at the EU level. In contrast, due to the steady growth of the amount of environmental legislation in the 1970s (see Chapter 1), environmental groups have only begun to organize themselves at the EU level two decades later than the business groups. This longer tradition and experience may favour the business side (Knill and Liefferink 2007).

Third, as a general rule in politics, the *nature of the interest* represented by an interest group affects its potential to be influential. Concentrated interests tend to organize and mobilize more easily than diffuse interests do (Olson 1965). Applied to the environmental area, this rule of thumb implies that environmental interests are more difficult to mobilize than 'economic' (in the sense of 'business') interests are. Indeed, while the benefits of most environmental policy measures are diffuse for everyone, their costs are generally concentrated upon a limited number of companies. As a result, environmental NGOs are confronted with a free-rider problem, which makes mobilization more problematic. Consequently, '[o]rganizations representing "diffuse interests", such as environmental NGOs [...], perform significantly worse in achieving their preferences than the main business groups, representing "concentrated interests"' (Bunea 2013: 567). However, although the political system of the EU is biased in favour of economic and concentrated interests (Beyers et al. 2008), successful mobilization of diffuse interests is no longer unusual in the EU. In other words, business interest groups are not always and by definition more influential than environmental NGOs are (Grant 2012).

As mentioned above, interest groups are active in all stages of the policy-making process, from the prelegislative stage (during the consultations organized by the Commission) to the implementation stage (at the domestic level). As far as the influence of interest groups in environmental policy-making is concerned, it is argued that this influence is likely to be the strongest in the early stages of the policy-making process, namely when the preferences of policy-makers are not yet fully developed – or at least made public (Adelle and Anderson 2012; Mazey and Richardson 2006). The policy preparation stage and the consultation period organized by the Commission offer thus the best opportunities for interest groups to influence the content of forthcoming European environmental policies (Bouwen 2009).

Hence, it comes as no surprise that both environmental NGOs and business groups tend to focus their lobby activities on the prelegislative stage and, consequently, on the European Commission (Bunea 2013; 2014). The main purpose of this strategy is to ensure that the policy proposal already goes in the direction of their interests before it enters the legislative pipeline under the ordinary legislative procedure and before it arrives in the European Parliament and the Council (see Chapter 4). However, in this prelegislative stage too, business interests seem to dominate environmental interests. Environmental NGOs often complain that, although they are regularly invited by the European Commission to participate in its consultation processes, they do not receive as much actual attention from the Commission as business lobby groups (Adelle and Anderson 2012; Heard-Laureote 2010). However, studies also show that the early stages of the policy-making process are the ones where environmental NGOs can have the highest level of influence. Another stage in which they are likely to be able to exert considerable influence is the implementation stage, where they can perform their watchdog function (see above) (Long and Lörinczi 2009).

Next to the European Commission, the European Parliament has increasingly become an attractive target for interest groups in the environmental area (Coen 2009). As explained in Chapters 1 and 3, the ever-increasing legislative powers of the EP in environmental affairs are obviously the main explanatory factor for this evolution. With the EP having veto power under the ordinary legislative procedure, it now pays off to lobby the EP as well (Rasmussen 2015). Whereas the EP was for a long time seen as an institution that was primarily open to environmental NGOs and to diffuse environmental interest representation, this has changed in parallel with the EP's growing powers. Environmental NGOs and business lobby groups alike now lobby the EP and none of them now seems to have significantly better access than any other. This makes the EP nowadays much more an 'environmental pragmatist' than the 'environmental champion' it was previously said to be (Rasmussen 2012: 239; Smith 2008) (see also Chapter 3). Within the EP, particularly the rapporteur, who drafts the report in the ENVI Committee and represents the EP in the trilogue negotiations with the Council and the Commission (see Chapter 4), and the shadow rapporteurs have become the subject of an intensified attention by lobby groups.

By contrast, the Council is the institution in the ordinary legislative procedure which experiences the least pressure from interest groups in the environmental field. However, the national governments are likely to be strongly approached before they go to Brussels when particular interests of national companies are at stake. The following quote is illustrative in this regard: 'if a Council working group on vehicle pollution is meeting and contains a civil servant from the Swedish government, the civil servant will certainly have been lobbied by Volvo and Saab and will be fully aware of the ways in which the Swedish motor vehicle industry might be affected by any proposed EU legislation' (Mazey and Richardson 2006: 255).

Conclusions

Having examined the role that environmental NGOs and business lobby groups play in EU environmental policy-making, this chapter complements the two previous ones in completing the picture of environmental policy-making in the EU. European environmental policies are not only made within the institutional triangle, but also in interaction with non-state actors representing particular interests. This chapter has shown that the representation of both diffuse environmental interests and concentrated economic interests is part and parcel in day-to-day environmental policy-making in the EU, but that this is – contrary to what is often claimed in popular media – not by definition problematic. Interest groups can provide legitimacy and expertise to the policy-making process and their input is often explicitly demanded by the European institutions, particularly the European Commission. What might be problematic, though, is the bias that seems to exist in favour of (the interests represented by) business lobby groups compared to environmental NGOs.

This chapter concludes our discussion of environmental policy-making in the EU and what the main characteristics of EU environmental *politics* are. The next chapters will extensively examine the content and effects of the output of the policy-making process, namely the *policies* as such, and evaluate them. The next chapter gives an overview of the various environmental policy instruments and how they are applied in the EU. This is followed by Chapter 7, which delves deeper into the 'traditional' subdomains of European environmental policies (waste and product; air; water; nature protection and biodiversity; soil; and noise policies). The two next chapters then examine in a more detailed way two more politicized European environmental policy issues, each with a very important international dimension: GMOs and climate change.

Chapter 6

Environmental Policy Instruments

Whereas the previous chapters discussed the politics and the policy-making processes behind EU environmental policy, the current and the following chapters focus on the policy content. Before turning to a substantive discussion of the main policy elements and political dynamics of various environmental subdomains in Chapters 7 to 9, this chapter is devoted to the instruments of EU environmental policy.

A discussion of policy instruments is a vital part of any policy analysis. Not only does the choice of certain types of instruments constitute an essential aspect of governing, instruments also form the main link between the EU's steering activities and the impact of its policies on the ground (Jordan et al. 2013). As this chapter will show, the choices the EU makes with regard to environmental policy instruments are characterized by a particular dynamism. Flexible use of the wide range of policy instruments that the EU has developed over time has been necessary to advance the EU's environmental agenda and to overcome institutional and political obstacles. The discussion of the EU's environmental policy instruments will reveal an evolution that is essential for understanding today's achievements and challenges in this domain.

Policy instruments are 'the actual means or devices governments [here, the EU institutions] have at their disposal for implementing policies, and among which they must select in formulating policy' (Howlett and Ramesh 2003: 87) and they 'define how, who and within which organizational structures to do things' in order to address environmental problems (Lenschow et al. 2005: 805). To analyse policy instruments, it is useful to look at different *types* of instruments. While there are several competing typologies of policy instruments (Wurzel et al. 2013), we use a classification that distinguishes instruments according to the type of resource mobilized by them (such as authority, money or information). The following sections consecutively discuss regulatory, planning, market-based and information instruments. Table 6.1 gives an overview of these types of environmental policy instruments, their operationalization and their functions.

EU environmental policy is thus conducted through widely varying types of policy instruments. Most of them are adopted by means of legislative acts, but others do not require a legislative act to be adopted. The main difference between legislative and non-legislative policies is that legislation is legally binding and that it is adopted through an interaction between the Commission, the Council and

Table 6.1 *Types of environmental instruments*

type of instrument	instruments	functions
regulatory instruments	- usually legislative acts	- imposing obligations, prohibitions or restrictions - introducing standards
planning instruments	- Environmental Action Programmes - Strategies - Communications (e.g. green papers, white papers, roadmaps)	- orienting policy-making
market-based instruments	- taxes - risk liability schemes - subsidies - tradable allowances - green public procurement	- sanctioning or rewarding behaviour through market mechanisms
information instruments	- information campaigns - labelling - impact assessments	- stimulating changes in preferences and behaviour of the public - generating information for policy formulation and evaluation

the European Parliament (usually through the ordinary legislative procedure, see Chapter 4), whereas non-legislative policies do not necessarily require the involvement of all institutions and are not legally binding. The main types of legislative acts used in EU environmental policy – regulations, directives and decisions – are presented in Box 6.1.

Two remarks with regard to legislative acts in the environmental field are worth mentioning. First, legislative acts are often further refined and implemented at the EU level through so-called implementing acts and delegated acts, which are adopted through a comitology procedure (see Chapter 4). Second, EU environmental policy is in a constant state of flux. EU institutions are involved in a continuous process of amending and revising parts of the extensive legislative body, in order to consolidate it, to adapt it to changing circumstances or new international environmental agreements, or to make it more efficient (Axelrod et al. 2011). Chapter 7 provides substantial evidence on how progress in environmental policy-making, for instance in waste or water policies, is to a significant extent driven by the revision of legislative instruments.

Regulatory instruments

As demonstrated by the steady increase in both the quantity and the scope of environmental legislation (see Figure 1.1), environmental policy is nowadays one of the largest policy domains in the EU. Regulatory instruments are the most commonly used tools in EU environmental policy. Through regulatory instruments, 'general norms for certain types of activities' are set (Lelieveldt and Princen 2011: 182). Most of them are adopted by means of legislative acts.

The initial logic behind governing through regulatory instruments was the harmonization of environmental standards between the member states. Before 1987, when there was no legal basis for environmental measures, the EU adopted legislation on environmental issues principally in order to complete or strengthen the common market (see Chapter 1). Common European environmental standards were thus meant to diminish competition distortion and trade impediments between member states. This harmonization logic remains omnipresent in the (still wide) use of regulatory instruments today. That contributes to the EU's reputation for being a 'regulatory state' (Majone 1994), which refers to the interventionist logic in environmental policy (Jordan et al. 2013; Wurzel et al. 2013).

Box 6.1   Types of legislative acts used for EU environmental policy

- *Regulations* are legislative acts that have general application, are binding in their entirety, and directly applicable in all member states. This means that they automatically have the force of law within the EU, without needing legislative or executive action by the member states (such as transposition into national law). Normally, they take legal effect a few days after they have been published in the EU's Official Journal. Regulations are particularly suited to imposing technical standards or creating a uniform legal framework that does not allow for differentiation between member states (Axelrod et al. 2011). For that reason, they have been applied in waste and product policies (for instance the REACH Regulation, 1927/2006). Otherwise, regulations are used to set up administrative structures or institutional procedures (for instance to introduce eco-labels, see below) or to transpose obligations imposed by multilateral environmental agreements into the EU legal order (for instance the Regulation on Ozone Depleting Substances, 1005/2009). Regulations are rare in a number of environmental policy areas, such as in air or water policy (Krämer 2012a).
- *Directives* are used more frequently than regulations in the environmental domain. They need to be transposed by member states after they have been adopted by the EU, meaning that each member state has to adopt national law in which it determines how the objectives of the directive will be implemented at the domestic level (see Chapter 4). Directives are in principle less detailed than regulations. They only determine the results to be achieved, but leave it to the discretion of member states how to get there. Directives are chosen as the legislative instrument when differences between member states (for instance in terms of natural conditions or legal systems) are too large for a 'one size fits all' approach. For that reason, they are particularly suited for harmonization, and have thus become the number one instrument of environmental policy (Jans

and Vedder 2012; Krämer 2012a; Wurzel et al. 2013). However, it is generally acknowledged that the practical differences between choosing a regulation or a directive as the legislative instrument should not be exaggerated (Nugent 2010), mainly because directives have become increasingly detailed and because some regulations do not have a direct effect in practice (Krämer 2012a; Lelieveldt and Princen 2011).

In many areas of environmental policy, it has appeared that the EU could go further if it imposed only a binding end result, but left as much flexibility as possible in the means to achieve it. That is why in 1976 the EU introduced the *framework directive* as a new tool. Framework directives define only the essential elements of a policy, such as long-term environmental goals, but they leave out all other details, such as specific substances or technical particularities (Wurzel et al. 2013). Those are deferred to so-called daughter directives, which are negotiated and adopted subsequently. The advantage of framework directives lies mostly in their ability to advance the body of environmental legislation in Europe, while postponing often thorny discussions about particular issues to later stages (Halpern 2010). They can also be used to simplify legislation, by bringing existing pieces under a single new umbrella (such as the Water Framework Directive, 2000/60, see Chapter 7). This can also stimulate member states to adopt a more integrated approach in their environmental legislation, as framework directives leave them with a great deal of implementation flexibility (Axelrod et al. 2011).

- Being rather an administrative instrument (Nugent 2010), *decisions* are only binding upon those to whom they are addressed (for example all member states, one or a couple of member states, individuals or companies). Being very numerous but also technical in nature, they are, for instance, used to authorize grants from an environmental fund, to establish a committee or to ratify international environmental agreements (see Chapter 10) (Krämer 2012a).

Regulatory policy instruments serve a twofold function in the environmental field, as examples in the following chapters will extensively illustrate. First, they can be applied to impose obligations, prohibitions or restrictions on member states, and – in the case of decisions – on companies or private persons within the EU (Halpern 2010; Holzinger et al. 2006; Lee 2014). For instance, under the End of Life Vehicles Directive (2000/53), member states must ensure that producers (or importers) of vehicles take back their products once they have become waste (Jans and Vedder 2012). Or, under the REACH Regulation (1907/2006), companies are obliged to notify their national authorities 60 days before they intend to put new chemicals onto the European market (Krämer 2012a). The use of regulatory instruments is often accompanied by some form of monitoring, reporting or inspection, either at member state or EU level.

Second, in the large majority of the cases, regulatory instruments in EU environmental policy are used to introduce standards, following the harmonization logic of the 1970s (Jordan et al. 2013). Product specifications were among the earliest standards, followed by environmental quality and emission standards (for instance, in water or air policy, see Chapter 7). As the EU gained more powers in the environmental domain, it also introduced process standards, dealing with the required use of specific methods, procedures or reference documents in production processes. Such process standards account for nearly half of all standards used in environmental policy (Halpern 2010; Holzinger et al. 2006; Lee 2014). Standardization is thus not only meant to control pollution and to protect the environment, but also to centralize information at EU level and give EU institutions more steering capacity.

Certain standards are adopted with regard to the use of 'best available technology' (BAT) (Krämer 2012a). The standards in regulatory policies containing BAT provisions are binding with regard to the methods that are used (for example how to determine emission limit values), rather than to the result that is achieved. Consequently, they are an additional way of allowing member states leeway during the implementation phase. The technologies in question are not included in the legislation, but defined through comitology procedures (see Chapter 4) (Lee et al. 2012). The use of BAT in environmental policies did not initially yield the desired outcomes because political compromises were prioritized ahead of objective, technological criteria, for instance for the definition of industrial emission values. More recently, however, economic and other considerations related to specific countries or installations have become one of the central principles in pollution control policies, increasing the effectiveness of BAT provisions (Krämer 2012a).

Concerning the imposition of standards, it is important to note that harmonization by the EU is used to introduce a threshold, but that member states can always perform better than that threshold. This is in fact explicitly foreseen in the Treaty, since Article 193 TFEU states that the adopted environmental legislation 'shall not prevent any Member State from maintaining or introducing more stringent protective measures' (see Box 1.2). Such practice is referred to as 'gold plating' and it can take different shapes. In its purest form, gold plating means that member states define stricter standards when they transpose directives into domestic legislation. But gold plating also happens when implementation is finalized well before the deadline or when not all the opportunities to invoke exceptions are exploited (HM Government 2011). However, instances of gold plating have been rare in environmental politics, even in Europe. On the contrary, several EU member states adopt an explicit 'no gold plating' strategy, or have done so in the past (Jans and Squintini 2009). They believe that such a strategy would harm their competitiveness or impose administrative burdens, or they use a no gold plating strategy to show their political opposition against either strict environmental protection or the imposition of EU regulation.

Planning instruments

Planning instruments install new planning structures to orient policy-making. The most important of those in the environmental field are Environmental Action Programmes (EAPs), strategies and communications. Importantly, and in contrast to most regulatory policy instruments, many planning instruments are non-legislative in nature (with the EAPs being the exception since 1993). This means that they are not legally binding and that they are not adopted through the ordinary legislative procedure. Strategies are usually adopted by the European Council. Communications are always Commission documents, but they can initially be requested by the Council and are often discussed and sometimes endorsed by the Council and the European Parliament afterwards.

First, *EAPs* are the main planning instruments of EU environmental policy. As mentioned in Chapter 1, the first EAP was developed in 1973, when a legal basis for environmental policy was still lacking. Since the entry into force of the Maastricht Treaty in 1993, with four EAPs having already been published at that time, EAPs have a Treaty basis. They outline the priority goals for environmental action in the EU, the measures to achieve those objectives and their timeframe (Krämer 2012a). In doing so, they give direction to the work of the European Commission, which is the first mover in the policy-making process (see Chapters 3 and 4). They also give a good indication of the opinion of the institutions on the direction for EU environmental policy in the future. An overview of the seven EAPs is presented in Box 6.2 (based on Holzinger et al. 2006; Jans and Vedder 2012).

Second, *strategies* are less stringent planning instruments than EAPs. With a specific focus on sustainable development, the EU Sustainable Development Strategy (EUSDS) was developed in 2001, in preparation for the 2002 World Summit on Sustainable Development (Tanasescu 2006), and renewed in 2006. The EUSDS formulates key objectives in a number of issue areas in order to streamline sustainable development policies both within the European Commission and among member states, and it also associates European goals with the global agenda (see Chapter 7). The EUSDS has no binding character and should be thought of as a soft steering instrument. It relies, for instance, on peer review between member states and on cooperation procedures similar to the open method of coordination (von Homeyer 2009; Spangenberg 2010). A set of sustainable development indicators was created to give Eurostat the task of monitoring the EUSDS and member states needed to report on their individual progress.

After 2010, when the Europe 2020 strategy was launched, an effort was made to include sustainable development concerns in that socio-economic strategy and the EUSDS was not renewed. Europe 2020 is the EU's overall growth strategy that is based on its ambition to achieve smart, sustainable and inclusive growth for the 2010–2020 period. The inclusion of environmental and social goals was a response to a common criticism of the Lisbon strategy, Europe 2020's predecessor for the period 2000–2010. Europe 2020 includes five headline targets, including the 20-20-20 climate and energy objectives already adopted in 2007: a 20 per cent reduction of greenhouse gas emissions, a 20 per cent target for renewables in the EU's energy mix, and a 20 per cent increase in the EU's energy efficiency (see Chapter 9). Europe 2020 also advanced seven so-called flagship initiatives, meant to boost growth and jobs in specific areas related to those headline targets. One of them dealt with resource efficiency, aiming to achieve a more efficient use of natural resources (see Chapters 1 and 7).

Third, *communications* are non-binding documents without a Treaty basis, adopted by the Commission. They are intended to communicate the Commission's position on a particular issue to the other institutions, the public and other stakeholders, as well as the policy options that the Commission considers desirable to deal with that issue (Krämer 2012a). It can thus have a function similar to the 'policy notes' of ministers in some member states, as the Commission, seeking to anticipate developments, signals its intentions with regard to future policies and as it aims to develop societal and political support for them. Indeed, communications are important because legislative proposals by the European Commission in the years that follow are often based upon the choices signalled in those documents. That is why interest groups also take extensive account of those non-binding documents and why public consultations are widely used (see Chapters 3 and 5).

Communications appear under different headings. They can take the form of Green Papers, which can be regarded as draft policy plans that are used for public consultations, and White Papers, which are the updated version after such consultations. In 2011, the Commission published a number of 'roadmaps' in the environmental domain. They defined 2050 as a long-term time horizon, which was new in EU policy-making. This policy innovation followed on from the EU's climate agenda. In order to reach the global goal of limiting global warming to two degrees Celsius (see Chapters 9 and 10), the European Council decided in October 2009 that the EU should aim for an 80 to 95 per cent reduction of greenhouse gases in 2050 (compared to 1990 levels). That decision supplemented the EU's previously agreed climate and energy objectives for 2020 with a long-term dimension. The Commission's newly created DG Climate Action then expanded the long-term goal by issuing the 'Roadmap for Moving to a Competitive Low Carbon Economy in 2050' (European Commission 2011b). That Communication proposed a way to share the efforts of emission reductions between different sectors and policy domains between 2011 and 2050. Other DGs followed with similar roadmaps for

Box 6.2 The seven Environmental Action Programmes

1st EAP (1973–1976): 'Programme of environmental action of the European Communities' – Official Journal C 112, 20/12/1973

The original EAP was the first attempt to streamline EU environmental policy actions in the absence of a Treaty basis (see Chapter 1). It introduced some of the important policy principles, such as the preventive action and the polluter pays principles (see Box 1.1). The proposed actions were mostly remedial and targeted the reduction of pollution and nuisances.

2nd EAP (1977–1981): 'European Community Action Programme on the Environment (1977 to 1981)' – Official Journal C 139, 13/06/1977

Released only four years after its predecessor, the second EAP was above all an update of the first, but expanded the scope of the principles, objectives and areas for prioritized action.

3rd EAP (1982–1986): 'Action Programme of the European Communities on the environment (1982 to 1986)' – Official Journal C 46, 17/02/1983

The third EAP is interesting as it introduced a number of new principles, such as the environmental integration principle (see Box 1.1 and Chapter 7). It also proved to be the first manifestation of a shift towards a preventive (instead of a remedial) approach to environmental policy-making, by stating that economic and social development should avoid creating environmental problems. It also started to encourage the use of economic policy instruments.

4th EAP (1987–1992): 'EEC Fourth Environmental Action Programme (1987 to 1992)' – Official Journal C 328, 07/12/1987

In a number of priority areas, the fourth EAP focused on setting strict standards and on preparing industry sectors for those standards. It also gave further impetus to the development of economic instruments.

5th EAP (1993–2000): 'Towards Sustainability. The European Community Programme of policy and action in relation to the environment and sustainable development' – Official Journal C 138, 17/05/1993

The fifth EAP marks a turning point, as it was the first Programme after the instrument had been integrated in the Treaty. It was also the first Programme with a substantive title ('Towards Sustainability'), explicitly referring to the 1992 Rio Summit (see Chapter 2). Perhaps because of the focus on sustainable development and the integrative character of that concept, the fifth EAP reads more as a real strategy than as a list of proposed measures. It also included references to the use of a broader range of instruments in environmental policy, including information instruments (see below).

6th EAP (2001–2012): 'Environment 2010: Our Future, Our Choice' – Official Journal L 242, 10/09/2002

Based on a detailed review of the fifth EAP and on increasing concerns about the implementation deficit in environmental policy, this Programme focused much more on the revision and better implementation of existing legislation. It also called for the adoption of thematic strategies in four key policy areas (climate change, biodiversity, health and quality of life, and natural resources and waste).

7th EAP (2014–2020): 'Living well, within the limits of our planet' – Official Journal L 354, 28/12/2013

The current EAP is set in the framework of the Europe 2020 strategy and builds upon the long-term objectives that have been formulated with regard to climate change, resource efficiency, transport, innovation and others. It includes a vision for 2050, by when the EU should have achieved a transition towards a resource-efficient and low-carbon economy. It also stresses that economic development and well-being should therefore be decoupled from environmental degradation and waste generation.

the same time horizon. DG Environment prepared the 'Roadmap to a Resource Efficient Europe' (European Commission 2011c) – which makes this the only one of the seven flagship initiatives of Europe 2020 to look beyond 2020 – and DG Energy drafted the 'Energy Roadmap 2050' (European Commission 2011d). The new 'White Paper on transport', adopted in the same period, also looks to 2050 (European Commission 2011e). Likewise, the seventh EAP (see Box 6.2) frames the EU's environmental challenges in a 2050 vision.

These recent Communications suggest a trend towards more long-term policy design in EU environmental policy. It signals awareness inside the European Commission that a new approach is needed to deal with long-term policy challenges, which are defined as 'public policy issues that last at least one human generation, exhibit deep uncertainty exacerbated by the depth of time, and engender public goods aspects both at the stage of problem generation as well as at the response stage' (Sprinz 2009: 2). Focusing on long-term policy design can be considered as a break-through as long-term policies are hard to adopt in democratic political systems because of uncertainty and the short-term time horizons of politicians related to electoral cycles (European Environment Agency 2011; Hendriks 2009; Lempert et al. 2009; Sprinz 2012). Some suggest that the EU is better placed than national democratic systems to deal with certain long-term challenges, because the European Commission is mandated to defend the general public interest and is free of short-term electoral deadlines (Hix and Høyland 2011; Skjærseth et al. 2013). The adoption of a 2050 perspective in EU environmental policy-making is related to the growing salience of a discourse of sustainability transitions in European politics. Indeed, EU discourse is increasingly punctuated with language that refers to the need for fundamental transformations of the systems shaping our production and consumption patterns. The adoption of a long-term time horizon is one of the most distinctive features of the theoretical transition framework (Happaerts 2016; Voss et al. 2009).

Finally, planning instruments are regularly created at member state level, as part of the implementation of European policies. In the environmental domain, legislation often demands the creation of planning cycles within national administrations. The output of those planning cycles is an important source of information flowing to the European level.

Market-based instruments

Market-based instruments (also called economic instruments) use money or market mechanisms as their main resource. They are punitive (for example taxes, fines), rewarding (for example funds, subsidies) or they regard governmental actors as clients, consumers and investors (Baker and Eckerberg 2008; Howlett and Ramesh 2003). Economic instruments are used for various reasons (Halpern 2010). Normatively, it is the logical application of the polluter pays principle (see Box 1.1). By having to pay taxes or buy permits, the polluter not only contributes to the costs of avoiding environmental damage, but also that of cleaning up existing pollution. However, not all economic instruments (for example subsidies) follow that logic (Holzinger et al. 2006). Economic instruments are also much more flexible in adapting to changing circumstances than regulatory instruments are. Furthermore, they are favoured because of their cost-effectiveness. The rationale here is that costs are minimized because as long as it is cheaper to invest in the avoidance of environmental pollution than to pay taxes or permits, private actors will do so (Holzinger et al. 2006; Lee 2014). The preference for incentivizing business to adopt pollution-avoiding procedures by such economic arguments instead of with direct regulation is the main reason why market-based instruments became appealing in the EU in the mid-1980s. That is why their use was promoted by the third and fourth EAP (see Box 6.2). The potential range of market-based instruments is wide: taxes, risk liability schemes, subsidies, tradable allowances and green public procurement. However, except for tradable allowances, the application of these instruments at EU level is quite restricted. That is mainly due to institutional barriers (the unanimity requirement in many cases) and the lack of willingness by member states to transfer key national competences (such as taxation) to the European level.

First, *taxes* are the most traditional of economic instruments. In EU environmental policy, the Commission has launched proposals to impose a carbon tax (Axelrod et al. 2011; Holzinger et al. 2006; Wurzel et al. 2013). It was one of the first concrete proposals to deal with the problem of climate change in the late 1980s and early 1990s. But the proposal failed because of a lack of agreement in the Council, where unanimity is needed for decisions on taxation (see Box 1.2 and Chapter 3). Member states such as the UK opposed the creation of a tax at EU level. The prospect of a veto in the Council has discouraged the Commission from proposing other environmental taxes, and is seen as the main reason why no 'eco-taxes' exist at EU level today (Holzinger et al. 2006; Krämer 2012a). The experience of the failed carbon tax, however, is considered to have paved the way for the Emissions Trading Scheme (see Chapter 9) (Wurzel et al. 2013). The only exception to an EU environmental tax is the Energy Tax Directive (2003/96), which imposes a minimal harmonization of tax rates on energy products, including those coming from fossil fuels (Axelrod et al. 2011; Wurzel et al. 2013).

Second, the polluter pays principle can also be achieved through *risk liability schemes*. The EU adopted the Environmental Liability Directive (2004/35), which forces polluters to pay for remedying environmental damage when they breach environmental legislation (Lee 2014). The Directive does not deal with personal injuries, damages or economic losses, but exclusively with environmental damages (Krämer 2012a). The responsibility for assigning the competent authority to make the scheme work in practice lies with member states (Jans and Vedder 2012).

Third, a number of market-based mechanisms fall under the category of *subsidies*. The EU has, however, no general fund that is used to finance the environmental policy. An attempt to introduce such an environmental fund failed in the early 1980s (Krämer 2012a). What comes closest to a fund for environmental issues is the Financial Instrument for the Environment (LIFE). The LIFE programme was created in 1992 to support environmental activities in the member states and in the EU's neighbourhood as well. It co-funds environmental projects with a European added value, focused on nature protection, clean technologies, pilot applications and others. These projects are established and executed by public authorities (often local or regional actors in the member states), NGOs and private actors. Since 2007, the LIFE programme has included a strand on biodiversity, thus functioning as a funding mechanism for the Natura 2000 network (see Chapter 7). A climate action strand was added in 2014. Between 1992 and 2015, LIFE co-financed more than 4000 projects for approximately €3.5 billion (European Commission 2014g). The total budget for the 2014–2017 LIFE work programme includes €1.1 billion under the sub-programme for Environment and €0.36 billion under the sub-programme for Climate Action. Some common criticisms on the LIFE programme state that it entails only a modest amount of money compared to the environmental challenges the EU is facing, and that the approval of projects follows a logic of distribution among member states instead of being based on objective quality criteria (Krämer 2012a).

One of the implications of the lack of a comprehensive funding mechanism is that financing environmental issues relies to a large extent on existing EU funds that form part of other policy domains. The most important ones are the regional funds, traditionally one of the biggest chunks of EU expenditure. However, the EU's cohesion policy has in the past often been perceived as a problem rather than a solution for the European environment. That opinion in large part arises from the fact that the use of regional funding is mainly left to the discretion of member states, meaning that the weight attributed to the environment depends on its importance in national policy (Krämer 2012a). That is gradually changing though, mostly because of the salience of the EU's climate agenda. For the period between 2014 and 2020, one of the four focus areas of cohesion policy is 'supporting the shift towards a low-carbon economy'. As a consequence, a minimum share of each region's allocation of the European Regional Development Fund (ERDF) – between 12 and 20 per cent, depending on the category of the region – must be invested in climate-related measures, such as renewable energy projects or clean transport technologies. That share accounts for more than €23 billion over those seven years (European Commission 2012a). This is part of a broader strategy of mainstreaming climate action in all EU policy areas, including by earmarking a minimum of 20 per cent of the total 2014–2020 Multiannual Financial Framework, which amounts to €180 billion euro for climate-related measures (European Commission 2014h).

Fourth, another economic instrument that can be used in environmental policy is issuing *tradable allowances*. Through such a mechanism, actors (usually businesses or industrial installations) are given or can buy the right to pollute. Allowances that are not used can be sold on a specially created market (Wurzel 2012). This instrument therefore functions as an incentive for private actors to invest in less polluting innovations, both because of the cost of buying allowances and because of the prospect of generating revenue by selling unused allowances. The incentive increases when the system includes a mechanism whereby the total amount of allowances progressively decreases in time. The EU has put in place one of the best-known applications of this economic policy instrument in the field of climate policy, namely the EU Emissions Trading Scheme (EU ETS), which will be discussed in detail in Chapter 9.

Fifth, the fact that governments also act as clients and consumers on the market has given rise to a final type of market-based environmental policy instrument, namely *green public procurement*. The public sector in the EU holds an important leverage in that regard, as it spends the equivalent of 19 per cent of the EU's gross domestic product annually (European Commission 2014i). Green public procurement policies have become a popular tool in the context of sustainable development because of the potential impact of that leverage on the functioning of the market, but also because the use of such a tool can ensure that governments set a good example. The EU developed a policy on green public procurement as a follow-up to the renewed EUSDS (see above). It entails the formulation of common purchase criteria for different product groups (such as electricity, cars or mobile phones). The policy is voluntary, meaning that authorities in member states are free to choose whether they implement (parts of) it or not (European Commission 2010a; 2014i).

Among these five types of economic policy instruments, taxes are the most traditional type. The other four 'new market-based instruments' aim to internalize environmental externalities, such as emissions trading or green public procurement, and became popular towards the end of the 1990s (see below). They were regarded as effective tools for sustainable development and as welcome alternatives to the much-criticized instruments of direct regulation, which were said to be static and inefficient (Holzinger and Knill 2005; Lee 2014).

The discourse of the EU's environmental policy usually attributes a considerable weight to economic instruments. Mirroring the 'ecological modernization' and 'green economy' paradigms, which imply that greening industry through technological innovation is not only beneficial for the environment but also for the industry's competitiveness, the Commission enthusiastically promotes those instruments (see Chapter 1). More broadly, it 'frames' environmental issues as economic problems with economic solutions, especially during times of economic crisis, when it is harder to put purely environmental issues on the agenda.

A good example is resource efficiency (see Chapter 7). In the Roadmap towards a Resource Efficient Europe (see above) and in DG Environment's discourse on the topic, it is not the environmental impact of the EU's resource use that is presented as the main problem, but rather the volatility of commodity prices, the EU's dependence on imports and the market distortions that lead to short-sighted investments and hinder long-term innovation. The solution therefore lies in fixing the structural errors of the market, by focusing on price-setting, investment choices and support for innovations. As such, resource efficiency is presented as a strategy not for environmental protection, but for innovation, jobs and competitiveness (Happaerts 2014). The use of this economic policy framing actually follows from the Commission's tendency to invoke internal market competences in environmental policy-making. Even after the establishment of a legal basis for environmental policy in the 1980s, it is in relation to the internal market and, increasingly, to economic governance (for instance the recommendations attached to European Semester) that the EU's weight and influence on national policies is largest. Those tools enable the Commission to enlarge its room for manoeuvre in other policy areas (Pollack and Shaffer 2010).

Information instruments

With information instruments, the EU relies on information and communication measures to get things done. This type of policy instruments includes instruments that aim at generating information that can be used to monitor, evaluate or benchmark policies, or to stimulate changes in the preferences or behaviour of citizens and other societal actors (Howlett and Ramesh 2003).

Ever since the earliest days of environmental policy-making, several information instruments have been used at the EU level (Halpern 2010). A first type of instrument involving public information is the launch of *information campaigns* or communication strategies to publicize news about EU initiatives or engage the broader public in other ways. For instance, when the 2030 climate and energy framework was proposed by the Commission (see Chapter 9), a short movie explaining the framework in layman's terms was published on DG CLIMA's website (European Commission 2014j). Moreover, EU policies sometimes contain an appeal to citizens, for example to choose more sustainable lifestyles (Krämer 2012a).

Second, information for the public can also be provided through *labelling* specific products or services. Consumers are then encouraged to buy labelled products, which are considered to be more environmentally beneficial than products not bearing such a label (Axelrod et al. 2011). For instance, the EU adopted its own Eco-Label Regulation (now 66/2010) in 1992, mirroring the 'eco-label' schemes that had previously been elaborated in Germany and Austria. The development of such a system at the EU level was partly motivated by the need to avoid market distortions resulting from the divergent national systems that had sprouted up throughout Europe. The EU eco-label scheme labels products and services that are less environmentally harmful than comparable ones (Wurzel et al. 2013). Like the EU's green procurement policy, it is a voluntary scheme. Producers are not in any way obliged to use the label, or to adapt their products to its criteria, but the idea is that they are encouraged to do so since consumers find such labels increasingly important. The scheme has a low uptake because separate national eco-label schemes co-exist and compete with the European scheme (Krämer 2012a; Wurzel et al. 2013), although national eco-labels must be based on criteria that are at least as strict as the European ones (Jans and Vedder 2012). Another reason for the low uptake is that industry has preferred the so-called Eco-Management and Audit Scheme (EMAS).

EMAS is a voluntary scheme allowing companies and other organizations to evaluate, report and improve their environmental performance ('eco-auditing'). It was launched in 1993, partly because the EU feared the proliferation of diverging national schemes after some member states such as the UK have already moved far ahead (Wurzel et al. 2013). The EMAS Regulation (now 1221/2009) stipulates that organizations can receive an EMAS registration, and can thus use the EMAS label on their products when they fulfil a number of requirements such as carrying out environmental auditing (Jans and Vedder 2012). In this sense, the rationale behind EMAS is not only informative as it informs consumers about which companies comply with the EMAS Regulation and may thus be regarded as taking their environmental responsibility into account, but it also incentivizes businesses to adopt their own environmental criteria.

A third type of information and communication instruments is *impact assessments*. These are policy appraisals, meant to inform policy-makers about the impact of their decisions on the environment and on sustainable development, and to stimulate learning effects. The EU in 1985 adopted the Environmental Impact

Assessment (EIA) Directive (now 2014/52), which requires member states to evaluate systematically the environmental impacts, before they can authorize certain individual projects that are likely to have significant effects on the environment (Jans and Vedder 2012; Lee 2014). EIAs are not only meant to improve environmental protection (by preventing damage caused by badly prepared projects), but are also supposed to reduce fragmentation and conflicts with other policy domains. Moreover, they imply that more attention is given to participatory decision-making and planning processes. The legislation was expanded in 2001 with the Strategic Environmental Assessment (SEA) Directive (2001/42), which applies to appraisals of broader plans and programmes, rather than of individual projects. The aim behind the SEA Directive was to introduce an environmental reflex into the earliest planning stages (Lee 2014).

Commission attempts to make EIAs mandatory for all projects co-financed by EU funds were opposed by Southern member states (Krämer 2012a). Furthermore, the instruments of impact assessment have been criticized, for instance for their unbalanced procedure in favour of certain actors (mostly the developer) to the detriment of public bodies and other interest groups (Lee 2014). The EIA Directive was reviewed in 2014 in order to deal with some of those criticisms. The review took place in the context of a political debate on the possibility of shale gas fracking in Europe. The new Directive simplifies a number of procedures and gives more prominence to climate change and resource efficiency (European Commission 2014k), but it does not make EIAs mandatory for shale gas exploration or extraction projects.

Governing with new environmental policy instruments?

Just before the turn of the century, a debate emerged about 'new governance', or a change in the way in which governments could pursue their policy goals and interact with other stakeholders in order to do so (see Knill and Lenschow 2000; Jordan et al. 2003; Wurzel et al. 2013). Environmental policy, or environmental governance, was one of the key loci of this debate, and the search for so-called new environmental policy instruments was particularly pronounced in Europe. Those new instruments pertain to all the types of environmental policy instruments sketched in the previous sections. The best-known are economic instruments, such as eco-taxes and emissions trading, and information instruments such as eco-labels and environmental impact assessments (Wurzel et al. 2013).

There are a number of driving forces behind the debate about and adoption of new environmental policy instruments. The appeal of new governance was strongly related to a call for deregulation (Lee 2014). That did not necessarily lead to the disappearance of regulatory and legally binding instruments, but it did force public authorities throughout Europe to think about a more flexible and softer approach towards regulation (see Chapter 1). It also frames in a trend towards 'new public management'. That concept emerged in the 1980s and focuses on bureaucratic reforms intended to lead to a more efficient and effective public sector (Pollitt and Bouckaert 2011). The EU institutions did not escape this dynamic. The European Commission made various proposals for new instruments and governance approaches. Those reflected an effort to better include stakeholders in decision-making, to adopt more flexible approaches, and to give more freedom to member states in the implementation of environmental policy and taking national and regional differences more into account (Axelrod et al. 2011; Holzinger et al. 2006; Wurzel et al. 2013). The EU's response to these calls can be found, for instance, in the much-cited 2001 'White Paper on Governance' (European Commission 2001a). However, in environmental policy, references to more flexible instruments had already been included in the fifth EAP in 1993 (see above) (Holzinger et al. 2006).

Furthermore, the dynamic was driven by a consensus that the EU's environmental policy was structurally flawed and needed fixing. The implementation deficit (see Chapter 4) was the most frequently cited motive for the adoption of more flexible instruments, which were endowed with high hopes for better performance and delivery of environmental goals (Demmke 2001; Halpern 2010 Holzinger et al. 2006; Knill and Lenschow 2000). It was also thought that, in the spirit of subsidiarity, more flexibility would help solve the large disparities in environmental quality not only across European regions, but also across sectors (Halpern 2010). New environmental policy instruments were thus also intended to fix the lack of integration of environmental issues into other sectors. Finally, the changes were favoured by an increasingly political debate about the limitations to the EU's policy-making capacity arising from the sole use 'interventionist' instruments (Holzinger et al. 2006).

Conclusions

Despite the popularity of some new environmental policy instruments in many European countries, this chapter has shown that the uptake of some of those instruments by the EU has been rather low. The EU has not adopted eco-taxes and the use of eco-labels and EMAS has been less popular than expected or in comparison to other jurisdictions. As mentioned, the biggest exception is the ETS, which is the largest scheme of emissions trading worldwide (Wettestad 2014). However, the modest application of new environmental policy instruments hides a stronger and older dynamic, namely the search for more and more flexibility in EU environmental policy-making. That trend started with the creation of framework directives and the introduction of BAT in the mid-1970s. Since then, the European institutions have constantly tried to strike the right balance between, on the one hand, direct regulation embodied in binding legislation, and, on the other hand, approaches that grant more freedom and flexibility, adopt a soft way of steering and bring a more context-oriented dimension to policy instruments (Demmke 2001; Halpern 2010; Holzinger et al. 2006).

It rests upon an 'ambiguous consensus' that the EU only imposes binding regulation when member states are left with enough discretion on how and when to achieve the goals set at EU level (Halpern 2010; Holzinger et al. 2006). The consequence of this consensus is that, on the one hand, legislative instruments with an interventionist logic remain predominant, but that, on the other hand, the instrument mix of EU environmental policy is actually quite varied and highly dynamic (Halpern 2010; Jordan et al. 2013; Lee 2014). Recent examples of dynamism and inventiveness include the Commission's anticipatory use of communications (including Green Papers, White Papers and Roadmaps) and the introduction of a long-term time horizon in environmental policy. Other examples demonstrate that, when the political space for new EU-wide instruments is too limited, the EU introduces voluntary policies, such as green public procurement or eco-labelling. In all those cases, the EU manifests a clear ability to 'muddle through' (Halpern 2010: 45) and to achieve partial but steady progress in its environmental activities.

The dynamism in policy instrumentation is to a significant extent due to the creativity manifested by the European Commission (Demmke 2001), but it is also the fruit of emulation of national policies and, as shown throughout this book, of the EU's embeddedness in global dynamics. The creation of the framework directive, for instance, bears strong similarities with the regime-protocol approach that has become popular in multilateral environmental agreements since the 1970s and 1980s. Here, framework conventions contain general principles and governance arrangements, while specific commitments are deferred to 'daughter' protocols. The Convention on Long-Range Transboundary Air Pollution (CLRTAP, 1979) as a framework convention and the Helsinki Protocol of Sulphur Emissions (1985) is an early example of that dynamic. Furthermore, the Commission has not hesitated to look towards national policies for inspiration, and certain member states such as Germany and the UK have been particularly active in uploading their new policy instruments to the EU level.

The increasing flexibility of EU environmental policy and its dynamism with regard to policy instrumentation have helped the EU, as the next chapters will show, to expand its steering activities to all aspects of environmental policy, including new issues such as GMOs and climate change (Halpern 2010).

Chapter 7

Traditional Sectors of Environmental Policy

The current and the two following chapters focus on the policy characteristics and political dynamics of specific policy areas, in the traditional sectors of environmental policy (this chapter), on genetically modified organisms (Chapter 8) and on climate change (Chapter 9). After an initial phase of 'incidental' policy measures related to the environment but primarily adopted in the framework of the common market, the EU started to establish a more comprehensive environmental policy in the 1970s (see Chapter 1). From those early beginnings, a sectorial or issue-based approach was developed, meaning that separate policies were adopted for specific environmental issues, such as air, water or nature protection.

Two factors drove the development of those issue-based environmental policies at EU level: societal concerns about environmental pollution and the aim to harmonize environmental standards between member states. First, very visible forms of air and water pollution, linked to industrialization, and its impact on human health and the environment, caused societal concerns and stimulated political action on the environment in the 1970s. As a result, environmental policy-making was mainly induced by the fight against pollution. Also at the international level, the same concerns about pollution and human health triggered action on the environment, for instance with the organization of the first UN summit on the issue, the United Nations Conference on the Human Environment (UNCHE) in Stockholm in 1972 (see Chapter 2). Second, the EU's early environmental policies aspired to produce common standards, especially with regard to water and air quality. The developments took place at a time when only a few member states (such as Germany or the Netherlands) had already initiated national environmental policies, and others (such as Belgium) had not yet taken much action in that domain (Jänicke and Weidner 1997).

This chapter first gives an overview of the main issue-based environmental policies at EU level. They are waste, water, air, nature protection and biodiversity, noise and soil policies. Our aim is not to present an exhaustive outline of past and current legislation (comprehensive overviews of those policies can be found in for instance Jans and Vedder 2012; Krämer 2012a), but rather to describe the origins and basic characteristics of the policies, their main political developments since the 1970s and the interplay with global environmental politics. Thereafter, attention is paid to some transversal strategies for sustainable development that the EU has initiated since the 1990s, following the global promotion of the sustainable development concept. Major trends are presented in the concluding section.

Waste and product policy

As wealthy and high consumption societies, the EU member states have generated ever more waste in recent decades (on average about 5 tonnes of solid waste annually for every citizen) (Eurostat 2014). It is obvious that the treatment and disposal of this waste (including a large proportion of hazardous waste) has become a major challenge. The dominant methods of burning waste in incinerators or dumping it into landfills create environmental damage. Burning (hazardous) waste causes air pollution, soil pollution, hazardous residues and also health risks. Landfills cause air, water and soil pollution and are responsible for carbon dioxide and methane emissions, as well as for releasing chemicals and pesticides into the ground(water), all with obvious consequences for human health and ecosystems.

The seriousness and magnitude of the problem has made waste prevention and management one of the top priorities of the EU's environmental policy. Determining and enforcing standards for waste treatment was one of the first topics of the EU's environmental policy before a legal basis for environmental action was established (European Commission 2005a; Hildebrand 1993). The first legislative initiatives were taken in 1975, with the adoption of the original Waste Framework Directive (75/442). The EU did not impose binding targets or strict treatment obligations on member states (with the exception of waste oil). Instead, policies were largely restricted to administrative and reporting requirements (Fischer 2011).

Waste policy has evolved significantly since the 1970s. It received an important boost after 'natural resources and waste' was incorporated as one of the four priorities of the sixth Environment Action Programme (see Box 6.2), which broadened the policy's focus and heightened its ambition. The sixth EAP was followed in 2005 by a Thematic Strategy on the Prevention and Recycling of Waste (European Commission 2005b). It promoted the vision of the EU as a recycling society, and it laid the foundation for the renewal of the Waste Framework Directive in 2008 (2008/98), which defines the basic strategic policy options, objectives and principles of today's EU waste policy. The renewed Framework Directive established a European waste hierarchy, whereby waste prevention is regarded as the priority (followed by reuse, recycling, recovery including through incineration and landfill). The idea behind the prevention priority is that reducing both the amount and hazardousness of waste will make disposal easier and less costly. As well as emphasizing the importance of prevention, the Waste Framework Directive also introduced prevention obligations and mandatory recycling targets (Fischer 2011).

As a result of these developments, the waste *acquis* now consist of a comprehensive set of framework legislation (the Waste Framework Directive), waste management and treatment legislation (for instance on emission standards related to incineration or on landfill restrictions) and legislation on specific waste streams (for instance of batteries, end-of-life vehicles, electrical and electronic waste or packaging waste). It imposes binding minimum recycling targets, but does not contain quantitative targets for reduction or reuse. The importance of the EU's waste policy is illustrated by the fact that in many member states, waste management systems derive solely from EU obligations (Fischer 2011). The evolution in the EU's waste policy reflects a changed vision and the consideration of more complex challenges. With the basic measures to mitigate environmental and health impacts in place, the waste policy now deals to an increasing extent with different economic interests and sustainability concerns, and waste is increasingly seen as an economically valuable resource (European Commission 2014l).

There is a substantive body of international agreements dealing with waste management, particularly within the framework of the Organisation for Economic Co-operation and Development (OECD) (such as the 1986 Decision on the export of hazardous waste to non-OECD countries) and the UN (such as the 1989

Basel Convention on the Transboundary Movement of Hazardous Wastes and Substances). However, those international regimes were not a strong driver of EU waste policy, which largely predates them. The international agreements focus mostly on reducing the release of substances, on eliminating the most harmful materials and on controlling their trade.

Since the late 1990s, the EU's waste policy has demonstrated a growing interface with the broadening EU product policy (Happaerts 2014). The EU has designed legislation for specific product groups, mostly to limit their impact on human health and the environment. Examples include the Directive on the Restriction of Hazardous Substances (RoHS), which bans the use of certain chemicals in electrical and electronic equipment (2011/65) and the Waste of Electrical and Electronic Equipment (WEEE) Directive, which determines the responsibilities of producers of electrical and electronic equipment (2012/19). Furthermore, in an attempt to develop an integrated product policy, information and economic instruments were developed to influence consumer choices, influence the market and incite self-regulation by private actors (see Chapter 6). The eco-label, EMAS and the green public procurement policy, also discussed in the previous chapter, are prime examples. In addition, energy labelling, substance bans and product design guidelines are used in the EU's product policy. A well-known example is the Ecodesign Directive (2009/125). Formally an instrument of industrial policy, it regulates the performance of energy-using and energy-related products, and ultimately aims to ban the most inefficient products from the European market.

One of the cornerstones of the EU's product policy is the REACH Regulation (1907/2006), which governs the use of substances in the chemicals sector. One of the most hotly debated environmental policy initiatives ever adopted by the EU, it was the result of a hard compromise between the strict protection of human and environmental health and the interests of one of Europe's key industrial sectors. In essence, the Regulation increases the responsibility of the chemical sector by introducing serious checks on the environmental and health consequences of the use of chemicals. The Regulation is based on the *registration, evaluation, authorization* and *restriction* of chemicals in light of environmental and health objectives. The production and use of chemicals is authorized by the European Commission, after an extensive registration and evaluation procedure in which the specially created European Chemicals Agency (ECHA) has a prominent role (see Chapter 3). After authorization, restrictions can be proposed by member states, the Commission or ECHA when there is an unacceptable risk to the environment or human health. When such urgent risks occur, member states can take action under a safeguard clause (Jans and Vedder 2012). The precautionary principle underlies REACH, as the use of chemical substances (and their amounts) is only permitted when convincing information is available pertaining to their safety (Hansen et al. 2007) (see also Chapter 8).

The EU's product policy has been evolving towards focusing on the environmental impact of products throughout their entire life-cycle. Since 2010 both waste and product policies have been framed under the umbrella of 'resource efficiency'. Driven by the global economic crisis that erupted in 2008 and multiple commodity price shocks in the second half of the 2000s, and motivated by the EU's considerable dependence on the import of resources, the European Commission has increasingly focused on the economic governance of raw materials. In that context, it defined resource efficiency as one of the seven flagship initiatives of the Europe 2020 strategy (see Chapter 6). Inspired by the idea that a more sustainable use of natural resources, originally an environmental issue, could weigh on the EU's economic agenda in times of crisis, 2009–2014 Environment Commissioner Potočnik chose resource efficiency as his new 'grand story', after he lost the competence for climate change to the newly created function of the Climate Action Commissioner in 2010 (Happaerts 2016).

In that context, the Commission undertook a substantive review of EU waste policy. The resulting legislative proposal, which was presented in the final months of the Barroso II Commission's term as Commissioner's Potočnik's main legacy, contained new and more stringent targets for the recycling of various waste streams, and a 0 per cent landfilling rate for recyclable waste by 2025 (European Commission 2014m). The proposal was set in a broader package, which also contained communications on other issues such as green employment, under the general heading 'the circular economy'. This new concept, which has become popular in business and policy-making circles (European Resource Efficiency Platform 2014), focuses on a strategy to achieve resource efficiency by keeping resources continuously within the economy, creating new added value even after products have reached the end of their life, and thus eliminating waste (European Commission 2014l). As set out in Chapter 1, the legislative proposal was scrapped by the incoming

Juncker Commission in early 2015, but this decision attracted opposition from the European Parliament, the Environment Council, specific business interests and civil society. This pressure forced First Vice-President Timmermans to promise that a new package would be tabled by the end of 2015. The new package is supposed to be more ambitious and include many other dimensions besides waste policy. The focus on market-based solutions and economic gains, already included in the resource efficiency flagship, is expected to be enhanced. The notion of 'the circular economy' is therefore likely to dominate the EU's waste and product policies in coming years.

Air policy

Air pollution was one of the earliest issues to cause strong environmental concerns, both in Europe and elsewhere. In 1968, a Swedish study demonstrated the link between the acidification of Scandinavian lakes and rivers and heavy industrial pollution originating from the UK and Central Europe (Darst 2001). Concerns for the impact on forests soon followed (Krämer 2012a; Meyer 2005). Subsequently, in the 1970s and 1980s, the fight against 'smoke stacks' became central in the EU's environmental policy. Acid rain was the first priority issue, but was quickly accompanied by the global concern for the decay of the ozone layer, which involves a less visible aspect of transboundary air pollution. During the 1990s, attention shifted towards other forms of air pollution, especially those related to urban air quality, which have major health impacts (Meyer 2005). The EU's policy interventions then focused on small particles, volatile organic compounds and other substances. Besides seeking to improve air quality, the EU invests heavily in the regulation of greenhouse gas emissions, as part of the fight against global climate change (see Chapter 9).

Air policy in the EU follows the waves of the global environmental agenda. In the 1970s and 1980s, that agenda was dominated by two main issues, namely acid rain and ozone layer protection. The regional Convention on Long-Range Transboundary Air Pollution (CLRTAP, 1979) and its Protocols, negotiated under the UN Economic Commission for Europe (UNECE), have been a major driving force for fighting acid rain. The UN-wide Vienna Convention for the Protection of the Ozone Layer (1985) has played a similar role in the global attempt to protect the ozone layer. On acid rain, the Scandinavian countries, at that time not members of the EEC, were important leading countries. The Swedish study mentioned above on the link between the acidification of lakes and rivers and heavy industrial pollution was one of the factors that pushed Sweden to host the UNCHE in 1972 (Wettestad 2002).

The current EU air policies have a broad scope and comprehensive goals. They broadly address two challenges: improving air quality (for human health and the environment as a whole) on the one hand, and restricting the emission of pollutants on the other. Air quality was first tackled by the Air Quality Framework Directive (96/62) and its four daughter directives relating to sulphur dioxide, nitrogen dioxide and oxides of nitrogen, particulate matter and lead (1999/30); benzene and carbon monoxide (2000/69); ozone (2002/3); and arsenic, cadmium, mercury, nickel and polycyclic aromatic hydrocarbons (2004/107). They set common rules and define minimum standards for clean air throughout the Union (Meyer 2005). In 2008, those rules were merged in the new Ambient Air Quality Directive (2008/50), which is one of the most comprehensive policies on air quality worldwide. However, it also weakened a number of previous requirements. For instance, air quality standards no longer have to be respected throughout the entire territory of member states and multiple options for delaying implementation were included (Krämer 2012a).

For the restriction of emissions, the main legislative instrument is the National Emission Ceilings Directive (2001/81), which covers four air pollutants of crucial importance for human health (sulphur dioxide, nitrogen oxides, volatile organic compounds and ammonia). It is based on the concept of the 'carrying capacity' of ecosystems, and defines interim objectives (initially for 2010 and later renewed for 2020) that the EU must achieve to keep pollution below dangerous levels (Meyer 2005). The use of emission ceilings closely resembles the operation of one of the Protocols of the CLRTAP (Jans and Vedder 2012; Krämer 2012a). Emission legislation is complementary to air quality legislation, as it provides the tools to secure the reductions that are necessary for improving ambient air quality (Meyer 2005). Subsequent efforts to reach more stringent standards for certain pollutants faced resistance from industry and were blocked in the Council (Krämer 2012a). A more recent legislative proposal, which introduces two additional pollutants (particulate matter and methane) and sets new emission ceilings for 2020 and 2030, was tabled in 2013 by the Commission (European Commission 2013d).

Besides tackling general air quality and major pollutants, the EU's air policy was integrated into transport and energy policies. The EU defined limits on the emissions of air pollutants from, for example, combustion plants, waste incineration facilities, vehicles and ships (Krämer 2012a). Some of those policies were adopted as early as 1970 yet have been updated since then (Axelrod et al. 2011).

As the result of EU legislation and reasonably good national implementation in the member states, much progress has been made in reducing air pollutants such as sulphur dioxide, lead, nitrogen oxides, carbon monoxide and benzene, resulting in a fairly effective fight against heavy industrial pollution and acid rain. However, despite significant and durable reductions in some harmful emissions, air quality continues to be a problem, especially in urban settings and densely populated and industrial areas of Europe. Summer or photochemical smog, caused mainly by ground-level ozone, regularly exceeds safe health limits. The same is true for particulate matter, which, as it presents a health risk, is of increasing concern. In addition, new areas of interest have arisen, such as emissions from shipping, the connection with climate change and the difficult challenge of getting a grip on everyday means of transport such as car and lorry traffic (Krämer 2012a).

Water policy

Water is a fundamental element of healthy ecosystems and a necessary basis for human health. Clean water and reliable access to it are constant concerns of EU citizens (European Commission 2012b), but water quality is still problematic in several EU member states (European Environment Agency 2015), especially in densely populated and industrial areas (such as Belgium) and in some Central and Eastern European member states (such as the Czech Republic or Bulgaria). In other member states water quantity and droughts have caused major concerns, particularly given the prospect of future climate change effects (for instance in Spain, Greece or Italy). That is why water protection is one of the EU's ongoing environmental priorities.

EU water legislation started in the 1970s with the Directive concerning the quality required for surface water intended for the abstraction of drinking water in the member states (75/440) and the Directive on pollution caused by certain dangerous substances discharged into the aquatic environment of the Community (76/464), which was *de facto* the EU's first framework directive (Wright and Fritsch 2011). Those two directives focused on the protection of surface water against discharges from industrial and domestic sources and on the monitoring and treatment of the quality of surface water. They had a significant impact on the development of national water programmes and on investment in the infrastructure for water treatment. In subsequent decades, water legislation was amended and complemented by new directives that addressed other forms of water pollution (for instance nitrates from agriculture).

Much of the existing legislation was later integrated into the Water Framework Directive (2000/60), which is still the most important instrument in the EU's water policy. The Water Framework Directive is innovative in a number of ways. First, building on the principles of integrated water management, it prescribes that groundwater and surface water have to reach a 'good status' by 2015, which refers to chemical criteria (common across the EU) and to ecological criteria (that differ across ecosystems, but are independent from their socio-economic impact). Second, the Water Framework Directive includes targets on water quantity and on the ecological potential of non-natural waters. Water pricing and the cost recovery of water services are considered important tools for achieving those objectives. Third, a great deal of attention is given to the participation of various stakeholders in its implementation, from the formulation of plans to the monitoring of results (Tolentino 2013). Finally, the Water Framework Directive introduced the pioneering river basin approach (Jans and Vedder 2012). That approach defines the scales for water management according to natural rather than administrative boundaries. Within each river basin, governments must produce a single river basin management plan.

As a result of the river basin approach, the scope of the Water Framework Directive exceeds the twenty-eight EU member states. As an example, in the Danube river basin, the most international river basin in the world with nineteen riparian states, water governance was already carried out through a cooperative framework within the International Commission for the Protection of the Danube River (ICPDR), which today includes five non-EU member states (Bosnia and Herzegovina, Serbia, Montenegro, Moldova and Ukraine) alongside nine EU member states and the EU itself. After the adoption of the Water Framework Directive, the ICPDR was established as the coordination platform for the implementation of the Framework Directive for the Danube basin. As a consequence, all the countries within the ICPDR framework regardless of the EU membership have undertaken measures to implement the Water Framework Directive throughout the entire basin.

With its focus on integrated water management, the Water Framework Directive repealed and integrated other pieces of more specific legislation, such as the Fish Water Directive (78/659). In other cases, particular 'stand-alone' directives remain in force, because they address specific concerns. Examples are the Urban Wastewater Directive (98/15), which obliges agglomerations of a certain size to connect households to wastewater treatment systems; the Floods Directive (2007/60), designed to reduce the risks and damage of floods after some catastrophic floods along the Danube and Elbe rivers in 2002; and the Marine Water Strategy Framework Directive (2008/56), which requires EU member states to cooperate with their neighbours within various marine regions (Jans and Vedder 2012).

EU water policy now covers the domains of river basin management, drinking water quality, water pollution, bathing water, urban wastewater, the marine environment and coasts, flood risk management, and water scarcity and drought (Jans and Vedder 2012). The policies are based on three concerns: the quality (relating to human health and biodiversity), availability and safety of water. But despite several decades of comprehensive policy-making, water pollution and related health risks remain an issue in Europe (European Environment Agency 2015). That is largely due to the substantial implementation deficit that characterizes EU water policy (Krämer 2012a) (see Chapter 4). Moreover, the current set of legislation seems ill-prepared for the problems of water scarcity that are likely to be manifested in Europe, especially around the Mediterranean, where climate change is expected to decrease precipitation and river flow (EEA 2012; Krämer 2012a).

Nature protection and biodiversity policy

Biodiversity – the variety of animals, plants and other elements of the living environment on earth – is essential to sustain life, forms the foundation of our food system, provides societies with clean air and water, and is the basis for energy sources and raw materials. In more recent years those ecosystems have been economically quantified – in terms of the monetary value of their goods and services – and have turned out to be an irreplaceable part of our economic system. Yet, the ecosystem is equally important for immaterial values such as aesthetic pleasure, artistic inspiration and recreation. For all those reasons the EU has developed policies to halt biodiversity loss and protect nature. Such policies are needed because much of Europe's natural capital is being depleted by growing production and consumption patterns and alteration of landscapes.

Nature protection policies are not as well developed as some other areas of environmental protection in the EU. Especially before the Single European Act introduced a legal basis for EU environmental policy, it was difficult to progress on the issue, mainly because common market concerns could not easily be invoked to protect nature as a collective good (Jans and Vedder 2012). Nevertheless, an early European system for nature protection was gradually put in place, building on the Birds Directive and the Habitats Directive.

The Birds Directive (79/409) created a scheme of protection for all wild bird species naturally occurring in Europe. It was a response to the 1970s reality of a sharp decline in Europe's bird species, caused by a combination of factors including hunting and pollution, but mostly by loss of habitats and unsustainable land use. It was also a recognition of the obvious fact that protecting bird species requires transboundary action, although the expansion of EU competences into wildlife protection was faced with member state opposition (Baker 2003). The Birds Directive places great emphasis on the protection of habitats for endangered as well as migratory species, especially through the establishment of a coherent network of Special Protection Areas (SPAs) comprising the most suitable territories for these species (Jans and Vedder 2012).

Since 1994, all SPAs form part of Natura 2000, a network of protected sites comprising about 18 per cent of the EU's land area (making it the largest network of protected areas in the world), which was established by the Habitats Directive (92/43). The impact of that Directive, which focuses not only on protected sites but also on species protection, is enormous. It has led to the protection of over 1000 animals and plant species and more than 200 'Special Areas of Conservation' (i.e. habitat types, such as special types of forests, meadows or wetlands) (Axelrod et al. 2011). Besides setting up the Natura 2000 network, the Habitats Directive has an important impact on land use practices in the member states. Most areas that are designated under the Habitats or the Birds Directives cannot be used for any other purposes. Member states often challenge this restriction, for example in the case of projects for harbour extensions, industrial zone development or coastal development.

In the early 1990s, the focus of the EU's nature protection policy shifted towards biodiversity. With the entry into force of the Convention on Biological Diversity (CBD) in 1993, biodiversity conservation became an international legal obligation for the EU. The initial European response to the CBD was hesitant and fragmented, leaning mostly upon the creation of Natura 2000 and the adoption of the goal of 'no further deterioration of ecosystems and habitats necessary to maintain diversity of species and within species' in the fifth EAP (Baker 2003: 29). After 1998, the Commission addressed the lack of a coherent response by issuing a (non-binding) Biodiversity Strategy. A new strategy was adopted in 2011 with 2020 as the new time horizon (European Commission 2011f). It followed recent developments at the multilateral level, including the adoption of a new strategic plan to stop the loss of biodiversity by 2020 at the CBD's Conference of the Parties in Nagoya in 2010. The EU's new Biodiversity Strategy aims at halting the (still continuing) loss of biodiversity and degradation of ecosystems in the EU, and at restoring them insofar as is feasible, by 2020. It also formulates a long-term vision for 2050, when Europe's natural capital should be protected, valued and appropriately restored for biodiversity's intrinsic value and for their essential contribution to human well-being and economic prosperity. However, going beyond the creation of protected areas, the EU's ambitions will be difficult to attain without more attention to biodiversity in the member states and further integration of biodiversity objectives in policy areas as agriculture, energy and transport. That is, for instance, a thorny issue in the management of genetically modified organisms (see Chapter 8).

Soil policy

Soil performs various environmental and economic functions, for example in agricultural production, filtration of various substances or raw materials provision. Soil quality in the EU is threatened by soil sealing resulting from agricultural and building practices, widespread contamination by heavy metals and mineral oil, erosion due to inappropriate land use and other practices, salinization and desertification (European Environment Agency 2010). At the national level, only a few member states (such as the Netherlands) have their own soil protection legislation. At EU level, soil protection is, for the moment, dispersed throughout different environmental policy instruments including in directives on water, waste, chemicals, industrial pollution prevention, nature protection, pesticides and agriculture.

After the publication of the sixth EAP in the early 2000s, which announced a thematic strategy on soil to bring some coherence in EU policies (see Box 6.2), a Commission initiative was very slow in coming because of opposition from DG Enterprise (Krämer 2012a). The Soil Thematic Strategy and a proposal for a Soil Framework Directive were finally presented in 2006 (European Commission 2014n). The proposed Framework Directive would, for instance, have compelled governments to reuse brownfield sites. It would also have formalized a number of common goals and principles, leaving it to the member states to determine how best to protect and use soil. That would have been congruent with the very diverse physical realities of soil quality and use in Europe. Since 2006, however, a blocking minority of member states (principally consisting of Austria, France, Germany, Malta, the Netherlands and the UK) have prevented the approval of the proposed Framework Directive by the Council, invoking the high cost of implementation and subsidiarity principles as some of their objections (Krämer 2012a). Although the Council agreed on soil protection objectives as part of the 7th EAP in 2013, the lack of a compromise on the proposed Framework Directive caused the Commission to withdraw the proposal before the 2014 elections (European Commission 2014o).

Noise policy

Noise pollution is probably one of the most neglected environmental issues, and has been treated as a problem of second order by most member states and the EU alike. Nevertheless, recent estimates suggest that about 20 per cent of EU citizens are confronted on a regular basis with noise pollution at a level considered unhealthy. In addition, more than 150 million Europeans live or work in areas where the noise levels cause 'annoyance' during the daytime hours (European Commission 2011g).

EU policies before the mid-1990s were limited to either implementing international agreements in the case of aircrafts, or regulating – because of common market concerns – maximum sound levels for vehicles, airplanes and machines (Jans and Vedder 2012).

By the mid-1990s the Commission abandoned this exclusively common market perspective, and looked to protect citizens against exposure to noise levels that endanger their health and quality of life, thereby focusing on the environmental effects of noise (European Commission 1996; Jans and Vedder 2012). The result is the Environmental Noise Directive (2002/49), which is *de facto* a framework directive for noise policy, setting common goals and policy principles, with the overall objective of avoiding, preventing or reducing environmental noise (Jans and Vedder 2012; Krämer 2012a). It foresees a comprehensive and uniform system of monitoring noise pollution, resulting in 'strategic noise maps' for major roads, railways, airports and agglomerations. Those noise maps, developed by member states, will form the basis for an assessment of the number of European citizens who are bothered by noise and/or sleep-disturbed. While monitoring is left to the Commission, member states have to develop action plans to reduce noise where necessary and maintain environmental noise quality where it is considered good (Krämer 2012a).

Transversal strategies for sustainable development

The global promotion of the concept of sustainable development had a profound impact on the EU, which has always been a promoter of global negotiations on sustainable development (Van den Brande 2012). Very soon after the concept became prominent in the global debate, it was added as a central objective in the Treaty, not only for the EU in general (Art. 3 TEU) but also for its external action (Art. 21 TEU) (see Chapter 1). As in other jurisdictions, the sustainable development concept was at first considered to be an environmental policy affair, as is illustrated by the fact that it became the central concept of the fifth EAP ('Towards sustainability', 1993) (see Box 6.2). Subsequently, concrete initiatives were taken to integrate the principles of sustainable development transversally into other policy areas, through the promotion of environmental policy integration (EPI) on the one hand, and the adoption of a specific EU Sustainable Development Strategy (EUSDS) on the other hand.

Environmental policy integration

The logic behind the promotion of EPI is that, in order to achieve sustainable development, environmental concerns and objectives should be integrated in other sectorial policies, such as agriculture, energy or industrial policies. That is in effect a policy translation of the Brundtland Report's main message, which stated that environmental problems are part of all other societal challenges. EPI is especially appealing to industrialized countries, where economic and social policies are already well developed (Happaerts and Bruyninckx 2014). The principle is additionally attractive to the EU, where sectorial fragmentation in the Commission, the Council and the Parliament has been an important hindrance to comprehensive environmental policy-making (see Chapter 3).

Integration of environmental policy was formulated as a key objective as early as 1983, in the third EAP (Hertin and Berkhout 2003). It later figured prominently in the European Treaties, which state that 'environmental protection requirements must be integrated into the definition and implementation of the Union policies and activities, in particular with a view to promoting sustainable development' (Art. 11 TFEU). From the early 1990s onwards, a number of initiatives were taken within the European Commission to achieve EPI, such as the identification of 'environmental correspondents' within each Directorate-General. As those first measures produced few results, the European Council in 1998 launched the 'Cardiff process' as a new impetus towards the achievement of EPI (Hertin and Berkhout 2003). The most important initiative was requesting each Council formation to establish and implement its own environmental integration strategy in order to integrate environmental considerations into their respective activities.

The Cardiff process certainly advanced the discourse on EPI and promoted the idea that isolated environmental policies are not sufficient to tackle Europe's complex environmental challenges. But the process did not deliver meaningful results on the ground (Adelle and Russel 2013). To this day, EPI continues to be an EU objective, as the awareness grows that the problems of sustainable development are rooted in current day-to-day patterns of production and consumption. That is especially the case with regard to climate change, where progress depends heavily on policy changes in areas such as agriculture, energy or transport. That is why, within climate policy-making, 'climate policy integration' or mainstreaming is increasingly becoming a priority strategy (Dupont and Oberthür 2012).

The difficulty that any EPI initiative faces in producing meaningful results is related to the fact that some fundamental conflicts between environmental goals and certain other priorities have never disappeared. Despite the undeniable fact that the EU has achieved a decoupling of economic growth from specific forms of pollution (see Introduction) and despite all the good intentions and discursive commitments since the Brundtland Report (see Chapter 2), these conflicts are hard to eradicate as production and consumption patterns remain to a certain extent unsustainable, for instance in the fields of agriculture, energy and transport.

In the agricultural field, environmental standards and measures to protect animal welfare or human health are still often interpreted as a hindrance to the competitiveness of European farmers vis-à-vis their counterparts in other parts of the world where such standards are lower or non-existent (Favoino et al. 2000). The field of energy too often faces tensions with environmental policies. Despite the genuine efforts to promote energy efficiency and renewable energy, investments in natural gas infrastructure continue (Dupont and Oberthür 2012). Since decisions on the domestic energy mix remain a member state competence, insufficient steps have been taken to phase out environmentally harmful energy sources such as coal or to deal with hazardous waste of nuclear energy. Finally, transport has proven to be one of the hardest sectors to decouple environmental pressures from economic welfare (European Environment Agency 2015). This is due to the rebound effect, which occurs when the efficiency gains of products and services are outweighed by their increased consumption, and, in the transport system, to an insufficient shift of passenger and freight transport away from road towards more sustainable modes such as rail and inland waterways.

These tensions between environmental policy and other policy areas, as well as the lack of fundamental changes in those sectors, explain why initiatives such as EPI face difficulties in progressing and delivering. They also make it clear why European policy-makers try intensively to frame their environmental initiatives, such as the circular economy, as policies that will bring economic growth, jobs and competitiveness.

Sustainable Development Strategy

The second initiative to integrate sustainable development concerns into EU policies is the EU Sustainable Development Strategy. At the global level, the disappointment over the implementation gap after the 1992 Rio Summit became a critical issue towards the end of the 1990s (see Chapter 2). Governments therefore set 2002 as a new deadline for the development of national sustainable development strategies (United Nations General Assembly Special Session 1997). Such strategies, one of the measures included in Agenda 21, were meant to integrate sustainable development in policy-making and to harmonize existing plans and strategies (Meadowcroft 2007). In many cases, governments used them as a starting point to develop a sustainable development policy. In that context, the EU developed its own EUSDS in preparation for the 2002 World Summit on Sustainable Development in Johannesburg (Tanasescu 2006). That happened at the time when the Cardiff process was perceived to be failing. It also needed to display the EU's leadership with regard to sustainable development at the global level.

Through the formulation of objectives and actions in key issue areas (such as clean energy and the management of natural resources), the EUSDS provided a framework for the promotion of the EU's overarching objective of sustainable development (European Commission 2001b). It also aspired to increase the vertical policy integration of sustainable development between the EU level and the member states (Steurer and Hametner 2013), which were implementing the Rio commitments with varying enthusiasm. At the same time, the EUSDS was considered to be a necessary environmental add-on to the Lisbon strategy, the EU's main socio-economic strategy between 2000 and 2010 that aspired to make Europe the most competitive region in an era of globalization. The EUSDS was renewed in 2006, with a slight change in themes. By adding sustainable consumption and production as a priority, the EU acknowledged that unsustainable consumption and production patterns are at the core of the sustainability problem and require integrated policy approaches. The renewed EUSDS also linked European goals more explicitly to the global development agenda (Council of the European Union 2006).

Coordinated by the Commission's Secretariat-General, the EUSDS was mostly based on non-legislative measures and on cooperation procedures similar to the open method of coordination (von Homeyer 2009; Spangenberg 2010). However, it never received much political attention and was rather disconnected from the Lisbon strategy. When Europe 2020, the EU's new socio-economic strategy, was launched in 2010, an effort was made to include sustainable development concerns directly into Europe 2020 (see Chapter 6). That strategy now aims at 'smart, sustainable and inclusive growth' (European Commission 2010b) and advances resource efficiency as one of the ways to operationalize the 'sustainable growth' ambition.

The impact of transversal policies such as EPI and the EUSDS is smaller and much more diffuse than the impact of binding, issue-based environmental policies. Nevertheless, those transversal strategies can have an added value that goes beyond discursive changes or the promotion of important principles (such as long-term policy-making or the precautionary principle). When studying specific policies in detail, one often uncovers an intricate interaction between sectorial and transversal policies. An example is the field of waste and natural resources. As the EU's waste policy was faced with new complex challenges, it was the 2001 EUSDS that pleaded for a new vision of the connections between natural resources, waste and economic growth. It proposed the development of an integrated product policy, which gave an impetus to subsequent waste and product policies in the EU. Later, the renewed 2006 EUSDS mentioned for the first time the concept of resource efficiency. It helped to advance the development of a comprehensive European resource policy, situated within the context of global consumption and production patterns (Happaerts 2014).

Conclusions

The first results of the development of EU environmental policy since the 1970s were basic policies to fight pollution in specific environmental domains, such as water, air, waste and nature. Those issue-based policies remain fundamental EU priorities. Though basic in their origin, they have evolved into comprehensive, well-developed and far-reaching policies. With an enormous body of legislation that is binding on twenty-eight member states, these supranational environmental policies are undoubtedly unique.

The EU has developed its environmental policy in close interaction with the global environmental agenda. On the one hand, multilateral agreements on environmental issues and transversal concepts have an immediate impact on policy-making in the EU. That is shown by the examples of air policy, biodiversity and sustainable development, among others. It is clear that the EU has constantly tried to present itself as an early implementer of, and loyal party to, international agreements. On the other hand, the EU has tried to adopt a leadership position, not only in designing internal environmental policies, but also as a negotiator in those multilateral frameworks (see Chapter 10). One of the best examples of how those leadership ambitions have shaped EU policies is climate change (see Chapter 9), but also the innovative choices made in water policy and other domains illustrate how the EU wants to be ahead of the pack.

The overview of issue-based policies related to fighting pollution and protecting nature in this chapter demonstrated that enormous progress has been made in several domains. Many manifestations of environmental pollution have been halted and reduced thanks to these (often end-of-pipe) policies. However, sectorial and isolated environmental policies in the EU are now showing their limits. New challenges have arisen that cannot be tackled by simple issue-based policies. As shown in multiple instances above, contemporary environmental problems are inherent to current consumption and production patterns, and thus deeply rooted in our systems of food, mobility, energy, housing and so on. Therefore, further environmental progress does not depend solely on the improvement of environmental policy and its implementation, but on fundamental changes in the policies that form part of those societal systems.

Chapter 8

GMO Policy

Genetically modified organisms (GMOs) are defined by the EU as 'organisms whose genetic material (DNA) has been altered not by reproduction and/or natural recombination, but by the introduction of a modified gene or a gene from another variety or species' (European Commission 2014p). Agro-industry is the main developer and user of GMOs, for a number of reasons including better protection against fungi, insects and pests, better adaptation to temperatures, humidity or drought, and higher yields. But critics insist that GMOs can be harmful for the environment and human health, and that above anything else they serve higher profits for GMO developers. The quarrel between the supporters and the critics of GMOs not only characterizes the societal debate on GMOs in Europe, but it also has a crucial impact on EU policy-making processes relating to GMOs.

Only a very small portion of the global production and use of GMOs occurs in the EU. Less than 6 per cent of land used for GMO cultivation worldwide is within the EU (Reuters 2013), where at the time of writing only one GMO crop (genetically modified maize MON 810) is cultivated – although this number is likely to rise following the adoption of a new legislative framework in 2015 (see below). As this chapter will demonstrate, the low level of GMO use in Europe is the consequence of the EU's restrictive policies on the production and use of GMOs. The EU's record stands in stark contrast with many other parts of the world, where the use and production of GMOs has been increasingly rapid and pervasive. The land area used for GMO crops was 175 million hectares worldwide in 2013, mainly used for soy bean, cotton and maize (James 2013). This is a nearly one hundred-fold increase in 18 years. GMOs are grown in about thirty countries and used in food and feed in an additional thirty. The early adopters of GMO technology have been the United States, Brazil, Argentina and Canada, yet other countries, mainly in Asia, are rapidly following. The main global industrial players include companies such as Monsanto, BASF, Syngenta, Bayer and Dupont.

EU policies on GMOs are for many reasons interesting, controversial and of global significance. First, the EU's *de facto* position against the broad production, use and spreading of GMOs is the result of a strong interpretation of the precautionary principle, which basically states that GMOs can only be approved where there is scientific certainty on their harmlessness (Laïdi 2010). This clearly opposes US policies on the issue, which are based on an approach that only allows restrictions in the case of scientific evidence of harm (Gupta and Falkner 2006; Pollack and Shaffer 2010; Tiberghien 2009). The rationale behind the US GMO policy is basically that if a genetically modified *product* does not differ from its conventional counterpart, it should be regulated in the same way. This contrasts with the EU approach, which also takes the production *process* into account in its regulatory choices. The different approach by the EU and the United States has made GMOs a contentious issue in the EU–US negotiations on the Transatlantic Trade and Investment Partnership (TTIP). In addition, the EU's policy has led to serious trade conflicts with the most important countries that do allow the broad use of GMOs.

Second, GMO policy-making is rather atypical compared to other environmental policies as GMOs are also linked to agricultural and health policies and so policy-makers from these areas are also involved in the policy-making process. In the Commission, for instance, GMO policies are the responsibility of DG Health and Food Safety (DG SANTE). Also the procedure through which GMOs are authorized is very specific, with a significant role attributed to an independent agency and a complicated comitology procedure that *de facto* leaves a good deal of autonomy to the Commission as the final decision-maker in the GMO authorization process, even if a large number of member states is opposed to that.

Third, the agro and food industries, which are largely in favour of introducing GMOs in Europe, have so far not been very successful in the EU's GMO policy-making process and have thus not ensured that GMOs were authorized for cultivation in Europe. This counterbalances the general assumption that business lobbies are likely to prevail above environmental NGOs in environmental policy-making (see Chapter 5). However, the most recent changes in the EU's legislative framework on GMOs, which might open the door for more GMO cultivation in the EU, are seen by GMO opponents as a victory for business lobbies.

This chapter discusses the EU's policies on the production and use of GMOs, as well as the rationales behind them. First, it introduces the precautionary principle as the main policy principle of the EU's GMO policy and outlines the societal debates on the risks of GMOs. Second, the EU's GMO policy framework is analysed. This section also describes the most recent amendment of the GMO legislation of 2015, which followed a period of almost 15 years of highly contentious debate. In a third section, we explain how the EU's GMO policies relate to major international developments in the field of biodiversity and trade politics. We conclude by highlighting the particularities of the EU's GMO policy.

The precautionary principle and the contested nature of GMOs

The precautionary principle

The precautionary principle originated out of pre-World War II German law, where it is referred to as the *Vorsorgeprinzip* (O'Riordan and Cameron 1994). The principle in essence means that new products, processes or materials should not be introduced into production or consumption systems unless it is certain that they do not cause unwanted damage to humans or the environment (de Sadeleer 2009). More colloquially: it is better to be safe than sorry. Remarkably, the precautionary principle entered the field of environmental politics when scientific knowledge about the environment expanded. With this improved knowledge, it became increasingly clear that the complex interactions and long-term impacts of environmental phenomena posed a particular challenge to the policymakers who decided what was safe for people (health-wise) and also to nature. Moreover, the introduction of new technologies, products, materials (mainly chemicals) and production processes created additional uncertainties about their impact. The precautionary principle has become one of the cornerstones of the EU's environmental policies, for instance in the REACH Regulation (see Chapter 7).

According to the European Commission, 'the precautionary principle applies where scientific evidence is insufficient, inconclusive or uncertain and preliminary scientific evaluation indicates that there are reasonable grounds for concern that the potentially dangerous effects on the environment, human, animal or plant health may be inconsistent with the high level of protection chosen by the EU' (European Commission 2000). One of the difficulties when applying the precautionary principle is that often there exists a considerable grey area for interpretation. The main question is which level of risk is considered 'acceptable' by a society. Scientists can indeed, with standardized methodologies, determine what the levels of objective risks and uncertainties are. However, how acceptable these risks are is a societal and political matter. What is acceptable for one group might be totally out of the question for another group. Hence, although the precautionary principle is based on scientific evaluation and information, its implementation remains highly political (Weimer 2010). That explains, for example, why the EU and the United States draw fundamentally different conclusions from risk assessments on GMOs.

Ulrich Beck discusses these matters in his seminal book *Risk Society* (1992). The title refers to our modern society in which risks are linked to the use of technology and our reliance on complex systems of provision, such as energy, communication, food and the agricultural systems, which are all characterized by inherent risks. This means that incidents, breakdowns, undesirable side-effects and the incurred costs to society they imply are unavoidable. Besides relying on solid science and objective risk analysis, the best way to deal with these risks is to hold a serious social and political debate about the potential risks, their acceptability, the potential distribution of costs and benefits, and possible policy responses. Beck strongly advises not limiting the debate to scientists and technocrats. Although the latter provide indispensable knowledge and objectify the debate, which is fundamental in the light of the precautionary principle, 'normal' citizens and other societal stakeholders are just as important in the debate in order to identify the level of societal risk acceptance. The EU's approach to GMOs, which pays attention to both the scientific and the social perspective, illustrates that this is not just a theoretical debate.

The EU's GMO policies are based on a strict application of the precautionary principle, which makes them the most restrictive ones in the world. The following sections illustrate that this strong interpretation of the precautionary principle led to a *de facto* moratorium on the commercialization of GMOs between 1998 and 2004. Afterwards, the EU allowed some GMO presence in the food and feed system, thereby reflecting changing scientific as well as societal debates. However, a recent revision of the legislation, which was pushed by longstanding political controversies, again allows for more precaution, but this time applied at the national level.

The debate on the desirability of GMOs

GMOs are the object of intense debates in the European context. Discussions about the issue tend to be strongly polarized, mixed with emotions and often based on inconclusive evidence. They raise fundamental questions about the independence of scientific research and invariably refer to the essentially different position of the EU compared to other important countries in the agricultural and food system (such as the United States, Brazil or Argentina). There are several hundreds of lobby professionals on either side of the GMO fence attempting to influence the position of EU policy-makers on the issue.

For agro-industry, tens of billions of euros in seed and crop sales are at stake. For the environmental movements, nature is threatened in the most fundamental way by 'messing around' with its building blocks, that is, the genetic material of plants and animals. Opponents and proponents of the use of GMOs are entangled in a strongly polarized debate. There seems to be little middle ground on the issue. One of the complicating factors is the role of scientific evidence. Although essential for the precautionary principle, science has not managed to attain a neutral position in the eyes of either proponents or critics. Sources of doubt are the financing of research on GMOs, and whether full information is being made available, as well as issues of transparency. Scientific research thus plays a very important, but not uncontroversial, role in GMO politics. It falls outside the scope of this chapter to give a comprehensive overview of all the arguments and the scientific evidence used to corroborate them. We thus simply present the main arguments for and against the use of GMOs in the food and agricultural system.

Arguments pro GMO use

The case for GMO use can be summarized in a few central arguments:

- The most important argument favouring GMOs is that they *increase agricultural yields* (Schiffino and Varone 2005). This can be the case directly through improved genetic potential for fruit bearing. It can also occur indirectly because of improved resistance to pests and other plant diseases as this reduces crop loss and leads to a situation in which less land is needed to produce the same amount of food. Or, given the prospect of a growing population, the reasoning goes that GMOs will make it much easier to feed the world in the future. Related to this, studies have shown that on average GMO producing farmers have higher incomes (Klümper and Qaim 2014).

- Proponents claim that GMOs *are better quality and more nutritious* than non-modified crops. For example, with regard to rice, the Food and Agriculture Organization (FAO) explains that 'genes responsible for producing the precursor of vitamin A have been inserted into rice plants, which have higher levels of vitamin A in their grain. This is called Golden Rice. As rice feeds more than 50 per cent of the world's population, it could help reduce vitamin A deficiency, which is a serious problem in the developing world. Many other similar products aimed at bio-fortification are in the production pipeline' (Food and Agriculture Organization 2003).

- *Environmental benefits* are also mentioned as an argument for GMO use. Genetically modified plants could potentially grow with less water use, allow degraded agricultural land to revive, and adapt better to changing climatic conditions. Moreover, their resistance to diseases decreases the need for pesticides, fungicides and herbicides (CropLife International 2014; Klümper and Qaim 2014).

- Some proponents argue that genetically modified crops could be designed specifically for their potential as biofuels. This would contribute towards *finding solutions for key energy questions* in light of peak oil, and the transition towards a low-carbon society, and it reduces the tension between agricultural crops and biofuels (Goho 2008).

- Finally, those in favour of GMOs mention the *advantages for human health*, as genetic plant and crop engineering could contribute to the development of medicines (Locwin 2014).

In terms of risks, the main counterargument against those who are more critical of GMOs is that there is no scientific evidence that GMOs have caused any harm to humans or the environment. Here, the central position of the GMO proponents is that no single human being or animal has ever been harmed due to the consumption of GMO food or feed (Entine 2014).

Arguments against GMO use

The arguments against the use of GMO food and feed mainly come down to the following claims:

- Those who are against the use of GMOs are concerned about the *environmental risks* (Greenpeace 2014). Genetic engineering is said to be a too imprecise technology. It is deemed too risky to play with the fundamental building blocks of nature, based on a technology that has too many unknowns and uncertainties (Moreau 2014). The resulting environmental risks include unexpected and harmful gene interactions and/ or mutations, which may stimulate sleeper genes or deactivate genes. Those interactions and mutations may create unwanted effects in plants, animals or consumers and they may generate interactions between wild and genetically engineered species with uncontrollable results. This may have an impact on birds, insects and other species that feed with genetically altered plants or animals. Moreover, the 'unstoppable' nature of GMOs means that this is by definition a transboundary issue in which the deliberate release of GMOs in one country is not without consequences for the environment in other countries, which may have more reluctant preferences towards the use of GMOs.
- *Health concerns* are also a central argument against the use of GMOs. Uncertainty exists about the long-term effects of GMOs on human health, but also on the health of animals and plants in the ecosystem (many of which are also used by humans) (Institute for Responsible Technology 2015).
- Another set of arguments against the use of GMOs is related to *economic problems*. An agricultural and food system largely based on genetic modification could be controlled by a handful of multinational corporations in an oligopolistic market. Combined with the strict protection of intellectual property rights over seeds this would make farmers (globally) more dependent. They could, according to the critics, become *de facto* dependent consumers of genetic technology, rather than producers of food (Food and Agriculture Organization 2015).

- A last argument is that the large-scale introduction of GMOs can lead to a reduction of genetic variation (Greenpeace 2014). Traditional plants and species are then likely to disappear in favour of a limited number of species with supposedly superior genetic qualities. Consequently, thousands of years of traditional agricultural knowledge could be lost or disregarded.

The most important counterargument against the claim of proponents that GMOs could solve world famine is the reasoning that famine is not caused by a worldwide lack of food, but rather by structural socio-economic barriers (Shah 2010). From that perspective, the increasing dependency of small farmers on multinational corporations that develop GMOs could even aggravate those problems.

The EU's GMO policy framework

European legislation on GMOs has existed since 1990 (on the earliest developments see Daviter 2009; Morris and Spilane 2012). From the beginning, European GMO policies have been designed to protect human health and the environment, while simultaneously respecting the rules of the single market. The legislation deals with the release, cultivation, marketing, labelling, traceability and dissemination of GMOs both in food intended for human consumption and in animal feed. Furthermore, it concerns the implementation of the provisions on transboundary movements of GMOs laid down in the Cartagena Protocol on Biosafety, an international agreement under the Convention on Biological Diversity to which the EU is a party (see below). This again demonstrates the important interaction between European and international environmental policies.

After an original period of limited imports and cultivation of genetically modified varieties in the 1990s, a moratorium was *de facto* put in place between 1998 and 2004, which meant that no GMOs were authorized for cultivation in the EU in that period. That was the result of a group of member states (Denmark, France, Greece, Italy and Luxembourg) declaring that they would block any new GMO authorization until the Commission proposed stricter legislation. Their move was a consequence of public resistance against GMOs caused by food scandals such as the mad cow disease and the cloning of Dolly the sheep (Burns 2012b; Pollack and Shaffer 2010). The *de facto* moratorium triggered a serious trade conflict with the United States and other countries (see below).

The EU's market has in principle been reopened to new GMO products and applications in 2004 following the entry into force of three legislative acts: the Directive on the deliberate release into the environment of GMOs (2001/18), the Regulation on genetically modified food and feed (1829/2003) and the Regulation on the traceability and labelling of GMOs (1830/2003). In 2001, the Commission also issued guidelines on co-existence, which are – in contrast to the three legislative acts mentioned above – not legally binding and which were revised in 2010. However, the main controversies that have characterized the EU's GMO policy from the start persisted even after the adoption of these three pieces of legislation. In addition, the cleavage between member states that favour GMOs and those that are more sceptical sharpened even more. That is why Directive 2001/18 was revised in 2015 (2015/412), introducing a significant change in the procedure to authorize GMOs and giving more freedom to the member states. The main aspects of the EU's GMO policy framework are described below. They deal with deliberate release; the safeguard clause; food and feed; traceability and labelling; and co-existence.

Deliberate Release Directive

The Deliberative Release Directive, revised in 2015 (2015/412), is the central piece in the EU's regulatory framework. Except for the provisions on the cultivation of GMOs that give more powers to the member states, the greater part of the 2015 Directive still resembles its predecessor from 2001 (2001/18). The Directive applies to two types of activities. First, it deals with the experimental release of GMOs into the environment, referring to the introduction of GMOs into the environment for experimental purposes (for example to study the behaviour of the GMO in an open environment and its interactions with other organisms and the environment). Experimental releases of GMOs into the environment are mainly carried out for the purposes of research on novel varieties.

Second, the Directive regulates the placing on the market of GMOs, including the cultivation, import or transformation of GMOs into industrial products following positive results in the experimental stage. The authorization procedure provides for a common methodology to assess on a case-by-case basis the risks for health and for the environment associated with the release of GMOs, and a mechanism allowing the release of the GMOs to be modified, suspended or terminated when new information becomes available on the risks of such release. This last point is important since plant genetics is a fast evolving scientific field frequently producing new results on (potential) risks. These results can then be used to confirm or revise policy decisions in accordance with the precautionary principle. However, this has not yet occurred in practice.

The authorization procedure goes as follows (European Parliament 2015; Lee 2014): when a company intends to place GMO food or feed on the market, it has to submit an application, via the national authority in each member state, to the European Food Safety Authority (EFSA). This European agency provides scientific advice to the EU institutions and the public on food and feed safety and conducts independent risk assessments on GMOs (see Chapter 3). The company's application must include all the information that is relevant to the general objective of safety for human health and the environment. This means that a clear explanation of the purpose and scope (why the GMO is to be introduced), a monitoring plan and labelling proposal, and a detection method need to be included in the application. In light of the precautionary principle, and to ensure that the scientific underpinning for a valid opinion is solid, all relevant data, studies and analyses of the results known to the submitter have to be added to the application.

Based on its own scientific risk assessment and on a consultation with the member states and the Commission, EFSA conveys its opinion to the Commission within six months. To assure transparency, a complete list of pending applications is published on the EFSA website. If the opinion is favourable, it also contains concrete proposals for labelling, and appropriate conditions or restrictions for the placing on the market of the GMO product. An interesting feature, in the light of Beck's call for stronger public debate, is the fact that European citizens can make comments on the EFSA opinion. Once an EFSA opinion is available, the Commission opens a consultation on its website for 30 days. Then, the Commission analyses all the comments received and consults EFSA to determine whether they have an impact on the agency's opinion. The Commission subsequently formulates a draft decision and presents it to a specific comitology committee, the 'Standing Committee of Food Chain and Animal Health' (SCoFCAH), which is composed of member state officials.

The role of SCoFCAH in the implementation of the Deliberate Release Directive illustrates the importance of comitology in the EU's environmental politics. In this comitology process, the 'examination procedure' applies, allowing the Commission to take a decision when the member states in the SCoFCAH (or in the appeal committee) are not able to find a sufficiently large majority to adopt a positive or negative opinion on the proposed authorization (see Chapter 4). In practice, at the time of writing, the required qualified majority for taking decisions on GMO authorization has never actually been reached. As a result, the final decisions on the proposed authorizations have always been taken by the European Commission and regularly against the will of a large number of member states (Skogstad 2011). In other words, 'at the end of the day, therefore, it is the European Commission which is finally taking the decision on applications authorizing GMOs to be placed on the market, even though these are never endorsed by a qualified majority of the member states' (Christiansen and Polak 2009: 7). In that sense, comitology in the area of GMOs is exceptional since, in general, the relationship between the Commission and the member states in a comitology procedure is much more cooperative.

When genetically modified products are authorized, they are publicized through the Commission's register of genetically modified food and feed. Authorizations are granted for ten years and they are renewable for additional ten-year periods. The authorization often requires a post-market environmental monitoring plan (PMEM), which is important for following up the potential consequences after the introduction of the GMO in the food chain. PMEMs aim at identifying unanticipated adverse effects on the environment which could arise directly or indirectly from genetically modified plants.

Safeguard clause and new national discretion

Ever since the earliest European legislation on GMOs, member states have been able to invoke a so-called safeguard clause. It means that a member state may provisionally restrict or prohibit the use or sale of the genetically modified product that has been authorized by the EU on its territory. Several countries have invoked the safeguard clause, including Austria, France, Germany, Greece, Hungary and Luxembourg. The Commission has the right to resist the use of the clause, through comitology, but the member states can challenge that decision through QMV (Lee 2014).

Under the pre-2015 rules, member states had to provide additional scientific evidence that went beyond all the information that had already been used in the authorization process. Other, non-science based, considerations (for instance ethical or social considerations) could not justify the use of the safeguard clause. In other words, considerations based on the protection of the environment or on the risks to human health could not be used to invoke the safeguard clause if they were not based on new scientific findings. In that form, the clause led to much controversy. The Commission argued that member states used the safeguard clause improperly, namely for reasons other than the availability of new scientific knowledge or information. Yet the Council tended to reject the Commission's requests to overrule the national safeguard bans, because even member states that were more favourable towards GMOs (such as the Czech Republic, Portugal and Spain) recognized the right of other member states to install such a ban (Lee 2014; Pollack and Shaffer 2010). The Commission reacted with two strategies. First, it became more selective in the safeguard bans that it submitted to the Council for revision, in particular avoiding submitting proposals on abolishing imposed *cultivation* bans, which were typically upheld in the Council. For instance, in 2007 the Commission succeeded in having an Austrian ban on the marketing of GMO maize lifted by targeting only the ban on marketing and not the one on cultivation, thereby persuading sufficient member states to abstain during the vote (Pollack and Shaffer 2010). Second, the Commission started fighting both marketing and cultivation bans in cases before the Court of Justice of the EU (Poli 2013). So far, the Court has always confirmed the viewpoint of the Commission.

The revised 2015 Deliberate Release Directive is intended to end the 'improper' use of the safeguard clause by member states as well as the continuing conflicts (and Court cases) between the member states and the Commission. At the heart of the 2015 revision lies the decoupling of the GMO *trade* rules on the one hand and the GMO *cultivation* rules on the other hand. While the trade rules remain in the hands of the EU, thereby protecting the internal market, the member states' discretionary power in terms of cultivation rules are increased. The new rules foresee that the actual use of seeds for cultivation can be restricted or banned by individual member states, despite the granting of the authorization for marketing and trading. In that case, the prohibition of cultivation has to be justified on other than the environmental and health grounds invoked by EFSA (for example town and country planning, land use, socio-economic impact, avoiding GMO traces in conventional or organic products, or other environmental policy objectives). To adopt a restriction or ban, a member state can ask the producer to exclude (a part of) its territory from the cultivation scope. If the company disagrees, or even if the member state has not previously asked for any exclusion, the country is permitted to impose its ban anyway. The new bans only apply to seeds, not to processed food and feed products. And given the free movement of goods in the EU, seeds that have passed the authorization procedure may be freely traded on the market and transported even in those countries that do not allow their cultivation.

The 2015 revision was of great political importance, as it is the first area of regulation on which the EU has exercised its shared competence in such a way that it *de facto* moves back in part to member states (Poli 2013; Randour et al. 2014). By giving more leeway to the member states to decide on the cultivation of GMOs at the domestic level, this Directive indeed returns some powers to the member states that were previously exercised by the EU. The original legislation on deliberate release adopted in 1990 (Directive 90/220), which already contained the key elements of the authorization procedure, was much more decentralized than the legislation in force between 2001 and 2015 (Directive 2001/18), and gave a larger role to individual member states in authorizing GMOs (Pollack and Shaffer 2010).

Regulations on food and feed and on traceability and labelling

Directive 2015/412 is complemented by two other regulations that date back to 2003. First, the Regulation on Food and Feed (1829/2003) introduces more specific procedural rules in relation to food and feed to the authorization procedure. It also responds to concerns of consumers who prefer clear labelling of genetically modified food and feed, and to concerns of farmers who want to make informed choices as regards the composition and properties of feed.

In 2015, the European Commission issued a proposal to amend the 2003 Food and Feed Regulation (European Commission 2015a). The Commission proposed to allow individual member states to adopt opt-out measures as a result of which they could ban the use of GMOs that are approved by the EU in food or feed. This means that individual member states should be able to ban the use of a GMO on their territory, even if that GMO has been authorized at the EU level, thereby having undergone the risk assessment by EFSA and the comitology scrutiny (see above). In that sense, the proposal followed a rationale similar to that of the 2015 amendment to the Deliberate Release Directive, namely returning powers on the use of GMOs to the national level. Importantly, according to the proposal, a member state cannot invoke justifications related to health and the environment in its decision to opt out, as this would undermine the EFSA procedure. The Commission proposal has been critically received as many observers cast doubt on the extent to which the proposed legislation is compatible with the EU's internal market (which implies that a member state cannot simply close its border for a genetically modified product) and with its international obligations, including WTO rules (see below). After this proposal was rejected by the EP, its adoption has become very unlikely.

Second, the Regulation on the traceability and labelling of GMOs placed on the market (1830/2003) stipulates traceability and labelling requirements for food and feed that are derived from a GMO, such as tomato ketchup produced from a genetically modified tomato or flour produced from a genetically modified maize. *Traceability* is the ability to track GMOs and food/feed produced from GMOs at all stages of the supply chain. The Regulation makes it mandatory 'from farm to fork'. Traceability makes it possible to closely monitor the potential effects of genetically modified food/feed on the environment and on health, and potentially to withdraw products if an unexpected risk to human health or to the environment is detected. The traceability rules oblige everyone who places a genetically modified product on the market, or who receives a product placed on the market within the EU, to be able to identify their supplier and the companies to which the products have been supplied. Although these requirements are highly bureaucratic, they are in fact designed to reduce the need for sampling and testing of products. If GMOs are traced in a detailed way, there is not necessarily any need to sample or test products for the presence of GMOs.

Regulation 1830/2003 also sets out *labelling* requirements for genetically modified products. Labelling informs the consumers about the product, allowing them to make a conscious choice about the important matter of food. For pre-packaged products containing GMOs, labels must indicate: 'This product contains genetically modified organisms'. Since conventional food, feed and seed (which are not genetically modified) can be unintentionally contaminated by GMOs, for instance during the harvesting or transportation process, the legislation makes an exception for conventional products 'contaminated' by GMOs. The latter escape the traceability and labelling requirements if they contain less than 0.9 per cent traces of GMOs (Pollack and Shaffer 2010). The labelling system therefore does not ensure 'GMO-free' products. A number of member states have, however, introduced national 'GMO-free' labels, without resistance from the Commission (Krämer 2012a).

Co-existence

One of the most sensitive and difficult aspects of the EU's GMO policy refers to the rules on so-called co-existence. Since agriculture is an open-air activity, perfect segregation of the different agricultural production types is not possible in practice. Consequently, the cultivation of genetically modified crops is likely to have implications for agricultural production beyond the GMO fields. For example, pollen flow is not only a necessary natural phenomenon, it is also in practice very difficult to stop. This means that genetically modified plants can interfere – or 'co-exist' – in 'natural' ways with non-genetically modified crops. It may also have economic implications for farmers who want to produce traditional plants intended for food next to genetically modified crops, as the two types of crops are subject to different market dynamics. Co-existence measures aim to create adequate segregation between genetically modified and non-genetically modified production. They are intended to give farmers the practical choice between conventional, organic and genetically modified crop production in compliance with the applicable legal obligations for labelling and purity standards for those three distinct categories of food. Co-existence measures are needed during cultivation, harvest, transport, storage and processing.

Under the principle of subsidiarity, the competence to develop policies regarding co-existence lies with the member states. However, in 2010, the Commission issued a revised version of the 'Recommendation on guidelines for the development of national co-existence measures to avoid the unintended presence of GMOs in conventional and organic crops' (European Commission 2010c; Varela 2012). In contrast to the legislative acts on GMOs, the

Recommendation is not legally binding. It introduces the principle of proportionality, meaning that measures to avoid the presence of GMOs in other crops should be proportionate to the intended end result. Therefore, co-existence measures should 'avoid any unnecessary burden' for operators and should take local constraints into account (Lee 2014). While proponents claim that this Recommendation is motivated by reasons of efficiency and avoiding excessive costs in order to protect agricultural activities, opponents see this as a backdoor for lobby groups to minimize the measures (Pearsall 2013). They argue that it suffices to find political support for claims about the excessive costs of measures to have them watered down. The Recommendation also makes reference to the possibility of member states introducing 'GMO-free areas', meaning that GMO cultivation is forbidden in large areas of the territory because the climatic, topographic or other natural characteristics of a specific region would render less extreme measures ineffective (Dobbs 2011). The 2010 Recommendation was therefore a clear foretaste of the possibility of national restrictions and bans, which was subsequently re-introduced in the 2015 Deliberate Release Directive (see above).

Since the competences on co-existence are still national, the member states are not obliged to formulate co-existence legislation (Dobbs 2011). However, with some notable exceptions (such as Spain), most member states have done so. In order to monitor and support the co-existence policy, the Commission has set up the European Coexistence Bureau (ECoB), located at the Joint Research Centre, which is the Commission's in-house scientific service. The ECoB develops technical reference documents on best practices and provides member states with non-binding guidelines for technical co-existence measures. In addition, the Commission has also set up the Network Group for the Exchange and Coordination of Information Concerning Coexistence of Genetically Modified, Conventional and Organic Crops (COEX-NET), which brings together representatives from member states' administrations in charge of co-existence. COEX-NET fosters the exchange of information on the results of scientific studies as well as on best practices developed within national strategies for co-existence among the member states and the Commission. The institutional set-up on co-existence illustrates the complexity of policy-making on GMOs. It requires continuous follow-up, exchange of information, questioning of (un)certainties, economic and environmental balancing and (public) debate.

Strict regulation, but much dissent and discontent

Even after the recent reforms the overall policy framework of the EU on GMOs remains controversial and subject to much dissent and discontent. Following the adoption of the 2001 and 2003 legislation, the first genetically modified food product – maize MON 810 by Monsanto – was approved for cultivation in the EU in May 2004. It was only the second crop to be approved and is still, at the time of writing, the only one cultivated in the EU today, since the Amflora potato, approved in 2010, was later withdrawn by the producer BASF (Reuters 2013). By April 2015, the EU had made sixty-eight authorizations in total, but apart from MON 810 and the Amflora potato, the other sixty-six concern imported GMOs for food, additives or animal feed (for instance cotton, maize, soybean) rather than cultivation (European Commission 2015b).

Even before the 2015 Deliberate Release Directive entered into force, the implementation of the EU's GMO legislation had led to very different, almost opposing, national realities. Some member states have embraced GMO agriculture within the limits of the EU policies, while others have kept trying to further restrict and limit GMOs. Among the more enthusiastic adopters are the Czech Republic, Portugal, Romania, Slovakia and Spain. Spain is the largest producer of genetically modified crops in Europe with about 100,000 hectares of genetically modified maize planted in 2013 (James 2013). At the other end of the spectrum, we find the strongest opponents to GMO food in France and Germany. Other member states that have placed bans on the cultivation and sale of specific GMOs include Austria, Greece, Hungary and Luxembourg. These different stances reflect a combination of factors, including the structure of the domestic agricultural sector, preferences of the strongest agricultural organizations in the country, the ideological orientations of the parties in the government, domestic public opinion on the safety of food, and broader considerations on the meaning of the precautionary principle.

There is also much discontent on the part of business and environmental groups. Agro and food industries, which play in a globalized market, are faced with a rather liberal approach to GMOs in the United States, Canada, Brazil, China and other important agricultural countries and food markets, and at the same time with the highly restrictive policies of the EU, which they have not managed to fundamentally influence despite relentless lobbying efforts.

The 2015 revision of the legislation was also criticized by the bio-tech industry, which claims that it will increase the pressure on member states to give in to anti-GMO feelings in public opinion, as they can prohibit GMO cultivation upon non-scientific grounds (see above) (International Centre for Trade and Sustainable Development 2014).

Environmental NGOs and bio-agriculture organizations regard every step the EU takes to permit or introduce any form of GMO as a fundamental loss against nature. They have little faith in current risk assessments as they keep pointing to the large blind spots in knowledge and the long-term implications. The sensitivity of the issue on the side of NGOs is also illustrated by the fact that the environmental groups Avaaz and Greenpeace succeeded in collecting over one million signatures in pursuit of a European Citizens' Initiative (see Chapter 3). The petition followed the authorization of the Amflora potato in 2010 and called for a new moratorium on the cultivation of GMOs in the EU. Although it never formally qualified as a European Citizens' Initiative (because it was launched too early), it raised pressure on the Commission to pay renewed political attention to the issue. Environmental NGOs also raised concerns that the 2015 legislation paves the way for cultivation in member states more favourable to GMOs. In the past, a number of member states consistently hindered the authorization of seeds for cultivation in the EU through the safeguard procedure or via blockage in the comitology process. But with an easy GMO opt-out, they may have less reason to resist the authorization of seeds for cultivation, making it possible for more liberal member states to go ahead with GMO cultivation.

GMO policy in an international context

The international dimension of biodiversity protection

In the framework of the Convention on Biological Diversity (CBD) (see Chapter 7), the Cartagena Protocol on Biosafety was adopted in 2000 and entered into force in 2003. The Protocol, which is the first international agreement on the transboundary movement of GMOs, aims at ensuring that such transboundary movements (including trade) do not have adverse effects on biodiversity, on the environment in general and on human health (Kirsop 2002). It was negotiated in the first instance to meet the concerns of certain developing countries wanting protection against uninformed imports of GMOs into their territory (Oberthür and Gehring 2006). The Cartagena Protocol stipulates a procedure by which GMO exporters have to obtain an Advance Informed Agreement (AIA) (that is, an explicit consent based on a risk assessment) from the importer before certain GMOs can be exported (Falkner 2000). Moreover, it permits the restriction of GMO import (that is, not granting a consent) on the basis of precaution, as the precautionary principle is here too one of the guiding principles for risk assessments. Once an importer has decided to accept the GMOs, the exporter has to provide the exported GMOs with appropriate labelling and documentation requirements.

At the time when the Cartagena Protocol was negotiated, in the years running up to 2000, the EU strongly emphasized precaution and biosafety. It defended this position and the application of the precautionary principle in risk assessment in the negotiations on the Protocol (Delreux 2012b; Rhinard and Kaeding 2006). The Protocol favoured ecological precaution over trade and is therefore seen as one of the major successes of the EU's international environmental diplomacy (see Chapter 10). The negotiations on the Cartagena Protocol reinforced the EU's identity in biotechnology regulation and eventually became a tool that helped many developing countries to adopt the same model of a precautionary GMO policy (Falkner 2007).

After the EU ratified the Cartagena Protocol in 2002, it adopted the Regulation on transboundary movement of GMOs (1946/2003) to implement most of the Protocol's provisions. The Regulation requires European GMO exporters to notify non-EU import countries and transit countries. It forbids exports of products that have not been authorized within the EU and those without the express consent of the importer. Finally, member states must take the necessary measures to avoid unintentional transboundary movements of GMOs. Following the transparency principle, if there is any risk of this occurring, member states must consult with the affected state and inform the public, the Commission, the other member states, the relevant international organizations and the Biosafety Clearing House (that is, a monitoring and data gathering body set up by the Cartagena Protocol).

The international dimension of global and transatlantic trade

The EU and the United States have been in strong disagreement over the EU's policy on genetically modified foods, leading to transatlantic trade conflicts. At no time was this clearer than when in 2003 the United States – accompanied by Argentina, Canada, Egypt, Australia, New Zealand, Mexico, Chile, Colombia, El Salvador, Honduras, Peru and Uruguay – filed a formal complaint with the World Trade Organization (WTO) challenging the EU's *de facto* moratorium after months of negotiations trying to get it lifted voluntarily (Pollack and Shaffer 2010). These countries accused the EU, which blocked imports of their farm products through its longstanding GMO ban, of violating international trade agreements and WTO rules.

The United States had been confronted with a sharp decline in the export of some agricultural products to the EU. For example, American maize exports to the EU more than halved between 1998 and 2002 (Rigby 2004). Although several reasons can be adduced for this drop in trade numbers (including falling commodities prices and the strong dollar), American farm industry advocates blamed the EU's GMO ban in particular. Claiming that the EU's policies were breaching WTO rules, the United States and its allies argued that the EU's regulatory process was far too slow and its standards were unreasonable given that the overwhelming body of scientific evidence finds the crops safe (Hanrahan 2010). Besides trade arguments, other elements were also used in the GMO conflict. The United States even called the European position towards GMOs 'immoral', after some African countries (such as Zambia), which aligned with the EU position and the precautionary principle, refused US aid because it contained genetically modified food, although they were in the middle of a famine (Mupotola 2005).

In November 2006, the WTO Dispute Settlement Body (DSB) reported that the EU policies constituted an infringement of the WTO Sanitary and Phytosanitary (SPS) Agreement and ruled that EU restrictions on genetically engineered crops indeed violated international trade rules. With its *de facto* moratorium between 1998 and 2004 (that is, the period in which the EU authorized no GMOs and thus *de facto* also blocked the imports of new genetically modified crops), the EU had broken its international trade commitments. The WTO also found violations in the lengthy and delaying process of authorization and in the safeguard clause, which was found not to be based on an appropriate risk assessment (Winham 2009). However, as the EU had adopted new legislation in 2003 (see above), eventually ending the import ban, the WTO ruling had little immediate effect. The 2003 legislation was introduced in part to address concerns brought forward by the EU's adversaries in the trade dispute. However, as mentioned above, the EU has remained highly prudent (or restrictive) over the authorization of GMOs. The fact that the EU has not fundamentally changed its policies, or that policy outcomes (authorizations) have not been significantly affected has led GMO opponents like Friends of the Earth to state that the WTO ruling was 'no victory for the United States or the biotech companies. Countries still have the right to ban or suspend genetically modified foods and crops. Europe's only failure was the way they did it and not why they did it' (Friends of the Earth 2006).

Probably the most important outcome of the WTO ruling is that the EU has since 2006 engaged in regular bi-annual meetings with its trade partners (primarily the United States, Argentina and Canada) regarding the application of biotechnology to agriculture and related trade issues. These dialogues are aimed at an exchange of information contributing to avoiding unnecessary obstacles to trade, in the spirit of the WTO goals and objectives. However, they do not seem to have a major impact on EU action on individual product authorizations for GMOs.

The WTO ruling and the ensuing policy dialogues did not mean the end of the international GMO trade dispute. In the United States, the EU's policies are still considered to be protectionist (that is, a trade barrier against agricultural imports). Public and economic pressure from the United States on the EU only increased after the 2006 ruling. In 2010, American agricultural and food industry lobby groups argued that the EU was failing to comply with the ruling, since the very low rate of approvals showed that it had still not ended the moratorium (Palmer 2010). After initial (but later suspended) steps in 2008 to retaliate with trade sanctions, and after the United States had agreed at least twice to give the EU more time to comply with the ruling, the internal pressure on the US government to take a firmer stance was again increased. The American Farm Bureau Federation asked the Obama administration to 'initiate a retaliation proceeding against the EU' (American Farm Bureau Federation 2010).

When the EU in 2011 adopted a Regulation that harmonizes the implementation of the zero-tolerance policy on non-authorized GMOs material in feed imported from non-EU countries (619/2011), this did not ease the relationship with the United States and other GMO-exporting countries. The Regulation sets a technical zero at a level of 0.1 per cent for the presence of genetically modified material in feed. This is the lowest level of genetically modified material considered by the EU for the validation of quantitative methods. It means that animal feed imports from the United States and other countries with large GMO maize and soy agriculture are in practice almost impossible.

The United States is expected to raise the pressure on the EU in the context of the negotiations on the future EU–US free trade agreement, the Transatlantic Trade and Investment Partnership (TTIP), which are ongoing at the time of writing. This is a logical expectation from the US point of view, as it has always considered the EU's precautionary stance as a free trade restriction. The EU, however, counters these expectations. It is aware that prospects for a transatlantic trade agreement raise many concerns among European consumers and civil society. Food is one of the prime objects of their worries, with GMOs and chlorine-washed chickens as often-cited examples (Harris 2014). The European Commission is ensuring that measures to protect the environment or health – on which its GMO policy is based – are non-negotiable (European Commission 2014q).

Conclusions

The EU has set up a fairly complex and comprehensive system for the authorization of GMOs that covers all the possible parts of the production and consumption cycle, from the early research and development stage to the potential consequences for health and the environment. It is a carefully calibrated system aiming to balance prudence, societal concerns, scientific evidence, national preferences for implementation, and (limited) possibilities for business to introduce GMOs in the European food and agricultural system. It is based on scientific considerations, but also on checks and balances within the policy system, with important roles for the EU's main institutions, but also for comitology committees and agencies.

Member states have a substantial impact on the policy implementation, and some have taken strongly varying positions. Most recently, the scale has tipped again towards the member states, as a legislative review introduced more national leeway into the policies whether or not GMOs can be cultivated in a particular member state. It further institutionalizes the divided GMO market in Europe, which seems to be the price of allowing the more favourable member states to cultivate their GMOs (Lee 2014). This development is another example of the creative consensus-seeking of the

European Commission, which is forced to design legislation in the context of persistent and presumably irreconcilable divisions even if it means that it has to give powers back to the member states.

The EU's GMO policy is probably the most prominent example of strict implementation of the precautionary principle on such a large scale. Since the first legislation in 1990, the system has led to only sixty-eight authorizations, with only one single variety actually cultivated in the EU. For GMO opponents, these are sixty-eight too many. According to proponents, the system is *de facto* a very extensive and expensive way of banning GMOs from Europe, which is thus missing out on all the benefits of GMOs. The EU has placed itself in a somewhat isolated position internationally, firmly opposed to countries with large agricultural and food industries. Whereas the United States, Canada and most of the emerging economies in Asia and Latin America have embraced GMOs as an integral part of innovation in the agricultural and food sector, the EU has stuck to its position, namely precaution as the basis of authorization and introduction.

The trade disputes between the EU and its main agricultural and food trading partners continue to this day. This is largely reflective of the radically different policy choices – based on divergent public opinion, the differing impacts of lobby groups and fundamentally different views on health and environmental protection – that have been made in and outside Europe. Given the deep structural and political drivers of the EU's and other countries' policy options, it is unlikely that either side will change its position any time soon. This means that it is likely that the EU's GMO regulatory actions will remain controversial and hotly debated for a long time. The several hundreds of lobbyists on all sides of the issue are just as much a reflection of the strongly opposing views as they are of the enormous commercial interests in the outcomes of decisions.

Chapter 9

Climate Change Policy

The accumulated presence of carbon dioxide (CO_2) and some other gases in the atmosphere causes average global air temperature to rise, a phenomenon commonly referred to as the greenhouse effect. The sources of those gases are both man-made and natural, but it is the anthropogenic sources (that are activities in industry, transport, agriculture, etc.) that have been growing on a dramatic scale. The increase in global air temperature unleashed a number of unseen and far-reaching climatic changes. Climate change will have – and is indeed already having – a range of impacts on weather patterns, food production, biodiversity and other areas, and is the main cause of a rising sea level (European Environment Agency 2015). For those alarming reasons, the reduction of greenhouse gas emissions in order to reduce human-induced climate change (mitigation) as well as efforts to cope with the consequences of climate change that are already irreversible (adaptation) have become priorities in global and European environmental politics. In the 2000s, climate change overtook every other environmental problem in terms of public concern, political attention and official agenda space. Climate change also became the principal environmental problem to be linked to global security, as it reduces the access to natural resources and therefore increases the risk of violent conflict (Barnett and Adger 2007; Scheffran et al. 2012).

The EU has been the most enthusiastic supporter of global action on climate change (see Chapter 10). Internally, it has designed a comprehensive regulatory framework to tackle emissions within Europe, both with policies at the EU level as well as by imposing targets that need to be met by policies at the national level. Since it originated in the late 1990s, the EU's policy framework on climate change is more recent than EU policies in the other environmental subdomains (such as air, water or biodiversity policy) previously discussed in this book (see Chapter 7).

205

Examining the climate change policy of the EU is interesting for a number of reasons and not least because it has evolved in a short period of nearly two decades into the most salient environmental issue in the EU. Moreover, as will be discussed in Chapter 10, the EU has tried very hard to be a leader on the world stage in this field. This chapter will demonstrate that its external leadership ambitions and internal policy-making zeal are closely intertwined. Finally, climate change has become a controversial domain of EU policy-making, which regularly makes it to the level of heads of state and government in the European Council (see Chapter 3). Member states are often divided on the question of how far EU action to limit climate change should go. In addition, those same divisions develop fault lines within the Commission, for instance between DG Climate Action and sectorial DGs concerned with energy or transport (see Chapters 3 and 7). Nonetheless, those internal controversies have not prevented the EU from adopting an encompassing set of policies to fight climate change, which is today one of the world's most ambitious regulatory frameworks in this field.

The next section shows how climate change gradually shifted, over only two decades, from being one of many global environmental problems to becoming the number one priority issue of the EU's environmental agenda. Subsequently, the main choices that the EU has made in this area and their implications are described. They include the establishment of the EU's emissions trading system (ETS) and its attempts to steer policies by setting climate and energy targets and objectives for 2020, 2030 and 2050. We also discuss the results that the EU's climate policy has had in tackling climate change. Conclusions are presented in a final section.

Gradually overpowering environmental policies

In its earliest form, the topic of climate change became a small part of the EU's research policy in the late 1970s, around the time when the first (scientific) World Climate Conference was held (Jordan et al. 2012) (see Chapter 2). As scientific evidence grew and the issue became more politically salient, a number of member states initiated climate policies. Although certain 'environmental leaders' in the Environment Council, such as Denmark, Germany and the Netherlands (see Chapter 3), increasingly urged for common mitigation policies, action at EU level did not immediately follow

(Jordan et al. 2012). A first Communication from the Commission in 1988 took stock of the scientific evidence and advanced the first (very general) policy options (European Commission 1988). The options included mitigation measures in the energy, agriculture and forestry sectors and adaptation to sea level rise. Those first steps brought climate change onto the agenda of the European Council for the first time in 1990, on the eve of the second World Climate Conference (Oberthür and Pallemaerts 2010), and when preparations for the 1992 Rio Summit were ongoing. In the same year, the Environment Council agreed to stabilize carbon emissions by 2000 (at 1990 levels), which became the voluntary goal for the EU under the United Nations Framework Convention on Climate Change (UNFCCC) in 1992 (Anderson 2009; Schunz 2014).

The first tangible policy measures taken at EU level were adopted in the 1990s. They followed the general pattern of other regulatory environmental policy instruments of the EU and were focused on harmonization. Indeed, through the introduction of technical standards for the energy efficiency of household appliances and lighting systems, accompanied by a labelling system to inform consumers, the European Commission primarily based its proposed policies on the regulatory policy instruments with which it was most familiar (see Chapter 6) (Jordan et al. 2012; Oberthür and Pallemaerts 2010). But the EU also deviated from its traditional regulatory policy instrument mix in two ways. On the one hand, in 1991 the Commission proposed to launch an EU-wide carbon tax (see Chapter 6). However, this proposal became obsolete as it was not adopted by the Council and the Parliament. On the other hand, a small number of voluntary agreements were concluded with car manufacturers, in which they pledged to reduce carbon emissions by 25 per cent in exchange for the Commission's intention to refrain from proposing binding legislation on that topic (European Commission 2014r; Krämer 2012a).

Before 2000 all those isolated measures could not be considered a comprehensive set of climate policies. The most important development in those early days was that climate change was finally introduced onto the EU's political agenda, largely as a result of the developments at the global level and in the scientific world. But the EU's initial internal measures were modest, partly as a result of divisions between member states (Jordan et al. 2012) and they did not match the dimensions and ambition of its external climate policy at that time (Schunz 2014).

A new stimulus for climate policy development was given by the signing of the Kyoto Protocol in 1997. The Kyoto Protocol stipulated quantitative emission reduction targets for industrialized countries (so-called 'Annex I countries') and it established a number of market-based mechanisms that these countries could use to achieve their target. As far as the quantitative emission reduction targets were concerned, the EU accepted in Kyoto a common greenhouse gas reduction target of 8 per cent by 2012 (compared to 1990 levels). In contrast to the United States, for instance, the EU opted to fulfil its Kyoto commitments by substantive internal achievements. This led to two major developments in the EU: the EU's first internal burden-sharing agreement and the launch of the European Climate Change Programme in 2000.

First, in the 1998 burden-sharing agreement (Council of the European Union 1998), the commitments of the fifteen member states were laid down in order to collectively achieve the 8 per cent target. National commitments varied from a 28 per cent reduction (Luxembourg) to a permitted increase in emissions of 27 per cent (Portugal). In the calculation of these national commitments, emission trajectories and national capabilities were taken into account (Schunz 2014), which would not be the case when a new agreement (then called 'effort-sharing') was negotiated later on in 2009 (see below).

Second, the European Climate Change Programme was a package of policy proposals, which ultimately led to the adoption of the Energy Performance of Buildings Directive (2002/91), the Biofuel Directive (2003/30), the Combined Heat and Power Directive (2004/8), the Energy Service Directive (2006/32), the F-gases Regulation (842/2006) and the Mobile Air Conditioning Directive (2006/40).

The other major element of the Kyoto Protocol, the establishment of market-based mechanisms, had an important impact on the development of the EU's climate policies. The European Commission started to push for the development of market-based instruments to drive the EU's climate policy (Jordan et al. 2012). One of these so-called flexible mechanisms that can be used for implementation of the Kyoto Protocol is emissions trading. The other two are the Clean Development Mechanism (CDM) and Joint Implementation (JI), which are used to exchange emission allowances between the parties to the Kyoto Protocol, respectively between industrialized and developing countries in the case of the

CDM, and among industrialized countries in the case of JI. The EU jumped on the bandwagon of the market-based instruments, and the adoption of the ETS Directive (2003/87) in 2003 was the direct result (see below). It is remarkable that emission trading became the cornerstone of the EU's climate policies, as the EU was actually opposed to the use of market mechanisms in the global regime in the run-up to Kyoto. These market-based instruments mainly reflected the US approach (Damro and Luaces Méndez 2003). This position changed in a fundamental way when the Kyoto Protocol had to be implemented. This policy change, induced by political developments at the international level, provides a good example of how the external context influences internal EU policies.

The entry into force of the Kyoto Protocol in 2005 and the leadership that the EU showed in that process (see Chapter 10) intensified the political momentum for climate change policies in the EU. After 2005, the gap between the EU's external leadership and internal climate policy progressively narrowed (Oberthür and Pallemaerts 2010). Moreover, in this period climate change basically became the EU's number one environmental priority, externally as well as internally. The dominant weight of climate change in EU environment policy was especially manifested with the creation of DG Climate Action and the Commissioner for Climate Action in 2009, when the Barroso II Commission took office (see Chapter 3). More recently, critical observers have been warning that the attention given to climate change is disproportionate in relation to other environmental policy issues and that the EU's climate change policy, to a large extent because of its strong institutional anchorage, is overpowering all other EU environmental policies.

In short, throughout the years climate change evolved in the EU from a rather marginal topic of research policy to a mature environmental issue and later on to the highest priority of the EU's environmental agenda. As the next section will show, the EU has succeeded in building a strong legal framework for the reduction of greenhouse gas emissions from various sources in Europe, combined with a leadership position on the global stage (see Chapter 10). However, it is also becoming increasingly difficult for the EU to make progress in climate policy-making in recent years (see Chapter 1). The enlargement waves with Central and Eastern European countries, with their more difficult economic situation and worse environmental performance, have resulted in more concessions being needed to strike climate deals. The economic crisis that has hit Europe since the end of the 2000s, combined with austerity policies and recurring calls for less regulation, has inhibited its ability to formulate ambitious climate goals. Likewise, since 2009 cracks have appeared in the EU's international leadership position and its relative bargaining power in the global climate change negotiations is decreasing.

Main elements of the EU's climate policy

The EU has developed a wide range of policies resulting in a complex climate policy landscape. The substantive elements of that landscape are discussed in this section. We first examine the Emission Trading System, which is the cornerstone instrument of the EU's climate policy. We then look at the EU's climate targets for 2020 and the various elements of the legislative package that was drafted to achieve those targets. We subsequently turn to the long-term objectives for 2050 and relate those to the challenge of integrating climate policy concerns into policy fields beyond the environment. Finally, we cast a glance at the EU's plans for 2030, the most recent piece of the political puzzle, and at other ongoing developments that are important for an understanding of where the EU is going with its climate policy.

EU Emission Trading System (ETS)

Development of a European emissions trading system
Based on the flexible mechanism approach of the Kyoto Protocol, the ETS was created in 2003 and has been in force since 2005. It is a cap-and-trade system for greenhouse gas emissions, combining the adoption of a quantitative limit on emissions ('cap') and the set-up of a market where emission allowances can be bought and sold ('trade'). An allowance is a permit granting the right to emit a specific volume of greenhouse gases. Such an emission trading system, for which the global regulatory framework was created by the Kyoto Protocol, implies the creation of a market for emission allowances. Each emitter included in the system needs to hold an allowance for each unit of CO_2 it emits. The economic mechanisms of the market should then play their role so that efficient emitters are rewarded and can sell their surplus of allowances, while large emitters are sanctioned by needing to buy additional allowances on the market.

The ETS applies to over 11,000 installations across the EU – including power stations and emission-intensive combustion plants and factories – and covers about 45 per cent of all EU greenhouse gas emissions. As explained above, the fact that the European Commission, despite its initial scepticism in the 1990s, has embraced emissions trading as the cornerstone instrument of the EU's internal climate policy, shows the strong influence of the external context. Besides being the largest emissions trading system in operation in the world, the EU ETS is now also the most elaborated market-based instrument of the EU's environment policy (see Chapter 6).

So far, the ETS has been developed in three phases: 2005–2007, 2008–2012 and 2013–2020. While the second and third phases coincide with the two commitment periods of the Kyoto Protocol, the first was seen as a pilot phase or 'trial run' (Anderson 2009). In that pilot phase (and also to an overwhelming degree in phase two) emission allowances were given away for free, distributed by the member states through National Allocation Plans (Wettestad 2014). Such a decentralized approach, in which member states retain great flexibility in the execution of EU legislation, is often used when the Commission needs to find ways to strengthen EU level policies without taking too much control away from the member states. A number of changes were introduced for the second trading period (European Commission 2014s). The use of certain CDM and JI credits on the ETS market was allowed, which was intended as a first step towards developing a more global market. Nitrous oxide (laughing gas) emissions were included in the system and the overall cap of allowances was reduced by approximately 6.5 per cent. Simultaneously, a number of member states (Austria, the Czech Republic, Germany, Lithuania, the Netherlands and the UK) started to organize auctions for the distribution of emission allowances, instead of giving all of them away for free.

Problems and reform
Since the inception of the ETS, its functioning has been fraught with problems. The oversupply of emission allowances in the market has been by far the biggest challenge. As a result of overly generous allocations by member states and of initial guesswork (as reliable estimates of emissions were lacking), the availability of allowances has exceeded the demands (Anderson 2009; European Commission 2014s; Wettestad 2014). That has dramatically brought down the price of a tonne of CO_2, as a result of which the incentives for companies to invest in climate-friendly measures have been minimized. Problems were aggravated by the outbreak of the financial-economic crisis, which caused emissions to drop as a result of lower economic activity (for instance, steel production dropped by 25 per cent in

2009), and thus put further stress on the demand for emission allowances (Wettestad 2014).

Another issue that has plagued the ETS is the increasingly touted concern of Europe's energy-intensive industries (for example paper, cement, chemicals, steel) that the system would harm their international competitiveness. The departure of those industries from Europe to countries with less strict climate policies would be a blow to the EU's economy. Also, it would not solve climate change, as it would lead to merely relocating the source of those industrial emissions elsewhere (so-called carbon leakage).

In 2008, four main improvements were made to the ETS in preparation for the 2013–2020 trading period. They were part of the so-called 2020 climate and energy package (see below). First, the individual caps set by member states were replaced by a single EU-wide cap, administered by the Commission. The overall EU cap shrinks each year by 1.74 per cent (Wettestad 2014). Second, auctioning (at EU level) became the default method for allocating allowances to the industry for the majority of emissions (Oberthür and Pallemaerts 2010). Third, those allowances that are still given for free are allocated on the basis of an assessment of the risk on carbon leakage. In practice, this means that the free allowances for the 2013–2020 period are mainly being given to those energy-intensive industries whose departure from the EU would cause significant carbon leakage. This has been seen as an effective strategy to keep the energy-intensive industries on board and to ensure their permanence in Europe (Eliassen et al. 2010). A fourth change brought additional gases and new sectors (such as the petrochemicals and aluminium sectors) into the ETS. From 2012 onwards, emissions from aviation are also included in the ETS (see Box 9.1).

Between 2011 and 2015, the Commission launched three initiatives for structural reform of the ETS, primarily to address the ongoing problem of an allowance surplus on the market. First, the use of credits that companies could buy from certain CDM projects in non-Annex I countries and include in the ETS is now banned (European Commission 2011h). The rationale behind this decision was to address environmental concerns (Wettestad 2014), but it also fits in a strategy to lower the substantial quantity of CDM allowances overflowing the market (because of significant offsetting by, for instance, the iron and steel sectors). Second, an amendment to the EU ETS Auctioning Regulation (176/2014) was agreed early 2014.

It allows the Commission to postpone the auctioning of 900 million allowances, originally expected to be released between 2014 and 2016, to 2019–2020 (European Commission 2014t). This decision, referred to as 'backloading', is intended to be a temporary measure to ease the surplus problem at the start of the third trading period. Third, as a more structural and long-term solution for the allowance surplus, a market stability reserve (MSR) will be created from 2019 onwards. Such a reserve allows for withdrawing a certain number of allowances from the market and to place them in the reserve if the total number of allowances on the market surpasses a particular threshold. By doing so, the MSR is meant to restore the carbon price and thus improve the market functioning of the ETS (Council of the European Union 2015a; European Commission 2014t).

The ETS and the EU's climate diplomacy

Despite widespread criticism of the functioning of the ETS, the system has been promoted by the Commission as its cornerstone instrument of climate policy (Delbeke 2006), and is often presented as one of its main successes. One of the main reasons is that, after the ETS's creation, similar emission trading systems have been initiated elsewhere. Indeed, emissions trading has become a popular instrument for tackling climate change through a market-based approach and has been applied in, for instance, Australia and Switzerland (European Commission 2014u). Moreover, around the world, several subnational and local emission schemes have been set up, such as those in Canada, Japan and the United States (Biedenkopf 2012; Chaloux and Paquin 2012; Niederhafner 2013). The system has also been tested through pilot projects in five cities and two provinces of China, and will be rolled out on a national scale starting in 2016.

Each of those foreign emissions trading systems is to some degree inspired by the EU ETS, and in some cases EU officials have actively contributed to their development. That is an element of the EU's 'climate diplomacy', which relies to a large extent on the diffusion of the EU's policies beyond its borders (Börzel and Risse 2012; Lavenex and Schimmelfennig 2009a). The most significant target audience for the EU's climate diplomacy are the emerging political powers in Asia (Bruyninckx et al. 2013). In the case of China, no actor engages as prominently with the emerging giant on emissions trading as the EU (and its member states) (Biedenkopf and Torney 2014). The EU considers climate diplomacy, often founded on bilateral dialogues and capacity-building, not as an alternative but as an

---

Box 9.1   External consequences of including international aviation in the EU ETS

In contrast to the EU's bilateral diplomacy focused on exporting the emissions trading system to third countries, the ETS has also been detrimental for the EU's climate diplomacy, particularly when the aviation sector was included in the system in 2012 (Biedenkopf and Torney 2014). The issue of greenhouse gases from aviation – which contributes an increasing share to worldwide emissions, already amounting to 2 per cent – is not regulated in the Kyoto Protocol. The Kyoto Protocol provides that this emission problem is to be addressed in a global deal to be negotiated in the International Civil Aviation Organization (ICAO). Despite the EU being at the forefront of pushing for such a deal, the negotiations in ICAO are still deadlocked.

The EU reacted to this deadlock at the global level by including aviation in its own ETS at the EU level. Indeed, the Aviation Directive (2008/101) provides that all flights arriving at and departing from EU airports, including those operated by non-EU airlines, must fall under the ETS from 2012. This unilateral move exacerbated the opposition of the non-EU ICAO members and isolated the EU within the ICAO (Lindenthal 2014). The EU was alone in arguing that the EU ETS should

---

addition to the UN-led process of strengthening the global climate regime. As this bilateral cooperation is based on the achievements and instruments of the EU's internal policy, it underscores once again how that policy is intricately linked to the global leadership role that the EU aspires to play. In general, the EU's climate diplomacy aims to promote domestic policy change outside of Europe, and to increase other countries' willingness to commit to emission reduction targets in a global deal (Torney 2014a). In the specific case of the ETS, continued diffusion of this instrument is intended to lead to a gradual development of a global network of carbon markets (Biedenkopf and Torney 2014; European Commission 2014u).

2020 package

In March 2007, the European Council agreed to three goals known as the 20-20-20 targets. They entail a total reduction of greenhouse gas emissions by 20 per cent (from 1990 levels), a 20 per cent share

be a model for a global mechanism and it maintained that it had international law on its side (European Commission 2014t; Scott and Rajamani 2013). The other major powers, in contrast, denounced such unilateral acts as a violation of their sovereignty and an unlawful exercise of EU authority outside its borders.

As a reaction, China cancelled Airbus aircraft orders as a retaliatory measure. The resulting internal pressure from EU member states with Airbus industries (France, Germany, Spain and the UK) made the EU stance crumble. The EU then decided to 'freeze' the implementation of the Directive on the inclusion of international aviation in the EU ETS until the end of 2016, leaving only flights within the European Economic Area countries (that are the EU member states plus Norway, Iceland and Liechtenstein) in the system. The deal was settled only after an agreement within ICAO that the latter would develop a global agreement by the same deadline, to come into force after 2020 (Lindenthal 2014). The EU thus swallowed a diplomatic loss – having to suspend the implementation of agreed legislation after opposition from major trade partners – in exchange for a promise that an ICAO deal would be struck 23 years after the intention to do so was written into the Kyoto Protocol.

of renewable energy in the EU's energy consumption and a 20 per cent improvement in energy efficiency, all to be reached by 2020 (European Council 2007). To reach those targets, the so-called climate and energy package, consisting of four (and in practice six, as will be explained below), pieces of legislation, was agreed in December 2008.

The swift adoption of such quite ambitious targets and of a comprehensive legislative package shortly afterwards was the result of a combination of four factors. First, the general political context in Europe was favourable to stringent climate measures, as a result of a receptive public opinion (illustrated, for example, by the success of the 2006 documentary 'An Inconvenient Truth'), high oil prices and concerns about energy security following tensions between Russia and Ukraine (Eliassen et al. 2010). Second, the EU was resolved to show leadership on climate change, in the run-up to the Copenhagen climate change conference (see Chapter 10). It is no surprise that the 20-20-20 goals are designed to be easily communicated to a wide international audience. Leadership ambitions also explain the EU's promise to move to a 30 per cent reduction target if a future global agreement were to include comparable targets for other industrialized countries. Third, the momentum on climate change meant that the European Commission was determined to substantially strengthen the EU's internal climate policy. The Commission therefore prepared a comprehensive package in which everything was linked and that covered the totality of the EU's emissions (Oberthür and Pallemaerts 2010). A fourth and final factor explaining the relatively smooth adoption of the ambitious package was that the financial-economic crisis had not yet affected the EU (Eliassen et al. 2010). It was only after 2008 that the crisis would become a heavy burden on EU politics and policy.

These factors provided a fertile environment in which the actors in the legislative process could progress with remarkable speed (Anderson 2009). The German Presidency of the first half of 2007 (still responsible, at that time, for presiding the European Council as well), which was largely dedicated to environmental issues, secured a political agreement on the 20-20-20 targets in the March 2007 European Council (Anderson 2009; Eliassen et al. 2010). One and a half years later, the French Presidency also played a leading role in the negotiations on the climate and energy package. Supported by the Commission, it presented the legislative proposals as a take-it-or-leave-it package to the Council, ultimately leading to a unanimous political decision on the entire package by the European Council in December 2008 (Bocquillon and Dobbels 2014), which was quickly followed by final adoption by the European Parliament. Behind the scenes, the Commission eased the economic concerns of member states by calculating that costs would not be excessive and that they would be fairly distributed (Eliassen et al. 2010). And, most importantly, DG Environment ensured that the new policies were framed not only in a climate change narrative, but also in an energy security narrative. That was needed to guarantee the support of the new Central and Eastern European member states, which were burdened down by their dependency on foreign imports (Eliassen et al. 2010).

The first substantive element of the package was the Directive on the reform of the EU ETS (2009/29), which consisted of four improvements in preparation for its third trading period after 2012 (see above). As a result, the ETS became a much more harmonized system than before 2012. With an EU-wide cap based on auctioning, more power was given to the Commission, which now administers the entire system (Wettestad 2014). The changes also implied that national horse-trading over effort-sharing would cover an ever smaller share of the EU's emissions (Jordan et al. 2012). The centralized system that is now in place, without national controls over allocation, had been politically unachievable before, but member states realized that more harmonization was needed to overcome the ETS's structural problems (Anderson 2009).

The second element was the Effort Sharing Decision (406/2009) that imposes national emissions reduction targets for all member states. Those reductions relate to the sectors not covered by the ETS (transport, agriculture, buildings, etc.), that is, to a little more than half of the EU's greenhouse gas emissions. The individual targets for the member states range from -20 per cent (for Denmark, Ireland and Luxembourg) to +20 per cent (for Bulgaria), all compared to 2005 levels. The targets were set on the basis of the member states' GDP per capita. As a consequence, twelve of the thirteen newest member states are still allowed to increase their emissions. This calculation method, which differed from the one used for the 1998 burden-sharing agreement (see above), was specifically applied to accommodate the demand of those member states, which fought hard against ambitious individual targets and stressed the need for (literal) 'effort-sharing' (Eliassen et al. 2010; Oberthür and Pallemaerts 2010). For the EU as a whole, the effort-sharing Decision foresees a 10 per cent reduction of emissions in non-ETS sectors, whereas the ETS should lead to a 21 per cent reduction (compared to 2005 levels). Taken together, the two first elements of the package were needed to implement the target to reduce greenhouse gases by 20 per cent.

The third element of the package, the Renewable Energy Directive (2009/28), uses a similar differentiation to deliver the 20 per cent renewable energy target. This Directive assigns national targets for the share of renewable energy (from wind, wave, hydro, tidal, solar, geothermal and biomass sources) in the energy consumption of all member states. The individual targets, ranging from 10 per cent (for Malta) to 49 per cent (for Sweden), are calculated on the basis of each member state's starting point (its 2005 share of renewables) and its GDP (Lee 2014). Before this Directive entered into force, member states had indicative and fragmented targets for different forms of energy. The Renewable Energy Directive furthermore imposes for each member state a target of 10 per cent for the share of renewables in the energy used in the transport sector

(Oberthür and Pallemaerts 2010). That replaces an earlier, more specific target for biofuels, which had come under increased pressure because of mounting evidence on the environmental damage caused by biofuel production. In response to those criticisms, the Directive also specifies new sustainability criteria for biofuels (Kulovesi et al. 2011).

The fourth element was the Carbon Capture and Storage Directive (2009/31), which ensures that the technology to capture, store and transport carbon is used safely and responsibly and it regulates financial incentives for pilot activities. It was the first piece of legislation on this issue worldwide (Kulovesi et al. 2011; Oberthür and Pallemaerts 2010).

Besides these four elements, two other pieces of legislation were *de facto* added to the package when the European Parliament decided to vote on them on the same day as the other elements (Burns 2013; Oberthür and Pallemaerts 2010). The Commission had initially kept them outside of the package to shield them from the overarching impact assessment and to keep negotiations less complex (Eliassen et al. 2010). First, the revised Fuel Quality Directive (2009/30) amends some petrol and diesel specifications, requires fuel suppliers to reduce the greenhouse gas intensity of fuels used in road transport and establishes sustainability criteria for biofuels. Second, the Passenger Car Regulation (443/2009) imposes the first standard for greenhouse gas emissions from new passenger cars, at an average of 130 grams per kilometre by 2015 for the fleet of individual car manufacturers. This norm was later complemented by a 95 grams target (to be reached by 2021) by the much-debated revised Passenger Car Regulation (333/2014) (see Chapter 4).

Those six pieces of legislation correspond with two of the three 20-20-20 goals. The final target, improving energy efficiency by 20 per cent, was not directly addressed by legislation in the package, notwithstanding that the Passenger Car Regulation, as an unofficial part of the package, contributes strongly to the target of a 20 per cent increase in energy efficiency (Kulovesi et al. 2011). However, several other pieces of legislation can be seen as also contributing to that target. The existing legislation to promote energy end-use efficiency and the development of an energy services market (SAVE Directive 93/76) was replaced by the Energy Efficiency Directive (2012/27). It requires member states to adopt National Energy Efficiency Action Plans, in which they are to set indicative national energy efficiency targets for 2020, and it proposes measures to remove market barriers. Furthermore, several instruments related to the EU's product policy feature energy efficiency as an important criterion (see Chapter 7). For instance, the Ecodesign Directive (2009/125) and the Energy Labelling Directive (2010/30) regulate the performance and labelling of energy-using and energy-related products, with the aim of informing consumers and ultimately removing the most inefficient products from the market. In addition, specific legislation exists for the efficiency of specific products, such as light bulbs (Regulation 244/2009) or tyres (Regulation 1222/2009). The Energy Performance of Buildings Directive (2010/31) is of particular importance: it requires that after 2020 all new buildings in the EU shall be nearly zero-energy-consuming.

2050 Roadmap and climate policy integration

In the immediate run-up to the 2009 climate change conference in Copenhagen, and at a time when the main decision on the 2020 package had already been taken, the European Council decided, in October 2009, that the EU should aim for an 80 to 95 per cent reduction of greenhouse gases in 2050 (compared to 1990 levels). The heads of state and government thereby followed the recommendation of the Intergovernmental Panel on Climate Change (IPCC), which is the main scientific body of the UN working on climate change, on the action needed to achieve the so-called two degrees target. This target aims to keep global warming below two degrees Celsius higher than to pre-industrial levels. DG Climate Action, created at that time, drafted the Roadmap for Moving to a Competitive Low Carbon Economy in 2050 to demonstrate what the policy implications of such a target would be (European Commission 2011b) (see Chapter 6).

Using a backcasting methodology, the Roadmap departs from a situation where the EU's emissions would be 80 per cent lower in 2050 (thus focusing on the least ambitious end of the range envisaged). It then calculates how emissions should be reduced in the EU between 2012 and 2050 in order to arrive at that situation, taking into account the obstacles and opportunities of specific sectors (energy, transport, industry, households and services, agriculture and others). In such a scenario, the power sector should become completely decarbonized and should take action immediately, relying mostly on renewable energy sources but also taking into account carbon capture and storage technologies. The transport sector is initially allowed a certain grace period, taking into account the time needed to develop new vehicles, but should more than halve its emissions between 2025 and 2050. Industry, in contrast, follows a rather linear reduction path, in accordance with the shrinking cap of the ETS (see above).

Even if 80 to 95 per cent is only a political and not a legal objective, the significance of the 2050 perspective should not be underestimated. By attaching a long-term policy vision and guidelines to an existing legal framework, the Commission pioneered in visualizing the consequences of ambitious long-term climate action. Although the Commission stresses that the Roadmap's guidelines merely ensure that the most cost-effective paths are chosen for a low-carbon future, it actually demonstrates that the 2050 target cannot be reached by relying on existing instruments and technologies. Instead, new business models and practices will be required to achieve the fundamental transformation needed for an 80 per cent (and certainly 95 per cent) reduction of greenhouse gases.

The 2050 Roadmap also clearly shows that the EU's long-term target will not be achieved by the 'environmental' actors and policies alone. The outcome will largely be determined by the performance of other sectors, notably energy, transport and agriculture. This leads to a debate on 'climate policy integration', seen as a new or more specific form of environmental policy integration (see Chapter 7). Also known as 'climate mainstreaming' or 'climate proofing', this is a strategy whereby climate considerations are integrated in other policy areas in order to contribute to the EU's overall climate policy goals (Adelle and Russel 2013; Dupont and Oberthür 2012; Halpern et al. 2008; Hulme et al. 2009; Medarova-Bergstrom et al. 2011). The importance attached by the Commission to this strategy is illustrated by the fact that one of the three Directorates of DG Climate Action (Directorate C 'Mainstreaming Adaption & Low Carbon Technology') is dedicated in large part to integrating climate policy, adaptation criteria and low-carbon technologies into the objectives of the EU's various funds as well as into transport, industry and energy policies.

The earmarking of 20 per cent of the total 2014–2020 Multiannual Financial Framework for climate action implied a major step forward for climate policy integration (see Chapter 6). The success was attributed to Climate Action Commissioner Hedegaard's personal efforts, although she met fierce resistance from Energy Commissioner Oettinger (Schoenefeld 2014b). As a consequence of these efforts, climate action and low-carbon development are now accorded a high priority in important funding programmes within environmental and cohesion policy and in Horizon 2020, the EU's current framework programme for research and technological development. However, the content-related criteria for such 'climate-related spending' are very vague, and it is not guaranteed that all of it will contribute to the achievement of the EU's climate goals.

The processes and outcomes of climate policy integration in specific areas vary a great deal (Hulme et al. 2009; Medarova-Bergstrom et al. 2011). A crucial case is the energy policy field, into which climate concerns are insufficiently integrated (Dupont and Oberthür 2012). Although progress has been made with respect to the promotion of renewable energy, continued investment in natural gas infrastructure and the lack of prioritization of climate policy objectives in several energy subsectors mean that the EU's energy policy is not on a path towards decarbonization but risks a carbon lock-in. Early analyses suggest that climate policy integration in EU policy-making is still too weak. At the same time, paradoxically, observers have already warned against excessive climate policy integration. According to these critics, the attention paid to climate policy integration, which quickly exceeded that for environmental policy integration, suggests that climate change is dangerously overshadowing other environmental issues (Adelle and Russel 2013; Schoenefeld 2014b).

2030 framework and ongoing debates

Towards the end of the Barroso II Commission, evidence emerged that the EU would be on track to reach the targets it set for 2020 and that it might even overachieve (see below). The 2020 climate and energy package certainly contributed to that achievement. In addition, the EU had even defined a long-term objective for 2050 and indicated the road towards that horizon. However, the EU was required to add mid-term milestones to its climate policy, with 2030 as the next symbolic year, for three main reasons. First, although the climate and energy package certainly suffices to reach the 2020 targets, the regulatory framework that it put in place is not strong enough to ensure the far-reaching changes needed. The Commission realized that it had made a commitment to a long-term goal that will be impossible to reach if sectors such as transport and energy continue on their current paths. Outgoing Climate Action Commissioner Hedegaard was therefore determined to leave a mark by enshrining a 2030 target that would push the EU further down the track towards the 2050 objective. Second, the Commission wanted to make a strong statement to investors, who are already making long-term decisions, that the EU remains committed to an ambitious climate action, as no target after 2020 was as yet legally binding. Third, a new internal target would send a message of ambition to the EU's international partners, in preparation for the 2015 climate change conference in Paris, which was the next crucial meeting in the development of a new global climate deal. In that sense, the 2030 framework thus mirrors the 2020 package, which came together in time for the 2009 Copenhagen conference, then deemed equally important. The timing of the 2020 package and the 2030 framework show that internal climate policy developments cannot be seen as being disconnected from political developments at the international level.

The final decision on the 2030 framework, taken by the European Council in October 2014, contains three new targets to replace the 20-20-20 targets, but now scheduled to be met in 2030 (European Council 2014) (see Table 9.1). First, greenhouse gas emissions should be reduced by at least 40 per cent in 2030 (compared to 1990 levels). That entails a firmer reduction path for the ETS sectors (see below) and also a new effort-sharing agreement among member states for the non-ETS sectors. It was also decided that the 40 per cent could be raised when the outcome of the global negotiations on the post-Kyoto climate regime was known.

Second, the share of renewable energy in energy consumption should be raised to at least 27 per cent. In contrast to the renewable energy target in the 2020 package, the new target in the 2030 framework is only binding at the EU level and it is not subdivided into national binding targets. According to the Commission, this gives more leverage to deploy EU-wide instruments, principally a more integrated energy policy, to reach the targets (European Commission 2014j). However, while it avoids thorny negotiations over the division of this target among the member states, the lack of national targets also takes away a major incentive to invest in renewable energy in domestic policies. The current situation is that

Table 9.1 *Comparison of the 2020 and the 2030 targets*

	2020 *climate and energy package*	2030 *climate and energy framework*
year of adoption	2008	2014
year of achieving the target	2020	2030
link with the international level	run-up to 2009 Copenhagen conference	run-up to 2015 Paris conference
target greenhouse gas reduction	20% (binding) (30% under conditions)	at least 40% (binding)
target renewables	20% (binding)	at least 27% (binding at EU level)
target energy efficiency	20% (indicative)	at least 27% (indicative)

the 20 per cent target for 2020 will be reached at EU level, but only because of the good performance of a handful of member states (see below).

Third, energy efficiency should increase by at least 27 per cent by 2030 (compared to projections of future energy consumption based on the current criteria). This target deviates from the original Commission proposal, which advanced a 30 per cent target (European Commission 2014j). The negotiations on the energy efficiency target in the 2030 framework were complex and fastidious. Besides discussion on the level of the target, there was also much debate over whether it should be binding or not. In the end, it was decided that this target should again be indicative only, as the UK among others had demanded.

Reaching an agreement on a framework with targets for 2030 was a difficult endeavour, particularly in a context when the financial-economic crisis and austerity policies had been gravely affecting the EU, the growing Euroscepticism made ambitious policy proposals harder to swallow and concerns grew about the competitiveness of European industries that had to deal with the world's most ambitious climate policies (see Chapter 1). As the EU is gradually reducing its emissions, and as the 2050 horizon is slowly coming closer, each additional step forward is becoming more difficult than the previous one. In addition, the adoption of the framework was overshadowed by the crisis in Ukraine and the ensuing tensions between the EU and Russia, which is still one of the EU's main energy suppliers. This crisis pulled the discussions in two opposite directions. Those who back a low-carbon agenda used it to sharpen public concern for energy dependence and urged that more attention be accorded to energy efficiency and EU-produced renewable energy. For the opponents of high climate ambitions, it fuelled arguments that Europe's energy security should be valued above any other agenda, even if it means continued or increased investments in fossil fuels in certain member states.

In these discussions, the member states from Central and Eastern Europe were said to have hampered progress. This should be understood in the light of their still weak overall economic performance, their energy-inefficient industries and their political sensitivities vis-à-vis energy dependence from Russia. Poland, which gets its electricity primarily from coal, was seen as taking the lead against an ambitious framework. In the end these member states were unable to block all aspects of the Commission's proposal, but they did succeed in cutting off the sharpest edges (see below). Furthermore, one of the indirect consequences of this debate, mainly due to Poland, was that the Juncker Commission started to consider the 'Energy Union' as one of its most important political priorities (Euractiv 2014).

In February 2015, the Commission issued its Energy Union Strategy (European Commission 2015c). It was also a test of the new political set-up of the Juncker Commission, as the Strategy was jointly steered by Commissioner Maroš Šefčovič, Vice-President for the Energy Union, and Commissioner Miguel Arias Cañete for Energy and Climate Action (see Chapter 3). The Strategy's main aim is to reduce the energy dependence of the EU by strengthening its single voice in dealings with energy trading partners, by connecting national energy networks and by diversifying energy sources including through renewable energy. The Energy Union is a mix of new ambitions and 'repackaged' existing policies. While former Polish Prime Minister Donald Tusk (who pushed for an Energy Union before he became the European Council President) had initially hoped for a joint EU mechanism for negotiations with external energy suppliers, the Energy Union Strategy is limited to the commitment for increased transparency of agreements for the purchase of gas, albeit respecting the confidentiality of commercially sensitive information. The Strategy was accompanied by a Communication on interconnectors, which aims to advance the ambition to reinforce gas and electricity links between national energy markets (European Commission 2015d), and by a Communication that outlined the EU's ambitions for the climate conference in Paris at the end of 2015 (European Commission 2015e) (see Chapter 10). Doing so, the inherent climate dimension of the Energy Union was emphasized.

Although at the time of writing the governance and political steering of the 2030 framework have still to be elaborated, it is already clear that it will be characterized by two opposing trends. On the one hand, it will shift the level of responsibility somewhat more to the EU level, particularly by making the renewable energy target binding at the aggregate (European) level only and thus requiring the Commission to increasingly invest in developing policy measures to achieve it. On the other hand, the member states will gain more freedom in the implementation of the package. While no additional planning or reporting requirements were specified, the member states are now only responsible for achieving the national reduction target in the non-ETS sectors and are not bound at the national level by any other target.

Amidst the ongoing debates, it is important to underline that climate action continues to be the object of new legislation. The EU is indeed continuing to construct a regulatory framework for climate change. Climate change policies are thereby an exception compared to other environmental domains where proposals on new legislation have become rare since the late 2010s (see Chapter 1). One example is the new Passenger Car Regulation (333/2014), mentioned above (see also Chapter 4). Adopted despite institutional deadlock and objections from the German automotive industry, it imposes more stringent emission standards for passenger cars by 2021. A second example concerns fluorinated gases (so-called 'F-gases'). This particular and very powerful type of greenhouse gases, which can be found for instance in air conditioning and refrigeration, has been the object of a regulation and a directive since 2006 (see above). A new F-gases Regulation adopted in 2014 (517/2014) repeals the previous legislation and is aimed at cutting the emissions of these gases by two-thirds between 2014 and 2030. It does so by capping and reducing the total amount of F-gases that can be sold in Europe, by banning their use in new equipment whenever alternatives are available, and by preventing the emissions from existing or discarded equipment (European Commission 2014v). Third, new rules on the monitoring, reporting and verification of emissions from maritime transport were adopted. They should constitute a first step in reducing the emissions from the shipping sector, which accounts for about 3 per cent of the world's total and is until now practically free from any regulatory limitation (European Commission 2015f). These three examples show that tabling and adopting new legislation for climate change remained possible even in the more difficult political context that has prevented any other new environmental legislation in recent years.

Achievements and effectiveness

To what extent have EU climate policies been effective in combatting climate change? Effectiveness is often overlooked in analyses of the EU's climate policy, partly because specific results on the ground are extremely hard to assess when it comes to climate change, certainly in the short term. Nevertheless, in an area that is deemed so crucial to the EU's environmental policies, it is essential to look at the policy achievements as well. This section looks at the effectiveness of the EU's climate policy at different time horizons, insofar as data have already become available.

At the time of writing, preliminary data are available on countries' compliance with their targets for the first commitment period of the Kyoto Protocol (2008–2012). The EU had committed to a common reduction by 8 per cent (compared to 1990 levels) in the Kyoto Protocol, while all EU member states had individual targets based on the burden-sharing agreement of 1998 (see above). The preliminary data, which are subject to minor changes as purchases of emission credits could still be finalized and need to be assessed, indicate that the EU has overachieved on this target (Jordan et al. 2012). Moreover, all member states except Italy are set to meet their individual targets (European Environment Agency 2014a). This is to a large extent related to the popular use of the Kyoto Protocol's flexible mechanisms, which involve these targets being reached thanks to investments in other countries (through Joint Implementation and the Clean Development Mechanism) (Anderson 2009). Looking beyond the overall rather modest Kyoto targets, sound predictions can already be made about the achievement of the EU's 20-20-20 targets for 2020. A report prepared by the European Environment

Agency (2014b) demonstrates that the EU as a whole is on track to meet all three targets.

The fact that the EU is on track to achieve its self-imposed 2020 targets can be explained by three main factors. The first factor relates to the flexible nature of the implementation of the targets. Indeed, the three targets can only be regarded as having been achieved when they are realized at the overall EU level. Although two of the three targets (on emissions and on renewables) were translated into binding national targets, only nine member states are currently on track towards meeting all three targets, while at least eleven member states are having difficulties in meeting more than one of them (European Environment Agency 2014b). The Czech Republic, Greece and the UK belong to the first group, whereas Belgium, France and Germany are part of the second group. That means that each target will actually be reached only thanks to the overachievement of specific member states that compensates for the underachievement of the others. This experience with the 2020 targets also explains the political appeal of making the renewable energy target of the 2030 framework binding only at EU level (see above). The unfortunate paradox is, of course, that although some of the most cost-effective climate gains could still be made in the underperforming member states, their incentives to invest in climate measures are now reduced.

A second factor that explains why the 2020 targets may be relatively easily achieved is the financial-economic crisis that has hit Europe since 2008 (Jordan et al. 2012). The crisis, and the higher energy prices that initially accompanied it, have lowered the demand for energy in the EU in the short run, thus also bringing down energy-related greenhouse gas emissions. However, in the long run the economic crisis will probably have a doubly negative effect on the EU's climate performance. On the one hand, it has contributed to the surplus of allowances in the ETS, leading to the plummeting of the price of an allowance (see above). On the other hand, the crisis has markedly stalled the investments in renewable energy technologies in several member states (European Environment Agency 2014b).

As a third and final driver, there can be no doubt that the policies at EU and member state level have produced significant results in terms of promoting renewable energy technologies, implementing energy efficiency measures and achieving real emission reductions in specific economic sectors. These reductions of greenhouse gas emissions are shown in Figure 9.1. The European Commission also likes to underline that these reductions have been accompanied by a growing GDP (by 45 per cent between 1990 and 2012), and that the EU has thus achieved the decoupling of greenhouse gas emissions from its economic welfare (European Commission 2014w).

However, the current numbers do not only convey good news. The EEA has explained that, although the 2020 targets will be met (possibly even by some margin), more and stronger policy efforts are needed in order to accomplish the necessary steps to reach the more ambitious 2030 targets and the 2050 objectives. Indeed Figure 9.1 shows that the EU will only be able to achieve a 32 per cent reduction of greenhouse emissions by 2030 rather than the self-imposed 40 per cent. Stricter reduction measures are especially needed in the underperforming sectors of agriculture and transport, as well as in the energy sector, which needs to become almost entirely decarbonized by 2050. Moreover, even if the targets will now only be

FIGURE 9.1   *Greenhouse gas emissions in the EU*

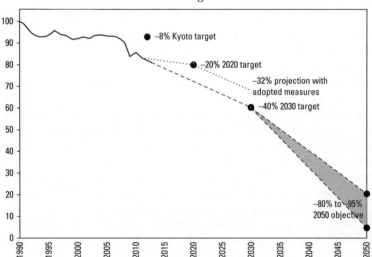

[full line: historic emissions; dotted line: projections taking into account adopted measures; dashed line: linear path to 2030 target and 2050 objective]

Source: based on European Environment Agency 2015: 94

binding at EU level, the most ambitious ones will not be met if the currently underachieving member states do not take additional measures (European Environment Agency 2014b).

Conclusions

This chapter has shown that the fight against climate change has evolved from a marginal issue to an overarching political priority for the EU. Concrete policy measures, in the form of climate legislation, have been adopted and long-term targets have been established. It is clear that the policies adopted initially, which consisted of efficiency measures and incremental steps aimed at picking the 'low-hanging fruit' (the easiest and least costly efficiency measures), will not suffice. On the contrary, the solution requires a major overhaul of some of the basic premises of the EU's policies in sectors such as energy, transport, agriculture and industry. Although the EU is far from an agreement on such implications, it has at least taken a bold and innovative step by visualizing them in the 2050 Roadmap, which follows from an agreement at the highest political level that an at least 80 per cent reduction of greenhouse gas emissions should be achieved by the middle of this century. Yet environmental policies alone cannot address the complexity of the climate change problem. The diffuse sources and uncertain impact of climate change make it a much harder problem to solve than most of the other environmental issues that the EU started tackling in the 1970s (see Chapter 7). The most difficult challenge with respect to climate change is that its solution ultimately requires fundamental changes of current production and consumption patterns, and therefore of investment choices, business models, consumer practices and even social norms.

The case of climate change also shows that the EU's internal and external environmental policies are deeply interwoven. Crucially, the climate negotiations at the global level have had a major impact on internal policy developments at the EU level. The establishment of the ETS is probably the example most illustrative of this development, but the EU also made progress in adopting more ambitious climate policies and targets in the run-up to the international climate change conferences that are considered crucial in the development of the global climate regime. That can largely be explained by the EU's desire to 'lead by example' at those global meetings (see Chapter 10). Before the mid-1990s, a large gap existed between the

EU's external leadership ambitions and its lack of an internal policy framework (Oberthür and Pallemaerts 2010). That changed during the 2000s, when the EU complemented its efforts to make the Kyoto Protocol enter into force and to implement it by developing a comprehensive EU climate policy. Now, having made significant achievements internally, the EU is faced with two other challenges. First, a lack of progress at the global level removes a major external incentive to move forward in Europe (Wettestad 2014). Second, the EU in the future needs increasingly to persuade its international partners to make similar choices in their domestic climate policies (for instance, by exporting its policy instruments). The EU's role in such international negotiations is the topic of the following chapter.

Chapter 10

The EU in International Environmental Politics

The EU is a major actor in international environmental politics. This chapter therefore focuses on the external dimension of EU environmental policy. Being a party to about fifty multilateral environmental agreements (MEAs) (European Commission 2015g), the EU plays a key role in international negotiations on a broad range of environmental issues such as air, climate change, biodiversity and biosafety, chemicals, soil, water, sustainable development, forests or oceans (for an overview of the literature on the EU in international environmental politics, see Groen and Oberthür 2012). Some of the MEAs to which the EU is a party are global in nature (negotiated under the auspices of the UN), while others are regional (mostly under the auspices of the United Nations Economic Commission for Europe, UNECE). Table 10.1 lists a selection of major MEAs to which the EU is a party.

The interaction between the EU and international environmental politics has a twofold dynamic, which shows that European and international environmental policies and politics are interwoven. On the one hand, as the EU is one of the main players at the negotiation table, it is able to co-shape the outcomes of international environmental negotiations – and thus the scope and the direction of global environmental governance. The extent to which the EU is able to be a policy-shaper at the international level varies from being an 'influential' actor (Rhinard and Kaeding 2006: 1024) in some negotiations and regimes (such as the Cartagena Protocol negotiations on biosafety, see Chapter 8) to being an actor which 'failed' to show global leadership (Bäckstrand and Elgström 2013: 1378) in other negotiations (with the 2009 Copenhagen climate change conference as the most notable example). On the other hand, developments at the international level have an impact on the EU and the environmental policies it adopts internally. Many internal

Table 10.1   *Major multilateral environmental agreements to which the EU is a party*

MEA	year of signature	issue
Barcelona Convention for the protection of the Mediterranean Sea against pollution	1976	oceans
Convention on Long-range Transboundary Air Pollution	1979	air
Bonn Convention on the Conservation of Migratory Species	1979	biodiversity
Vienna Convention on the Protection of the Ozone Layer	1985	air
Montreal Protocol on the Protection of the Ozone Layer	1987	air
Basel Convention on Hazardous Waste	1989	waste
Espoo Convention on Environmental Impact Assessment	1991	governance
UN Framework Convention on Climate Change	1992	climate change
Convention on Biological Diversity	1992	biodiversity
OSPAR Convention for the Protection of the marine environment of the North-East Atlantic	1992	oceans
UN Convention to Combat Desertification	1994	soil
Kyoto Protocol	1997	climate change
Aarhus Convention on public participation in environmental decision-making	1998	governance
Rotterdam PIC Convention	1998	chemicals
Cartagena Protocol on Biosafety	2000	biotechnology
Stockholm POPs Convention	2001	chemicals
Nagoya Protocol on Access and Benefit Sharing	2011	biodiversity
Minamata Convention on Mercury	2013	chemicals

environmental policies of the EU have indeed found their origins in the regulatory framework of MEAs. For instance, as explained in Chapter 9, the EU Emission Trading Scheme fits within the flexible mechanisms that were created by the Kyoto Protocol.

This chapter first opens the black box of the EU as international environmental negotiator. Focusing on how the EU functions internally when it acts externally, the first section discusses the legal framework of the EU's external environmental competences and its formal status in international environmental politics, the way the EU is externally represented (who speaks for the EU?) and the way internal coordination takes place (how is an EU position developed?). The second section then examines the EU's role in international environmental politics by focusing on its leadership ambitions, the extent to which these are achieved and the effectiveness of the EU as a global actor in the field of the environment. Particular attention is paid to the role of the EU in multilateral climate change negotiations, which have been the most politicized international environmental negotiations.

External representation and internal coordination

Status and external environmental competences

The main instruments of international environmental politics – MEAs that are generally negotiated under the auspices of international organizations – are still state-based. Since the EU is not a state, it was initially not self-evident that it could fully participate in these instruments. Particularly in the 1970s and 1980s, it has not been an easy task to be fully accepted by other countries as a negotiator of equal value. The reasons why the EEC or the EC were not immediately recognized as an authoritative actor around the international negotiation table were related to the complex and continuously evolving division of competences between the European and national levels, the lack of precedents for an actor without the formal status of a state fully participating in international negotiations and becoming a party to international agreements, and the (feeling of) uncertainty this generated for the external partners (Sbragia 1998). However, this struggle was won in the late 1980s and early 1990s. As a result, the EU is today fully recognized as an actor in international environmental politics by its international partners, as well as by the press and non-state actors. This holds true both for environmental agreements and for environmental negotiations.

First, the EU – and the (E)EC before the entry into force of the Lisbon Treaty in 2009 – possesses international legal personality, which enables it legally to become a party to environmental *agreements*. The EU then assumes the legal status of a so-called Regional Economic Integration Organization (REIO), which was a formula invented to enable the European Community to become a party to the LRTAP Convention in 1979 (Kuijper et al. 2013: 202). Second, the EU's legal status in international environmental *negotiations* is somewhat more complicated. In practice, the EU is considered a 'normal' negotiation partner during international environmental negotiation processes, as it is, for instance, fully allowed to speak or to table proposals. Many environmental negotiations take place in a UN context, where the EU is formally an observer, not a full member. Legally speaking, the main difference between an observer and a full member is that an observer has no voting rights. In practice, however, this lack of voting rights is not that important, since international environmental politics is characterized by a consensus logic and voting is very unusual. Moreover, the greater part of today's international environmental negotiations is conducted in Conferences or Meetings of the Parties (COPs or MOPs) to existing MEAs. COPs and MOPs are annual or bi-annual gatherings of the parties to an existing environmental agreement, organized for follow-up discussions. In many international environmental regimes, the COPs and MOPs are the main decision-making bodies. For instance, the global climate change negotiations are currently being conducted in the framework of the COPs to the United Nations Framework Convention on Climate Change (UNFCCC). Likewise, global negotiations on biodiversity take place in COPs of the Convention on Biological Diversity (CBD). As the EU is usually a formal party to the MEAs under the umbrella of which such COPs and MOPs are organized, it enjoys the same rights and status as the other parties. This means that in almost all day-to-day international environmental negotiations, the EU *de facto* acts as fully-fledged negotiation partner.

To be an actor in international environmental politics, the EU also needs external competences in the environmental field. As discussed in Chapter 1, the EU does indeed have competences on environmental issues. In the context of the EU's external environmental relations it is important to note that environmental competences are shared competences. This means that both the EU and the member states can adopt environmental legislation, but that the member states can only do so 'to the extent that the Union has not exercised its competence' (Art. 2§2 TFEU). Let us first examine where the EU's competences on external environmental affairs come from, followed by a discussion of the consequences of their shared nature.

The EU's external environmental competences can have two sources: either they are mentioned explicitly in the Treaty, or they are established through the case law of the Court of Justice of the EU (see Chapter 3). The first type are called 'express powers', the second 'implied powers' (Eeckhout 2011: 120–64). First, the Treaty of Rome (1957) contained only two policy fields with express external competences for the then EEC: trade policy and the conclusion of association agreements with third states. The Single European Act (SEA, 1986–1987) added express powers in the field of external environmental policy by the then Article 130r SEA, which is currently Article 191 TFEU (see Chapter 1). The Treaty of Lisbon (2009) reinforced this express power by adding a fourth objective for EU environmental policy, which explicitly deals with the external dimension of environmental policy, to Article 191§1 TFEU: 'promoting measures at international level to deal with regional or worldwide environmental problems, and in particular combating climate change' (see Box 1.2). The reference to climate change in this Treaty article is seen as a formalization of existing practices (de Jong and Schunz 2012), as a result of which it did not have an actual impact on the EU as an actor in international climate politics.

Second, and in parallel with the expansion of the EU's express powers, the EU's external environmental competences grew in a more indirect way, namely through the case law of the Court of Justice, leading to implied powers. During the 1970s, a series of Court cases broadened the scope of the EU's external (environmental) competences. Broadly speaking, these Court cases – of which the ERTA case (Case 22/70) is the most important one – created the doctrine of parallelism between internal and external EU competences (Kuijper et al. 2013: 1–21). This means that when the EU has internal competences on a particular issue, it is also allowed to conduct external relations in that domain and to become a party to international agreements covering these issues. Applied to the environmental field, it implies that the EU has *external* competence to conclude international agreements on those environmental issues that are already regulated by *internal* legislation.

No matter whether external environmental competences are express or implied powers, they are shared competences. Contrary to exclusive EU competences, where member states are no longer allowed to act (such as for instance in trade policy), shared competences still leave some room for political action to the member states. The Treaty also emphasizes the shared nature of *external* environmental competences in Article 191§4 TFEU, where it states that the EU and the member states can act internationally in their respective spheres of competence, as the EU's external environmental relations occur 'without prejudice to Member States' competence to negotiate in international bodies and to conclude international agreements' (see Box 1.2). The shared nature of external environmental competences largely affects – and complicates – the external representation of the EU in international environmental negotiations.

External representation

For the EU, MEAs are 'mixed agreements' because they touch upon shared environmental competences. Mixed agreements are international treaties to which both the EU and the member states are a party (Eeckhout 2011; Hillion and Koutrakos 2010; Wessel 2011). This implies that the EU and the member states formally participate alongside each other in international environmental negotiations. Apart from specifying that the member states and the EU should loyally cooperate, the EU Treaties do not specify how the entire EU – meaning the Union plus the member states – is to negotiate mixed agreements. It only deals with the external representation in the field of Union competences and it leaves out the member states' part of the shared competences. Legally speaking, when MEAs are negotiated, the EU representation follows a different logic for the EU part of the shared competences on the one hand and the member states' part on the other, leading to a system of 'dual representation': the European Commission represents the EU, and the rotating Presidency of the Council represents the member states.

On the one hand, Article 218§3 TFEU only provides for a procedure for the external representation of the EU part of the shared competences. It stipulates that the Commission submits a recommendation to the Council, which can then nominate a 'Union negotiator'. Under the Lisbon Treaty, this 'Union negotiator' must be the Commission, since Article 17§1 TEU stipulates that '[the Commission] shall ensure the Union's external representation'.

On the other hand, for the member state part of the shared competences, the member states usually opt to pool their voices and to delegate their negotiation authority to a common negotiator, in practice usually the member state holding the Presidency of the Environment Council. Whereas authorizing the Commission is a legal obligation, negotiating via the Presidency is a political choice, which is usually made by the member states to increase their bargaining power (Frieden 2004).

The shared nature of environmental competences does not in general prevent the EU from developing common positions in international environmental negotiations (Woolcock 2012). However, the lack of a clear stipulation in the Treaty on who represents the EU in cases of shared competences has repeatedly caused tensions between the Commission and the Council on the question of external representation. After the entry into force of the Lisbon Treaty these tensions were particularly evident. The Commission and the member states have each wanted to defend – and even to expand – their 'territory', a classic example of interinstitutional tensions based on bureaucratic rivalry (Dijkstra 2009). The Commission and the member states have in fact disagreed on the question whether the Lisbon Treaty changed the provisions on external representation in the environmental field or not. Having lost powers in the field of external relations (for instance to the European External Action Service or the EU Delegations which were established in the same period), the Commission sought to compensate for this by expanding its powers in external representation at the cost of the member states (Corthaut and Van Eeckhoutte 2012).

In the course of 2010, the Commission proposed a number of times that it should act as the sole negotiator in areas of shared competences, leaving no role anymore for the member states and/or the Presidency. The Commission used the argumentation that one of the political rationales behind the Lisbon Treaty was precisely to increase the coherence of the EU's external representation, that the Copenhagen climate conference of a few months before had proven that the old system did not work, and that the only way out was a kind of 'WTO formula' with the Commission being the sole negotiator. The member states, for their part, protected their pre-Lisbon territory and defended the status quo, arguing that the Lisbon Treaty did not change the external representation question in the environmental area (on the different interpretations of the effect of the Lisbon Treaty on the EU's external representation in environmental affairs, see e.g. Buck 2012 versus Thomson 2012). These interinstitutional tensions impeded the EU as international environmental negotiator during the months after the entry into force of the Lisbon Treaty, for instance during the first negotiation session on the Minamata Convention on mercury. However, this situation has been gradually resolved by adopting practical arrangements that *de facto* allowed the negotiators to do their job (Council of the European Union 2011; Delreux 2012a).

A negotiation arrangement based on dual representation is only applicable when the EU participates in international negotiations that are meant to result in legally binding treaties (such as MEAs). However, as will be discussed below, even in such treaty negotiations, the political practice often deviates from the formal provisions. Moreover, the dual representation dynamic does not characterize the EU's external representation in the majority of environmental negotiations which do not produce legally binding MEAs, but declarations, decisions or resolutions. The latter are only politically binding but not legally enforceable on the parties. This holds true for most COP and MOP decisions, as well as for results of high-level summits on sustainable development, such as Rio (1992), Johannesburg (2002) or Rio+20 (2012) (on the role of the EU at these summits, see Jupille and Caporaso 1998; Lightfoot and Burchell 2005; Lightfoot 2012). In such negotiations, the European Treaties do not foresee a formal procedure for appointing an EU negotiator. Consequently, Article 218 TFEU is not applicable, the dual representation arrangement does not necessarily hold and the formal negotiating role for the Commission is generally limited. The EU negotiation arrangements are then usually led by the rotating Presidency.

Another example is the series of international climate change negotiations which have taken place since the end of the 2000s in the run-up to the Paris climate change conference of 2015. These have been conducted without a formal mandate for the Commission and they are thus not covered by the Article 218 TFEU procedure. This might come as a surprise since the aim of the negotiations was to reach a legally binding climate treaty and since the EU clearly has competences on climate policy. It can be explained by the fact that the Commission 'believes it could win a legal dispute over competence on climate change in the European Court of Justice, but politically does not dare to pick such a fight' (van Schaik 2012: 11). The Commission indeed seems to be satisfied with the (influential) role it is *de facto* able to play in the climate negotiations even in the absence of a formal mandate. As a matter of fact, the European Commission is increasingly playing a bigger role on the international stage at the expense of the Presidency. This suggests that the balance may tip to the advantage of the Commission in the future at the expense of the Presidency (and thus the Council). That the Commission is taking a stronger stance is not a consequence of formal competence questions or of the entry into force of the Lisbon Treaty, but rather of the personality and the negotiation skills of the Climate Action Commissioner in the Barroso II Commission, 'the charismatic former Danish Minister Connie Hedegaard' (de Jong and Schunz 2012: 184) and of the institutionalization of the DG Climate Action since 2010 (see Chapter 3).

Although 'dual representation' (for negotiations leading to an MEA) or a looser Presidency-led formula is the representation arrangement to be expected from a formal perspective, these arrangements are not always used in practice. They are usually applied for making formal statements or for intervening in plenary negotiation settings, where webcasting and translation emphasize the official nature of the interventions. However, in the more technical preparatory negotiation settings, where the actual negotiation work takes place and the texts are drafted, a more informal external representation format is used. To understand the external representation of the EU in international environmental negotiations, 'a reference to legal competence is useful yet often insufficient for understanding practices that may diverge significantly from what formal rules would lead us to expect' (Jørgensen et al. 2011: 601). Because of the vagueness of the Treaty provisions, the complex distribution of competences and the need to settle interinstitutional tensions in a pragmatic way, the EU negotiation arrangement in MEA negotiations is often an *ad hoc* one, which is considered the most useful and feasible in a particular international negotiation session. The way the negotiation arrangement is precisely fleshed out depends on practicability and pragmatic considerations and the exact organization of the EU representation varies from negotiation session to negotiation session (Delreux 2011).

The most noticeable manifestation of the pragmatic interpretation of the EU negotiation arrangements is the deployment of the personal capabilities, expertise and know-how of the various actors in the EU, no matter what their institutional or national affiliation is (member state or Commission). This is chiefly evident in the phenomenon of so-called lead countries (or 'lead negotiators' in climate change negotiations). Here, member state and Commission representatives are able to 'take the lead' in the EU's external environmental policy-making, irrespective of their formal role in the decision-making process. Not only is the external representation of the EU in contact groups at the international level (and thus not at ministerial level or when cameras zoom in on negotiation sessions) subject to an informal division of labour between member states and the Commission, but also the preparation of EU positions is often driven by such an informal dynamic. In climate change negotiations, for instance, various so-called issue leads and issue coordinators from different member states and the Commission hold the pen when drafting EU positions. This informal system takes place under the formal authority of the Presidency, which still bears the final responsibility. The actors taking the lead are informally assigned a particular task because of specific skills or expertise they possess or because they want to be closely involved in the negotiations. In the context of climate change negotiations, this system has quickly become an uncontested informally institutionalized practice for the preparation and conduct of international environmental negotiations. This system of informally dividing the negotiation tasks has four benefits for the EU (Delreux and Van den Brande 2013). First, it allows the Presidency to share the burden of the negotiation task, since international environmental negotiations are often too complex and too dense to be appropriately handled only by the Presidency. Second, by applying the lead country system, the available expertise, know-how and experiences of twenty-nine actors (member states plus Commission) are pooled and utilized. Third, member states get the opportunity to be fully involved in the negotiations. Finally, this system guarantees continuity, since neither the preparation of EU positions nor the representation of the EU change every six months when another member state takes the Presidency seat.

Internal coordination

The position defended by the EU in international environmental negotiations is developed through internal coordination processes between the member states and the European Commission that take place at various levels. First of all, before the European negotiators leave Brussels for the international environmental conference, the internal coordination process is principally conducted in the Environment Council (see Chapter 3). This is also the case for climate negotiations. The fact that climate decision-making takes place in the environmental configuration of the Council is historically grown, but it is noteworthy since climate change is gradually becoming a foreign policy issue with a potential impact on security, energy dependence and development questions. This contrasts, for instance, with the situation in the United States, where the climate negotiations are conducted by the State Department. Only at the beginning of 2015 did climate diplomacy appear for the first time on the agenda of the Foreign Affairs Council. The Ministers of Foreign Affairs adopted a Climate Diplomacy Action Plan, prepared by the Commission and the EEAS and aiming to employ the diplomatic networks of the EU and the member states in the run-up to the Paris climate conference (Council of the European Union 2015b). This reflects the increasing awareness that a comprehensive environmental or climate diplomacy implies an integration of the environment into EU foreign policy as well as the mobilization of the entire range of European and national diplomatic resources.

The Council's centre of gravity for the EU's internal coordination is the Working Party on International Environmental Issues (WPIEI), composed of national experts from the member states (with Commission officials attending) (see Chapter 3). The WPIEI convenes in various configurations, such as the WPIEI Climate Change, the WPIEI Biodiversity or the WPIEI Global. For some international environmental negotiations, EU coordination is limited to the WPIEI, whereas for other negotiations the WPIEI only conducts the preparatory work for the Working Party on the Environment (WPE), COREPER I, and the ministerial meeting of the Environment Council. It is only the EU positions for the most politicized and salient negotiations, such as the annual climate change conferences, that take the form of Council Conclusions, adopted by the Environment Council, yet technically prepared by the WPIEI (and the WPE) and politically by COREPER I. The EU position for less salient negotiations is determined in EU position papers, agreed by the experts in the WPIEI and not discussed by the ministers. There is, however, an important exception: when the Commission is appointed as European negotiator in a case of negotiations leading to a legally binding agreement (under Article 218 TFEU, see above), the Commission also receives a mandate (formally 'negotiating directives') from the Council, which covers the main positions to be defended internationally.

During the course of an international negotiation session, internal coordination also takes place '*sur place*' in a WPIEI setting (Delreux 2011). In general, these meetings are organized every morning before the international negotiations start, but when negotiations evolve and become increasingly intense, they are also held in the evening or during lunchtime or whenever it is considered necessary. During the ministerial segments of international negotiations, coordination is also organized at the level of environment ministers, or even at the level of heads of state and government, in the few cases when leaders participate in these negotiations (such as the last day of the 2009 Copenhagen climate conference). These 'on the spot' coordination meetings provide the forum for determining and refining the EU positions, and for updating and adapting them according to the developments at the international level.

EU coordination meetings also have a disadvantage: they are very time-consuming. The time spent in internal coordination meetings – the so-called EU bunker (Afionis 2011: 346) – cannot be used for informal contacts with the negotiation partners, for instance to make the necessary package deals 'in the corridors'. Indeed, this EU 'navel-gazing' is therefore often said to undermine its external effectiveness and performance. In international climate change negotiations, the lack of outreach to third parties and of the construction of strategic alliances with them is often seen as a major factor that explains the decreasing leadership of the EU (Bäckstrand and Elgström 2013). This not only seems to be the case in international climate – and more broadly environmental – negotiations, but it is equally applicable to EU external relations in other policy domains (Degrand-Guillaud 2009; Elgström 2007).

In EU decision-making processes with regard to international environmental negotiations, some member states mostly remain inactive. They do not – or only very seldom – take the floor in WPIEI or coordination meetings and seem to acquiesce in the outcome of these meetings. Hence, EU decision-making is *de facto* driven by a limited number of member states, which have the capabilities and the necessary expertise to contribute, and – even more importantly – which are interested in or have an interest in these negotiations (Delreux 2011). Although the interested and closely involved member states vary according to the issue area at stake, member states such as Germany, Denmark, the Netherlands, Sweden or the UK are typically the ones that are frequently members of the group that drives the decision-making at the EU level, together with the Commission and the member state holding the rotating Presidency.

After a deal on an MEA has been reached at the international level, the agreement still has to be ratified (or 'concluded' in EU jargon) by the EU before its rights and duties become legally binding on the EU. Importantly, this ratification requirement only holds for legally binding agreements and, as a consequence, not for COP or MOP decisions. In the EU, international treaties are ratified by the Council and the European Parliament. Since ratification is characterized by a 'take it or leave it' logic, the Council and the Parliament cannot amend the MEA. This means that after an international negotiation session, the negotiated MEA needs to be accepted by the Council and the Parliament in order to become fully accepted by the EU. The ratification decision of the EU is often treated in a political package with the legislation that is needed to implement the MEA in EU law. Additionally, because MEAs are mixed agreements to which the EU and the member states are parties, the member states also need to ratify the agreement at their domestic level (generally with parliamentary approval).

The EU as leader in international environmental politics?

Tools and driving forces of environmental leadership

The EU is usually an advocate of strong environmentally friendly measures at the international level and it occupies a position in global environmental politics that is much more in favour of strong international environmental regulation than other countries (nowadays mainly the United States and the emerging powers). Therefore, the EU is often referred to as a leader in international environmental politics (Sbragia and Damro 1999; Zito 2005; Oberthür 2009; Kelemen 2010), particularly in international climate negotiations (Oberthür and Roche Kelly 2008; Schreurs and Tiberghien 2007; Wurzel and Connelly 2011). The fact that the EU aims to disseminate key environmental norms, such as sustainable development or the precautionary principle, also contributes to its leadership image (Bretherton and Vogler 2008; Vogler and Stephan 2007).

The EU's environmental leadership only began at the end of the 1980s. In the years before, the EU's role in international environmental politics was limited or rather the EU was behaving as a laggard, for instance in the negotiations on the Montreal Protocol on ozone layer protection (Vogler 2011). In the 1960s and 1970s, it was mainly the United States that was the leader in international environmental politics, but the United States and the EU have 'traded places' since the mid-1980s (Kelemen and Vogel 2010) (see Chapter 2). The EU's leadership in environmental affairs does not imply, however, that the EU defends the most ambitious and far-going position in every single environmental negotiation. For instance, the EU had a rather medium or even moderate-conservative position in the international negotiations that resulted in the Cartagena Protocol on Biosafety, the UNECE Protocol on Strategic Environmental Assessment or the Nagoya Protocol on Access and Benefit Sharing on genetic resources (see respectively Delreux 2012b; Delreux 2009; Oberthür and Rabitz 2014).

The EU's leadership in international environmental politics can be explained by three underlying dynamics. First, being a 'multi-lateral microcosm of the international system itself' (Oberthür and Roche Kelly 2008: 43), the EU has always been a frontrunner and advocate of multilateral cooperation and of a global order based on international rules. This not only holds true in the environmental domain, but it is a general characteristic of the EU's external relations where 'effective multilateralism' is a guiding principle (Drieskens and van Schaik 2014). The EU's adherence to multilateralism, on environmental policy but also beyond, is increasingly in contradiction with the sovereignty approaches of a number of emerging powers such as China.

Second, leading on international environmental affairs also contributes to the EU's aim of profiling itself as a civilian or 'soft' power (as opposed to a military power) (Scheipers and Sicurelli 2007). International environmental leadership plays an important role in shaping the EU's international identity and it enables the EU to distinguish itself from the United States and the emerging powers (Keukeleire and Delreux 2014).

Third, environmental leadership also serves the material interests of the EU. The EU's leading position at the international environmental scene may indeed also be prompted by the wish of (producers in) the member states to maintain a competitive position at the global market. The combination of an existing high level of environmental protection in the EU and the fact that European companies are subject to strong international competition in a globalized economy implies that it is in the EU's competitive interest that strong environmental standards also apply in third countries.

Therefore, the EU aims to create a level playing field by trying to export its own (relatively stringent) environmental legislation to the international level so that not only European producers, but also their global competitors, all need to meet similar standards (Kelemen 2010; Kelemen and Vogel 2010).

Besides its leadership role at the multilateral level, the EU is also promoting environmental norms outside its territory and jurisdiction in three other ways (Keukeleire and Delreux 2014). First, the EU has contributed to the dissemination of environmental policies and practices through its enlargement policy. Since the transposition of existing European legislation into the national legislation of candidate countries is a key condition for joining the EU, the EU has been able to spread its environmental standards to other European countries. This has been important in the accession waves in the past, such as the one of 2004–2007 to Central and Eastern Europe (see Braun 2014), and is still important in the current enlargement policies of the EU, particularly towards the Western Balkan countries.

Second, various bilateral (trade or association) agreements between the EU and third countries include environmental clauses, which generally consist of environmental standards that third countries need to meet in order to receive benefits from the EU (such as more favourable access to the EU market or financial aid and assistance). Likewise, third countries from the EU's broader neighbourhood often ratify MEAs to signal to the EU their compliance with environmental standards in the hope of becoming eligible for European rewards (Schulze and Tosun 2013). In the framework of the European Neighbourhood Policy (ENP), for instance, the EU has concluded 'Action Plans' with its Eastern and Southern neighbours in which technical assistance and funding on environmental matters are provided for. The 'more for more' rationale behind the ENP implies that the more a neighbouring country progresses in internal reforms according to what the EU wants (for instance in the areas of climate, water or hazardous chemicals policy), the more market access and financial assistance it will receive from the EU. These bilateral agreements are thus based upon the conditionality principle. However, the results are mixed and effectiveness of the conditionality depends on a range of domestic political and economic factors in the neighbouring countries (Keukeleire and Delreux 2014).

Third, EU environmental norms can also indirectly inspire third countries, which then base their newly developed environmental policies on the principles and norms employed by the EU. This type of 'external governance', defined as 'the expansion of EU rules beyond its borders' (Lavenex and Schimmelfennig 2009b: 807), is often overlooked as an instrument of the EU's external environmental policy, but it has nonetheless been an effective one towards the EU's neighbourhood (see Knill and Tosun 2009). EU environmental norms now 'diffuse' (Börzel and Risse 2012) even further as they have had an impact on recent developments in, for instance, China. The newly developed Chinese climate policies, for instance on emissions trading, were primarily the result of shifts in the political choices of domestic policy-makers, but in the formulation of their new policies they 'drew in part on ideas and policies from the EU' (Torney 2015: 114) (see Chapter 9).

Achievements and effectiveness of environmental leadership

It is clear that the EU has the ambition to be a leading actor in global environmental politics. But to what extent is the EU able to achieve its leadership ambitions and to be an effective and influential international environmental actor? The EU's track record in terms of effectiveness varies. Whereas the EU has succeeded in being a significant actor, for example in the negotiations on the Cartagena Protocol on biosafety (see Chapter 8) or on trade in hazardous chemicals, it has largely failed to leave its mark on the multilateral negotiations in the fields of forestry or sustainable development.

The picture is more positive for the EU when considering its effectiveness only in negotiations that have resulted in legally binding MEAs. When international environmental negotiations actually lead to an MEA, the international outcome is in general a quite good reflection of the EU's preferences (Delreux 2014). When negotiations fail to produce an MEA or when negotiations produce non-legally binding outcomes, the extent to which the EU achieves its pre-determined goals is usually much lower. Examples of negotiations that did not produce a MEA include the Copenhagen climate change conference or the negotiations on a global forestry treaty (Savaresi 2012). The Rio+20 Summit on sustainable development (see Chapter 2) is an example of a negotiation leading to a non-legally binding text, which was a disenchantment for the EU.

A number of factors related to the EU's status, competences, external representation and internal coordination (see above) ca explain why it is often difficult for the EU to influence the (outcome of the) negotiations. The shared nature of the external environmental competences means that member states still have some leeway or that they can sideline the EU in their bilateral contacts. Moreover, in an EU with twenty-eight member states, which have different economic systems, national sensitivities and potentially diverging interests, it is almost unavoidable that there will be different positions or that the EU will need a lot of internal coordination efforts to get the member states aligned. Although these difficulties certainly exist, it is rather remarkable that the EU is mostly able to overcome them and to develop a position that goes beyond the lowest common denominator.

However, the EU position has a tendency to suffer from two kinds of shortcomings that may undermine the EU's effectiveness. First, whereas the EU usually has detailed position papers on the various technical issues discussed in the negotiations, it often lacks the capacity to prioritize or to determine fallback positions in the endgame of the negotiations. One of the main reasons why the EU has a tendency to lose grip on the last stages of the negotiations when the real political deals are made is precisely a lack of strategic thinking about the final compromise and an inability to respond quickly and flexibly to last-minute proposals by its negotiation partners. Second, the EU positions are usually very much focused on its own objectives and tend to insufficiently take into account – and anticipate – the objectives of the negotiation partners (Woolcock 2012).

The cohesiveness of the EU's position often depends on the existence of internal legislation on the questions that are discussed at the international level. In many cases, the environmental topics on the agenda of the international negotiations are already regulated by EU policies, making it relatively easy for the EU to adopt a common position. Indeed, 'common internal policies tend to unify member state interests, so that all member states can be expected to support the internationalization of the internal level' (Oberthür 2011: 673). The existing legislation, which already implies a compromise between the member states, then serves as the basis of the EU position. It is often defined as the 'red lines', which may not be crossed by provisions in the MEA. This is because an MEA with provisions that conflict with existing EU legislation would imply a renegotiation of this legislation. In such a case, a delicate internal compromise would be put at risk and Pandora's Box would probably be reopened (Delreux 2014).

In global environmental negotiations, which usually take place under the auspices of existing UN Conventions, presenting a single common position is generally the most effective negotiation strategy of the EU. However, this does not necessarily mean that such a position has to be defended by a single spokesperson. The most effective negotiation arrangement is then to have multiple EU negotiators (Commission, Presidency, lead negotiators, etc.) who all take the floor on behalf of the EU and who defend the same European position. Former Climate Action Commissioner Hedegaard referred to such a strategy as follows: 'A lot of Europeans in the room is not a problem, but there is only an advantage if we sing from the same hymn sheet. We need to think about this and reflect on this very seriously, or we will lose our leadership role in the world' (in her hearing as candidate commissioner before the European Parliament in January 2010). By contrast, in regional environmental negotiations, where the EU negotiates with a limited number of (neighbouring) countries, such as in the UNECE, negotiating in a united way and presenting a common position may even be counterproductive for the EU. It may annoy the relatively few negotiation partners around the table, who may feel they have no say. In this sense, more EU unity 'can also invoke a negative reaction from negotiating partners. The EU acting as a bloc may cause irritation' (van Schaik 2013: 192).

Although there are indeed a number of internal complexities that can undermine the EU's effectiveness in international negotiations, the EU also faces structural dynamics over which it has no or less control. These dynamics are mostly related to the fact that the EU is usually the most demanding actor in such negotiations. In an international negotiation context characterized by a consensus requirement, conservative actors are more likely to be more effective than reformist actors for the simple reason that negotiators with a position close to the status quo have the veto power to block outcomes that are more ambitious. As a result, lowest common denominator outcomes are thus the most likely result of international environmental negotiations and such outcomes do not reflect the EU's leadership ambitions. This dynamic explains why the EU has been able to be an effective negotiator in the negotiations on the Cartagena Protocol on biosafety and on the Nagoya Protocol on access and benefit sharing (Delreux 2012b; Oberthür and Rabitz 2014). Here, the EU had a moderate position and was not the most demanding actor.

Another structural factor impeding the EU is its reduced leverage in international negotiations. In its attempt to 'lead by example', the EU has often already adopted the environmental measures internally that it is promoting at the international level. Apart from financial means, the EU often has little to offer to its negotiation partners as it has already unilaterally adopted the commitments it asks from third countries, which diminishes the EU's leverage and negotiation power (Woolcock 2012).

The EU's leadership in climate change politics

It is in the field of international climate change politics that the EU's leadership ambitions have chiefly been analysed. The EU has been a rather influential and effective climate negotiator in the second half of the 1990s and most of the 2000s, but the highly politicized Copenhagen climate change conference of 2009 constituted a major setback for the EU (Oberthür 2011). The EU is also seen by third countries as a leader in international climate change politics, with the exception of the Copenhagen conference and the EU's failed attempt to include international aviation in its Emissions Trading Scheme (see Box 9.1) (Torney 2014b).

In the 1990s, European leadership in climate change politics was shown through the EU's support for the Kyoto Protocol (Damro and Méndez 2003; Groenleer and van Schaik 2007). The Kyoto Protocol has even been said to represent a 'high point for EU global leadership' (Bäckstrand and Elgström 2013: 1376). The EU was particularly an advocate for a Protocol with strong emission reduction targets, but it was initially not in favour of the Kyoto market mechanisms such as emissions trading, which principally reflected the US approach, but which ironically later became the cornerstone of the EU's climate policies (see Chapter 9). The EU's diplomatic efforts to achieve the necessary threshold to get the Kyoto Protocol ratified and thus entering into force demonstrated its leadership role. This was primarily important after the United States withdrew from the Kyoto process. In this respect, the deal the EU reached with Russia on Russian ratification of the Kyoto Protocol in exchange for EU support for Russia's WTO membership bid is one of the EU's biggest diplomatic successes in this area (Bretherton and Vogler 2006; Parker and Karlsson 2010). Likewise, the EU campaigned for strong implementation rules for the Kyoto Protocol, notably in the so-called Marrakesh Accords of 2001.

The EU also tried to take on a leadership role in the second half of the 2000s on the post-2012 climate regime (that is, the negotiations on a global climate change regime to succeed the Kyoto Protocol regime, of which the first commitment period ended in 2012). The EU was the first major actor to propose strong internal targets with the 2020 climate and energy package (or the '20-20-20 objectives'), thereby aiming to lead by example (see Chapter 9) (Kulosevi 2012; Oberthür and Dupont 2011; Parker and Karlsson 2010). In another attempt at leadership, the EU pushed for the inclusion of the two degrees target (that is, limiting global warming to a maximum of two degrees Celsius above pre-industrial levels) as the basis of the post-2012 regime. This can be seen as one of the small number of EU achievements in recent climate talks.

The outcome of the 2009 Copenhagen conference was a clear indication that the EU's climate leadership in the current international power constellation has declined. The EU was excluded from the final talks between the emerging economies and the United States where the Copenhagen Accord was drafted and the content of that Copenhagen Accord was very disappointing for the EU (for a range of quotes from European politicians illustrating that disillusion, see van Schaik 2013: 140–141). Although the EU can be criticized for internal failures, such as the multiplicity of actors representing the EU in the endgame of the negotiations or the internal division on the question of whether the EU should move its position to a higher emission reduction target in order to give an impetus to the negotiations, it was primarily the external negotiation context that was unfavourable to the EU. It is indeed much more the changing external opportunity structure within which the EU has to act than its own internal organization that explains the EU's decreasing effectiveness and leadership in recent climate change negotiations (Bäckstrand and Elgström 2013; Groen et al. 2012; Groen and Niemann 2013; Oberthür 2011; van Schaik 2013).

Compared to climate negotiations in the 1990s, the balance of power has in fact evolved considerably at the international level. Whereas climate change politics in the Kyoto period was largely a transatlantic game where China and India were only 'interested bystanders' (Vogler 2011: 34), the emergence of the BASIC countries (a group of four emerging economies: Brazil, South Africa, India and China) as major actors in the negotiations has decreased the relative power of the EU since the 2000s. This trend was further reinforced by the economic stagnation as a result of the financial-economic crisis that has hit the European economy since the end of the 2000s (see Chapter 1). The relative share of these emerging countries in global greenhouse gas emissions is also growing sharply, which negatively affects the EU's weight in the negotiations too. Paradoxically, the EU's own internal climate policies have reduced its relative contribution to global greenhouse gas emissions from 19 per cent in 1990 to 11 per cent in 2012, but by having this effect they have also weakened the EU's relative power at the international level (Olivier et al. 2013). Moreover, it is a general rule of thumb in international negotiations characterized by a consensus requirement that the conservative players, such as the United States or the BASIC countries, are likely to have more bargaining power than the reformist players, such as the EU (Meunier 2005; Rhinard and Kaeding 2006). Consequently, the former can prevent the latter from achieving ambitious outcomes. In Copenhagen, the EU did not sufficiently take into account that the major players had rather conservative positions (van Schaik and Schunz 2012) and it went to this climate change conference with 'unrealistic expectations [and] a miscalculation of the geopolitical context' (Bäckstrand and Elgström 2013: 1382).

Since the end of the 2000s, all three pillars of the EU's external climate policies have come under pressure: multilateralism (other countries increasingly prefer informal gatherings such as the G20 or the Major Economies Forum [MEF] of the seventeen largest emitters for discussion of climate change to the more inclusive UN framework, see Happaerts 2015); a preference for legally binding instruments (others tend to be in favour of soft law outcomes, such as a pledge and review system) and environmental integrity (scientific reports by the Intergovernmental Panel on Climate Change show that the current measures are not sufficient to effectively tackle global warming). In terms of external climate policy effectiveness, the EU suffers from a mismatch between its ambitions and its ability to deliver. The EU has failed to export its own solutions to the multilateral level, proving that its 'leading by example' strategy simply did not work. The EU is still more able to influence the agenda of the climate change regime (such as the two degrees target) than the outcome.

Whereas the climate change conference of Copenhagen was a clear failure for EU leadership, the climate change conferences taking place in the years after Copenhagen – i.e. those in Cancun (2010), Durban (2011), Doha (2012), Warsaw (2013) and Lima

(2014) – indicate that the EU may have turned the corner and that it may have found a new role for itself in multilateral climate change negotiations. That new role now consists of a combination of defending ambitious – yet more concrete and pragmatic – preferences and attempting to play the role of bridge builder, coalition maker or mediator at the international level while trying to shift the balance as much as possible in the direction of its own preferences (Groen et al. 2012; Pavese and Torney 2012). The EU has, for instance, tried to build up alliances with the least developed countries and the Alliance of Small Island States (AOSIS), which resulted in the establishment of the so-called Cartagena Dialogue (van Schaik 2012). Its role in the post-Copenhagen climate change conferences is therefore described as that of a 'leadiator', a combination of a 'leader' and a 'mediator' (Bäckstrand and Elgström 2013). Particularly in Durban in 2011, the EU played a crucial role in gathering developed and developing countries together to commit themselves to reach an encompassing global deal to cut greenhouse gas emissions beyond 2020 (the so-called Durban Platform) by 2015.

Conclusions

In recent decades, the EU has developed into a major actor in global environmental politics. It has adopted a broad scope of environmental legislation, which has enabled the EU to lead by example at the international level and to show the world that a high level of environmental protection is compatible with economic growth and welfare. These enlarged competences have also given the EU the necessary legal basis to become an active party to all major multilateral environmental agreements. Simultaneously, the successive enlargement waves have amplified the EU's bargaining power, since it now represents twenty-eight states, more than 500 million citizens and a vast economic market.

The EU has not only adopted internally the most ambitious multilateral regulatory framework on environmental issues in the world, it also aspires to internationalize and export that level of environmental protection to third countries. Whereas the EU has known some diplomatic successes in the past in important areas such as biodiversity protection or the (first steps in the) fight against climate change, its leadership is today increasingly under pressure. This is related to power shifts at the international level that are pushing non-European actors to the forefront and to the structure of the international negotiations that tends to prevent much progress, as well as to obstacles in the EU's internal policy-making process. The extent to which the EU will be able to overcome these challenges depends on its ability to act strategically on the international stage, to make sure that the various member states and European institutions promote a similar message, to avoid major inconsistencies between its environmental diplomacy and its external relations in other environment-related areas, and to adapt flexibly to a changing world order where the EU's place is rapidly evolving.

List of Legislation

Decisions

Decision 406/2009 – '*Effort Sharing Decision*' – 'Decision No 406/2009/
EC of the European Parliament and of the Council of 23 April 2009 on
the effort of Member States to reduce their greenhouse gas emissions to
meet the Community's greenhouse gas emission reduction commitments
up to 2020', Official Journal, L140, 05/06/2009, pp. 136–148.

Directives

Directive 75/440 – '*Surface Water for Drinking Directive*' – 'Council
Directive 75/440/EEC of 16 June 1975 concerning the quality required
of surface water intended for the abstraction of drinking water in the
Member States', Official Journal, L194, 25/07/1975, pp. 26–31.

Directive 75/442 – '*Waste Framework Directive*' – 'Council Directive
75/442/EEC of 15 July 1975 on waste', Official Journal, L194,
25/07/1975, pp. 39–41.

Directive 76/464 – '*Dangerous Substances Directive*' – 'Council Directive
76/464/EEC of 4 May 1976 on pollution caused by certain dangerous
substances discharged into the aquatic environment of the Community',
Official Journal, L129, 18/05/1976, pp. 23–29.

Directive 78/659 – '*Fish Water Directive*' – 'Council Directive 78/659/
EEC of 18 July 1978 on the quality of fresh waters needing protection
or improvement in order to support fish life', Official Journal, L222,
14/08/1978, pp. 1–10.

Directive 79/409 – '*Birds Directive*' – 'Council Directive 79/409/EEC of
2 April 1979 on the conservation of wild birds', Official Journal, L103,
25/04/1979, pp. 1–18.

Directive 82/501 – '*Seveso Directive*' – 'Council Directive 82/501/EEC of
24 June 1982 on the major-accident hazards of certain industrial activities', Official Journal, L230, 05/08/1982, pp. 1–18.

Directive 90/220 – '*Deliberate Release Directive*' – 'Council Directive
90/220/EEC of 23 April 1990 on the deliberate release into the environment of genetically modified organisms', Official Journal, L117,
08/05/1990, pp. 15–27.

Directive 92/43 – '*Habitats Directive*' – 'Council Directive 92/43/EEC of
21 May 1992 on the conservation of natural habitats and of wild fauna
and flora', Official Journal, L206, 22/07/1992, pp. 7–50.

Directive 93/76 – '*SAVE Directive*' – 'Council Directive 93/76/EEC of 13 September 1993 to limit carbon dioxide emissions by improving energy efficiency (SAVE)', Official Journal, L237, 22/09/1993, pp. 28–30.

Directive 96/62 – '*Air Quality Framework Directive*' – 'Council Directive 96/62/EC of 27 September 1996 on ambient air quality assessment and management', Official Journal, L296, 21/11/1996, pp. 55–63.

Directive 98/15 – '*Urban Wastewater Directive*' – 'Commission Directive 98/15/EC of 27 February 1998 amending Council Directive 91/271/EEC with respect to certain requirements established in Annex I thereof (Text with EEA relevance)', Official Journal, L67, 07/03/1998, pp. 29–30.

Directive 1999/30 – '*First Daughter Directive to the Air Quality Framework Directive*' – 'Council Directive 1999/30/EC of 22 April 1999 relating to limit values for sulphur dioxide, nitrogen dioxide and oxides of nitrogen, particulate matter and lead in ambient air', Official Journal, L163, 29/06/1999, pp. 41–60.

Directive 2000/53 – '*End of Life Vehicles Directive*' – 'Directive 2000/53/EC of the European Parliament and of the Council of 18 September 2000 on end-of life vehicles', Official Journal, L269, 21/10/2000, pp. 34–43.

Directive 2000/60 – '*Water Framework Directive*' – 'Directive 2000/60/EC of the European Parliament and of the Council of 23 October 2000 establishing a framework for Community action in the field of water policy', Official Journal, L327, 22/12/2000, pp. 1–73.

Directive 2000/69 – '*Second Daughter Directive to the Air Quality Framework Directive*' – 'Directive 2000/69/EC of the European Parliament and of the Council of 16 November 2000 relating to limit values for benzene and carbon monoxide in ambient air', Official Journal, L313, 13/12/2000, pp. 12–21.

Directive 2001/18 – '*Deliberate Release Directive*' – 'Directive 2001/18/EC of the European Parliament and of the Council of 12 March 2001 on the deliberate release into the environment of genetically modified organisms and repealing Council Directive 90/220/EEC', Official Journal, L106, 17/04/2001, pp. 1–39.

Directive 2001/42 – '*Strategic Environmental Assessment Directive*' – 'Directive 2001/42/EC of the European Parliament and of the Council of 27 June 2001 on the assessment of the effects of certain plans and programmes on the environment', Official Journal, L197, 21/07/2001, pp. 30–37.

Directive 2001/81 – '*National Emission Ceilings Directive*' – 'Directive 2001/81/EC of the European Parliament and of the Council of 23 October 2001 on national emission ceilings for certain atmospheric pollutants', Official Journal, L309, 27/11/2001, pp. 22–30.

Directive 2002/3 – '*Third Daughter Directive to the Air Quality Framework Directive*' – 'Directive 2002/3/EC of the European Parliament and of the Council of 12 February 2002 relating to ozone in ambient air', Official Journal, L67, 09/03/2002, pp. 14–30.

Directive 2002/49 – '*Environmental Noise Directive*' – 'Directive 2002/49/ EC of the European Parliament and of the Council of 25 June 2002 relating to the assessment and management of environmental noise', Official Journal, L189, 18/07/2002, pp. 12–25.

Directive 2002/91 – '*Energy Performance of Buildings Directive*' – 'Directive 2002/91/EC of the European Parliament and of the Council of 16 December 2002 on the energy performance of buildings', Official Journal, L1, 04/01/2003, pp. 65–71.

Directive 2003/30 – '*Biofuel Directive*' – 'Directive 2003/30/EC of the European Parliament and of the Council of 8 May 2003 on the promotion of the use of biofuels or other renewable fuels for transport', Official Journal, L123, 17/05/2003, pp. 42–46.

Directive 2003/87 – '*ETS Directive*' – 'Directive 2003/87/EC of the European Parliament and of the Council of 13 October 2003 establishing a scheme for greenhouse gas emission allowance trading within the Community and amending Council Directive 96/61/EC (Text with EEA relevance)', Official Journal, L275, 25/10/2003, pp. 32–46.

Directive 2003/96 – '*Energy Tax Directive*' – 'Council Directive 2003/96/ EC of 27 October 2003 restructuring the Community framework for the taxation of energy products and electricity (Text with EEA relevance)', Official Journal, L283, 31/10/2003, pp. 51–70.

Directive 2004/8 – '*Combined Heat and Power Directive*' – 'Directive 2004/8/EC of the European Parliament and of the Council of 11 February 2004 on the promotion of cogeneration based on a useful heat demand in the internal energy market and amending Directive 92/42/ EEC', Official Journal, L52, 21/02/2004, pp. 50–60.

Directive 2004/35 – '*Environmental Liability Directive*' – 'Directive 2004/35/CE of the European Parliament and of the Council of 21 April 2004 on environmental liability with regard to the prevention and remedying of environmental damage', Official Journal, L143, 30/04/2004, pp. 56–75.

Directive 2004/107 – '*Fourth Daughter Directive to the Air Quality Framework Directive*' – 'Directive 2004/107/EC of the European Parliament and of the Council of 15 December 2004 relating to arsenic, cadmium, mercury, nickel and polycyclic aromatic hydrocarbons in ambient air', Official Journal, L23, 26/01/2005, pp. 3–16.

Directive 2006/32 – '*Energy Service Directive*' – 'Directive 2006/32/EC of the European Parliament and of the Council of 5 April 2006 on energy end-use efficiency and energy services and repealing Council Directive 93/76/EEC (Text with EEA relevance)', Official Journal, L114, 27/04/2006, pp. 64–85.

Directive 2006/40 – '*Mobile Air Conditioning Directive*' – 'Directive 2006/40/EC of the European Parliament and of the Council of 17 May 2006 relating to emissions from air conditioning systems in motor vehicles and amending Council Directive 70/156/EEC (Text with EEA relevance)', Official Journal, L161, 14/06/2006, pp. 12–18.

Directive 2007/60 – '*Floods Directive*' – 'Directive 2007/60/EC of the European Parliament and of the Council of 23 October 2007 on the assessment and management of flood risks (Text with EEA relevance)', Official Journal, L288, 06/11/2007, pp. 27–34.

Directive 2008/50 – '*Ambient Air Quality Directive*' – 'Directive 2008/50/EC of the European Parliament and of the Council of 21 May 2008 on ambient air quality and cleaner air for Europe', Official Journal, L152, 11/06/2008, pp. 1–44.

Directive 2008/56 – '*Marine Water Strategy Framework Directive*' – 'Directive 2008/56/EC of the European Parliament and of the 'Council of 17 June 2008 establishing a framework for community action in the field of marine environmental policy (Marine Strategy Framework Directive) (Text with EEA relevance)', Official Journal, L164, 25/06/2008, pp. 19–40.

Directive 2008/98 – '*Waste Framework Directive*' – 'Directive 2008/98/EC of the European Parliament and of the Council of 19 November 2008 on waste and repealing certain Directives (Text with EEA relevance)', Official Journal, L312, 22/11/2008, pp. 3–30.

Directive 2008/101 – '*Aviation Directive*' – 'Directive 2008/101/EC of the European Parliament and of the Council of 19 November 2008 amending Directive 2003/87/EC so as to include aviation activities in the scheme for greenhouse gas emission allowance trading within the Community (Text with EEA relevance)', Official Journal, L8, 13/01/2009, pp. 3–21.

Directive 2009/28 – '*Renewable Energy Directive*' – 'Directive 2009/28/EC of the European Parliament and of the Council of 23 April 2009 on the promotion of the use of energy from renewable sources and amending and subsequently repealing Directives 2001/77/EC and 2003/30/EC (Text with EEA relevance)', Official Journal, L140, 05/06/2009, pp. 16–62.

Directive 2009/29 – '*ETS Directive*' – 'Directive 2009/29/EC of the European Parliament and of the Council of 23 April 2009 amending Directive 2003/87/EC so as to improve and extend the greenhouse gas emission allowance trading scheme of the Community (Text with EEA relevance)', Official Journal, L140, 05/06/2009, pp. 63–87.

Directive 2009/30 – '*Fuel Quality Directive*' – 'Directive 2009/30/EC of the European Parliament and of the Council of 23 April 2009 amending Directive 98/70/EC as regards the specification of petrol, diesel and gas-oil and introducing a mechanism to monitor and reduce greenhouse gas emissions and amending Council Directive 1999/32/EC as regards the specification of fuel used by inland waterway vessels and repealing Directive 93/12/EEC (Text with EEA relevance)', Official Journal, L140, 05/06/2009, pp. 88–113.

Directive 2009/31 – '*Carbon Capture and Storage Directive*' – 'Directive 2009/31/EC of the European Parliament and of the Council of 23 April 2009 on the geological storage of carbon dioxide and amending Council Directive 85/337/EEC, European Parliament and Council Directives 2000/60/EC, 2001/80/EC, 2004/35/EC, 2006/12/EC, 2008/1/EC and Regulation (EC) No 1013/2006 (Text with EEA relevance)', Official Journal, L140, 05/06/2009, pp. 114–135.

Directive 2009/125 – '*Ecodesign Directive*' – 'Directive 2009/125/EC of the European Parliament and of the Council of 21 October 2009 establishing a framework for the setting of ecodesign requirements for energy-related products (Text with EEA relevance)', Official Journal, L285, 31/10/2009, pp. 10–35.

Directive 2010/30 – '*Energy Labelling Directive*' – 'Directive 2010/30/ EU of the European Parliament and of the Council of 19 May 2010 on the indication by labelling and standard product information of the consumption of energy and other resources by energy-related products (Text with EEA relevance)', Official Journal, L153, 18/06/2010, pp. 1–12.

Directive 2010/31 – '*Energy Performance of Buildings Directive*' – 'Directive 2010/31/EU of the European Parliament and of the Council of 19 May 2010 on the energy performance of buildings', Official Journal, L153, 18/06/2010, pp. 13–35.

Directive 2010/75 – '*Industrial Emissions Directive*' – 'Directive 2010/75/ EU of the European Parliament and of the Council of 24 November 2010 on industrial emissions (integrated pollution prevention and control) (Text with EEA relevance)', Official Journal, L334, 17/12/2010, pp. 17–119.

Directive 2011/65 – '*RoHS Directive*' – 'Directive 2011/65/EU of the European Parliament and of the Council of 8 June 2011 on the restriction of the use of certain hazardous substances in electrical and electronic equipment (Text with EEA relevance)', Official Journal, L174, 01/07/2011, pp. 88–110.

Directive 2011/92 – '*Environmental Impact Assessment Directive*' – 'Directive 2011/92/EU of the European Parliament and of the Council of 13 December 2011 on the assessment of the effects of certain public and private projects on the environment (Text with EEA relevance)', Official Journal, L26, 28/01/2012, pp. 1–21.

Directive 2012/19 – '*WEEE Directive*' – 'Directive 2012/19/EU of the European Parliament and of the Council of 4 July 2012 on waste electrical and electronic equipment (WEEE) (Text with EEA relevance)', Official Journal, L197, 24/07/2012, pp. 38–71.

Directive 2012/27 – '*Energy Efficiency Directive*' – 'Directive 2012/27/EU of the European Parliament and of the Council of 25 October 2012 on energy efficiency, amending Directives 2009/125/EC and 2010/30/EU and repeating Directives 2004/8/EC and 2006/32/EC (Text with EEA relevance)', Official Journal, L315, 14/11/2012, pp. 1–56.

Directive 2014/52 – *'Environmental Impact Assessment Directive'* – 'Directive 2014/52/EU of the European Parliament and of the Council of 16 April 2014 amending Directive 2011/92/EU on the assessment of the effects of certain public and private projects on the environment (Text with EEA relevance)', Official Journal, L124, 25/04/2014, pp. 1–18.

Directive 2015/412 – *'Deliberate Release Directive'* – 'Directive (EU) 2015/412 of the European Parliament and of the Council of 11 March 2015 amending Directive 2001/18/EC as regards the possibility for the Member States to restrict or prohibit the cultivation of genetically modified organisms (GMOs) in their territory (Text with EEA relevance)', Official Journal, L68, 13/03/2015, pp. 1–8.

Regulations

Regulation 1829/2003 – *'Food and Feed Regulation'* – 'Regulation (EC) No 1829/2003 of the European Parliament and of the Council of 22 September 2003 on genetically modified food and feed (Text with EEA relevance)', Official Journal, L268, 18/10/2003, pp. 1–23.

Regulation 1830/2003 – *'Traceability and Labelling Regulation'* – 'Regulation (EC) No 1830/2003 of the European Parliament and of the Council of 22 September 2003 concerning the traceability and labelling of genetically modified organisms and the traceability of food and feed products produced from genetically modified organisms and amending Directive 2001/18/EC', Official Journal, L268, 18/10/2003, pp. 24–28.

Regulation 1946/2003 – *'Transboundary Movement Regulation'* – 'Regulation (EC) No 1946/2003 of the European Parliament and of the Council of 15 July 2003 on transboundary movements of genetically modified organisms (Text with EEA relevance)', Official Journal, L287, 05/11/2003, pp. 1–10.

Regulation 842/2006 – *'F-gases Regulation'* – 'Regulation (EC) No 842/2006 of the European Parliament and of the Council of 17 May 2006 on certain fluorinated greenhouse gases (Text with EEA relevance)', Official Journal, L161, 14/06/2006, pp. 1–11.

Regulation 1907/2006 – *'REACH Regulation'* – 'Regulation (EC) No 1907/2006 of the European Parliament and of the Council of 18 December 2006 concerning the Registration, Evaluation, Authorisation and Restriction of Chemicals (REACH), establishing a European Chemicals Agency, amending Directive 1999/45/EC and repealing Council Regulation (EEC) No 793/93 and Commission Regulation (EC) No 1488/94 as well as Council Directive 76/769/EEC and Commission Directives 91/155/EEC, 93/67/EEC, 93/105/EC and 2000/21/EC', Official Journal, L396, 30/12/2006, pp. 1–849.

Regulation 244/2009 – '*Lighting Regulation*' – 'Commission Regulation (EC) No 244/2009 of 18 March 2009 implementing Directive 2005/32/EC of the European Parliament and of the Council with regard to ecodesign requirements for non-directional household lamps (Text with EEA relevance)', Official Journal, L76, 24/03/2009, pp. 3–16.

Regulation 401/2009 – '*Regulation on the EEA*' – 'Regulation (EC) No 401/2009 of the European Parliament and of the Council of 23 April 2009 on the European Environment Agency and the European Environment Information and Observation Network (Codified version)', Official Journal, L126, 21/05/2009, pp. 13–22.

Regulation 443/2009 – '*Passenger Car Regulation*' – 'Regulation (EC) No 443/2009 of the European Parliament and of the Council of 23 April 2009 setting emission performance standards for new passenger cars as part of the Community's integrated approach to reduce CO_2 emissions from light-duty vehicles (Text with EEA relevance)', Official Journal, L140, 05/06/2009, pp. 1–15.

Regulation 1005/2009 – '*Ozone Depleting Substances Regulation*' – 'Regulation (EC) No 1005/2009 of the European Parliament and of the Council of 16 September 2009 on substances that deplete the ozone layer (Text with EEA relevance)', Official Journal, L286, 31/10/2009, pp. 1–30.

Regulation 1221/2009 – '*EMAS Regulation*' – 'Regulation (EC) No 1221/2009 of the European Parliament and of the Council of 25 November 2009 on the voluntary participation by organisations in a Community eco-management and audit scheme (EMAS), repealing Regulation (EC) No 761/2001 and Commission Decisions 2001/681/EC and 2006/193/EC', Official Journal, L342, 22/12/2009, pp. 1–45.

Regulation 1222/2009 – '*Tyre Labelling Regulation*' – 'Regulation (EC) No 1222/2009 of the European Parliament and of the Council of 25 November 2009 on the labelling of tyres with respect to fuel efficiency and other essential parameters (Text with EEA relevance)', Official Journal, L342, 22/12/2009, pp. 46–58.

Regulation 66/2010 – '*Eco-Label Regulation*' – 'Regulation (EC) No 66/2010 of the European Parliament and of the Council of 25 November 2009 on the EU Ecolabel (Text with EEA relevance)', Official Journal, L27, 30/01/2010, pp. 1–19.

Regulation 182/2011 – '*Comitology Regulation*' – 'Regulation (EU) No 182/2011 of the European Parliament and of the Council of 16 February 2011 laying down the rules and general principles concerning mechanisms for control by Member States of the Commission's exercise of implementing powers', Official Journal, L55, 28/02/2011, pp. 13–18.

Regulation 619/2011 – '*Low Level Presence Regulation*' – 'Commission Regulation (EU) No 619/2011 of 24 June 2011 laying down the methods of sampling and analysis for the official control of feed as regards presence of genetically modified material for which an authorisation procedure is pending or the authorisation of which has expired (Text with EEA relevance)', Official Journal, L166, 25/06/2011, pp. 9–15.

Regulation 1257/2013 – *'Ship Recycling Regulation'* – 'Regulation (EU) No 1257/2013 of the European Parliament and of the Council of 20 November 2013 on ship recycling and amending Regulation (EC) No 1013/2006 and Directive 2009/16/EC (Text with EEA relevance)', Official Journal, L330, 10/12/2013, pp. 1–20.

Regulation 1293/2013 – *'LIFE Regulation'* – 'Regulation (EU) No 1293/2013 of the European Parliament and of the Council of 11 December 2013 on the establishment of a Programme for the Environment and Climate Action (LIFE) and repealing Regulation (EC) No 614/2007 (Text with EEA relevance)', Official Journal, L347, 20/12/2013, pp. 185–208.

Regulation 333/2014 – *'Passenger Car Regulation'* – 'Regulation (EU) No 333/2014 of the European Parliament and of the Council of 11 March 2014 amending Regulation (EC) No 443/2009 to define the modalities for reaching the 2020 target to reduce CO2 emissions from new passenger cars', Official Journal, L103, 05/04/2014, pp. 15–21.

Regulation 517/2014 – *'F-gases Regulation'* – 'Regulation (EU) No 517/2014 of the European Parliament and of the Council of 16 April 2014 on fluorinated greenhouse gases and repealing Regulation (EC) No 842/2006 (Text with EEA relevance)', Official Journal, L150, 20/05/2014, pp. 195–230.

References

Adelle C., Anderson J. (2012), 'Lobby Groups' in Jordan A., Adelle C. (eds.), *Environmental Policy in the EU: Actors, Institutions and Processes. Third edition*, Abingdon, Routledge, pp. 152–169.

Adelle C., Jordan A., Turnpenny J. (2012), 'Policy making' in Jordan A., Adelle C. (eds.), *Environmental Policy in the EU: Actors, Institutions and Processes. Third edition*, Abingdon, Routledge, pp. 209–226.

Adelle C., Russel D. (2013), 'Climate Policy Integration: a Case of Déjà Vu?', in *Environmental Policy and Governance*, 23: pp. 1–12.

Afionis S. (2011), 'The European Union as a negotiator in the international climate change regime' in *International Environmental Agreements*, 11(4): pp. 341–360.

American Farm Bureau Federation (2010), *Actions to increase U.S. agricultural exports*, http://www.fb.org/newsroom/nr/nr2010/07-26-10/TradeActions-4.doc (consulted August 2014).

Anderson J. (2009), 'Can Europe Catalyze Climate Action?', in *Current History*, March 2009: pp. 131–137.

Andersen S. (2012), *The Enforcement of EU Law. The Role of the European Commission*, Oxford, Oxford University Press.

Andersen M., Rasmussen L. (1998), 'The Making of Environmental Policy in the European Council' in *Journal of Common Market Studies*, 36(4): pp. 585–597.

Andresen S. (2007), 'The effectiveness of UN environmental institutions', in *International Environmental Agreements*, 7: pp. 317–336.

Axelrod R., Schreurs M., Vig N. (2011), 'Environmental Policy Making in the European Union' in Axelrod R., VanDeveer S., Downie D. (eds.), *The Global Environment. Institutions, law, and policy. Third edition*, Washington DC, QC Press, pp. 213–238.

Bäckstrand K., Elgström O. (2013), 'The EU's role in climate change negotiations: from leader to "leadiator"' in *Journal of European Public Policy*, 20(10): pp. 1369–1386.

Bailer S. (2014), 'An Agent Dependent on the EU Member States? The Determinants of the European Commission's Legislative Success in the European Union' in *Journal of European Integration*, 36(1): pp. 37–53.

Baker S. (2003), 'The dynamics of European Union biodiversity policy: interactive, functional and institutional logics', in *Environmental Politics*, 12(3): pp. 23–41.

Baker S., Eckerberg K. (2008), 'Economic instruments and the promotion of sustainable development' in Baker S., Eckerberg K. (eds.), *In Pursuit of Sustainable Development. New governance practices at the sub-national level in Europe*, New York, Routledge, pp. 50–73.

Barnett J., Adger W. (2007), 'Climate change, human security and violent conflict', in *Political Geography*, 26(6): pp. 639–655.

Barroso J. (2009), *Political Guidelines for the Next Commission*, http://ec.europa.eu/commission_2010-2014/president/pdf/press_20090903_en.pdf.

Bauer M., Jordan A., Green-Pedersen C., Héritier A. (2012), 'Dismantling Public Policy: Preferences, Strategies, and Effects', in Bauer M., Jordan A., Green-Pedersen C., Héritier A. (eds.), *Dismantling Public Policy. Preferences, Strategies, and Effects*, Oxford, Oxford University Press, pp. 203–226.

Beck U. (1992), *Risk Society. Towards a New Modernity*, London, SAGE Publications.

Benedetto G. (2005), 'Rapporteurs as legislative entrepreneurs: the dynamics of the codecision procedure in Europe's Parliament' in *Journal of European Public Policy*, 12(1): pp. 67–88.

Benson D., Adelle C. (2012), 'EU environmental policy after the Lisbon Treaty' in Jordan A., Adelle C. (eds.), *Environmental Policy in the EU: Actors, Institutions and Processes. Third edition*, Abingdon, Routledge, pp. 32–48.

Benson D., Jordan A. (2010), 'European Union environmental policy after the Lisbon Treaty: plus ça change, plus c'est la même chose?' in *Environmental Politics*, 19(3): pp. 468–474.

Beyers J. (2005), 'Multiple Embeddedness and Socialization in Europe: The Case of Council Officials' in *International Organization*, 59(4): pp. 899–936.

Beyers J., Eising R., Maloney W. (2008), 'Researching Interest Group Politics in Europe and Elsewhere: Much We Study, Little We Know?' in *West European Politics*, 31(6): pp. 1103–1128.

Biedenkopf K. (2012), *Emmissions Trading. A Transatlantic Journey for an Idea?*, KFG Working Paper Series, 45, Berlin, Freie Universität Berlin.

Biedenkopf K. (2015), 'The European Parliament in EU external climate governance' in Stavridis S., Irrera D. (eds.), *The European Parliament and its International Relations*, Abingdon, Routledge, pp. 92–108.

Biedenkopf K., Torney D. (2014), 'Cooperation on Greenhouse Gas Emissions Trading in EU-China Climate Diplomacy' in Reuter E., Men J. (eds.), *China-EU Green Cooperation*, Singapore, World Scientific, pp. 21–38.

Birnie P., Boyle A., Redgwell C. (2009), *International Law & the Environment*, Oxford, Oxford University Press.

Blom-Hansen J. (2011), *The EU Comitology System in Theory and Practice. Keeping an Eye on the Commission?*, Basingstoke, Palgrave.

Bocquillon P., Dobbels M. (2014), 'An elephant on the 13th floor of the Berlaymont? European Council and Commission relations in legislative agenda setting' in *Journal of European Public Policy*, 21(1): pp. 20–38.

Bomberg E. (2007), 'Policy learning in an enlarged European Union: environmental NGOs and new policy instruments' in *Journal of European Public Policy*, 14(2): pp. 248–268.

Börzel T. (2000), 'Why there is no "southern problem". On environmental leaders and laggards in the European Union' in *Journal of European Public Policy*, 7(1): pp. 141–162.

Börzel T. (2002), 'Pace-Setting, Foot-Dragging, and Fence-Sitting. Member State Responses to Europeanization' in *Journal of Common Market Studies*, 40(2): pp. 193–214.

Börzel T., Hofmann T., Panke D., Sprungk C. (2010), 'Obstinate and Inefficient: Why Member States Do Not Comply With European Law' in *Comparative Political Studies*, 43(11): pp. 1363–1390.

Börzel T., Risse T. (2012), 'From Europeanisation to diffusion: introduction', in *West European Politics*, 35(1): pp. 1–19.

Bouwen P. (2004), 'Exchanging access goods for access: A comparative study of business lobbying in the European Union institutions' in *European Journal of Political Research*, 43(3): pp. 337–369.

Bouwen P. (2009), 'The European Commission' in Coen D., Richardson J (eds.), *Lobbying the European Union: Institutions, Actors, and Issues* New York, Oxford University Press, pp. 19–38.

Brandsma G. (2013), *Controlling Comitology. Accountability in a Multi-Level System*, Basingstoke, Palgrave.

Braun M. (2014), *Europeanization of Environmental Policy in the New Europe. Beyond Conditionality*, Surrey, Ashgate.

Bretherton C., Vogler J. (2006), *The European Union as a Global Actor* Abingdon, Routledge.

Bretherton C., Vogler J. (2008), 'The European Union as a Sustainable Development Actor: the Case of External Fisheries Policy' in *Journal of European Integration*, 30(3): pp. 401–417.

Broscheid A., Coen D. (2007), 'Lobbying activity and fora creation in the EU: empirically exploring the nature of the policy good' in *Journal of European Public Policy*, 14(3): pp. 346–365.

Bruyninckx H. (2013), 'Globalisering, milieu en duurzame ontwikkeling' in Leuvens Onderzoeksnetwerk Duurzame Ontwikkeling (ed.), *Duurzame ontwikkeling. Een multidisciplinaire visie*, Leuven, Acco, pp. 229–242.

Bruyninckx H., Ye Q., Quang Thuan N., Belis D. (eds.) (2013), *The Governance of Climate Relations Between Europe and Asia* Cheltenham, Edward Elgar.

Buck M. (2012), 'The EU's representation in multilateral environmental negotiations after Lisbon' in Morgera E. (ed.), *The External Environmental Policy of the European Union. EU and International Law Perspectives*, Cambridge, Cambridge University Press, pp. 76–95.

Bunea A. (2013), 'Issues, preferences and ties: determinants of interest groups' preference attainment in the EU environmental policy' in *Journal of European Public Policy*, 20(4): pp. 552–570.

Bunea A. (2014), 'Explaining Interest Groups' Articulation of Policy Preferences in the European Commission's Open Consultations: An Analysis of the Environmental Policy Area' in *Journal of Common Market Studies*, 52(6): pp. 1224–1241.

Burns C. (2012a), 'The European Parliament' in Jordan A., Adelle C. (eds.), *Environmental Policy in the EU: Actors, Institutions and Processes*. *Third edition*, Abingdon, Routledge, pp. 132–151.

Burns C. (2012b), 'How and When Did We Get Here? An Historical Institutionalist Analysis of EU Biotechnology Policy', in *Journal of European Integration*, 34(4): pp. 341–357.

Burns C. (2013), 'Consensus and compromise become ordinary – but at what cost? A critical analysis of the impact of the changing norms of codecision upon European Parliament committees' in *Journal of European Public Policy*, 20(7): pp. 988–1005.

Burns C. (2014), *EU environmental policy in a time of austerity: dismantling or leading?*, paper presented at the ECPR Standing Group on the European Union conference, The Hague.

Burns C., Carter N., Davies G., Worsfold N. (2013), 'Still saving the earth? The European Parliament's environmental record' in *Environmental Politics*, 22(6): pp. 935–954.

Burns C., Carter N., Worsfold N. (2012), 'Enlargement and the Environment: The Changing Behaviour of the European Parliament' in *Journal of Common Market Studies*, 50(1): pp. 54–70.

Carson R. L. (1962), *Silent Spring*, London, Hamilton.

Chalmers A. (2012), 'Trading information for access: informational lobbying strategies and interest group access to the European Union' in *Journal of European Public Policy*, 20(1): pp. 39–58.

Chaloux A., Paquin S. (2012), 'Green Paradiplomacy in North America: Climate Change Regulation at Subnational level: Successes and Limits of the NEG-ECP' in Bruyninckx H., Happaerts S., Van den Brande K. (eds.), *Sustainable Development and Subnational Governments. Policy-Making and Multi-Level Interactions*, Basingstoke, Palgrave Macmillan, pp. 217–238.

Chasek P., Wagner L. (eds.) (2012), *The Roads from Rio. Lessons Learned from Twenty Years of Multilateral Environmental Negotiations*, New York, Routledge.

Christiansen T. (2006a), 'The European Commission. The European executive between continuity and change' in Richardson J. (ed.), *European Union. Power and policy-making*, New York, Routledge, pp. 99–120.

Christiansen T. (2006b), 'The Council of Ministers. Facilitating interaction and developing actorness in the EU' in Richardson J. (ed.), *European Union. Power and policy-making*, New York, Routledge, pp. 147–170.

Christiansen T., Polak J. (2009), 'Comitology between Political Decision-Making and Technocratic Governance: Regulating GMOs in the European Union', in *Eipascope*, 18(1): pp. 5–11.

Coen D. (2007), 'Empirical and theoretical studies in EU lobbying' in *Journal of European Public Policy*, 14(3): pp. 333–345.

Coen D. (2009), 'Business Lobbying in the European Union' in Coen D., Richardson J. (eds.), *Lobbying the European Union: Institutions, Actors, and Issues*, New York, Oxford University Press, pp. 145–168.

Coen D., Katsaitis A. (2013), 'Chameleon pluralism in the EU: an empirical study of the European Commission interest group density and diversity across policy domains' in *Journal of European Public Policy*, 20(8): pp. 1104–1119.

Corthaut T., Van Eeckhoutte D. (2012), 'Legal Aspects of EU Participation in Global Environmental Governance under the UN Umbrella' in Wouters J., Bruyninckx H., Basu S., Schunz S. (eds.), *The European Union and Multilateral Governance. Assessing EU Participation in United Nations Human Rights and Environmental Fora*, Basingstoke, Palgrave Macmillan, pp. 145–170.

Costello R., Thomson R. (2010), 'The policy impact of leadership in committees: Rapporteurs' influence on the European Parliament's opinions' in *European Union Politics*, 11(2): pp. 219–240.

Costello R., Thomson R. (2011), 'The nexus of bicameralism: Rapporteurs' impact on decision outcomes in the European Union' in *European Union Politics*, 12(3): pp. 337–357.

Costello R., Thomson R. (2013), 'The distribution of power among EU institutions: who wins under codecision and why?' in *Journal of European Public Policy*, 20(7): pp. 1025–1039.

Council of the European Union (1998), *Council conclusions of the 2106th Council meeting*, 09402/98.

Council of the European Union (2006), *Review of the EU Sustainable Development Strategy (EU SDS) – Renewed Strategy*, 10117/06.

Council of the European Union (2011), *EU statements in multilateral organisations – general arrangements*, 15901/11.

Council of the European Union (2015a), *Market stability reserve: Council takes important step towards the reform of EU Emissions Trading System*, http://www.consilium.europa.eu/en/press/press-releases/2015/05/05–reform-eu-emissions-trading-system/ (consulted May 2015).

Council of the European Union (2015b), *Outcome of the Council meeting. 3364th Council Meeting Foreign Affairs*, 5411/15.

CropLife International (2014), *Environmental Benefits*, http://biotech-benefits.croplife.org/impact_areas/environmental-benefits/ (consulted August 2014).

Damro C., Luaces Méndez P. (2003), 'Emissions trading at Kyoto: from EU resistance to Union innovation' in *Environmental Politics*, 12(2): pp. 71–94.

Darst R. (2001), *Smokestack Diplomacy. Cooperation and conflict in East-West environmental politics*, Cambridge, London, MIT Press.

Daviter F. (2009), 'Schattschneider in Brussels: How Policy Conflict Reshaped the Biotechnology Agenda in the European Union' in *West European Politics*, 32(6): pp. 1118–1139.

de Jong S., Schunz S. (2012), 'Coherence in European Union External Policy before and after the Lisbon Treaty: The Cases of Energy Security and Climate Change' in *European Foreign Affairs Review*, 17(2): pp. 165–188.

de Ruiter R., Neuhold C. (2012), 'Why Is Fast Track the Way to Go? Justifications for Early Agreement in the Co-Decision Procedure and Their Effects' in *European Law Journal*, 18(4): pp. 536–554.

de Sadeleer N. (2009), 'The Precautionary Principle as a Device for Greater Environmental Protection: Lessons from EC Courts' in *Review of European Community and International Environmental Law*, 18(1): pp. 3–10.

de Schoutheete P. (2006), 'The European Council' in Peterson J., Shackleton M. (eds.), *The Institutions of the European Union*, New York, Oxford University Press, pp. 37–59.

Degrand-Guillaud A. (2009), 'Characteristics of and Recommendations for EU Coordination at the UN' in *European Foreign Affairs Review*, 14(4): pp. 607–622.

Dehousse R., Fernández Pasarín A., Plaza J. (2014), 'How consensual is comitology?' in *Journal of European Public Policy*, 21(6): pp. 842–859.

Delbeke J. (2006), 'The Emissions Trading Scheme (ETS): The cornerstone of the EU's implementation of the Kyoto Protocol' in Delbeke J. (ed.) *EU Environmental Law. The EU Greenhouse Gas Emissions Trading Scheme*, Deventer, Claeys & Casteels, pp. 1–13.

Delreux T. (2009), 'The EU in Environmental Negotiations in UNECE: An Analysis of its Role in the Aarhus Convention and the SEA Protocol Negotiations' in *Review of European Community and International Environmental Law*, 18(3): pp. 328–337.

Delreux T. (2011), *The EU as International Environmental Negotiator*, Surrey, Ashgate.

Delreux T. (2012a), 'The Rotating Presidency and the EU's External Representation in Environmental Affairs: the Case of Climate Change and Biodiversity Negotiations' in *Journal of Contemporary European Research*, 8(2): pp. 210–227.

Delreux T. (2012b), 'The EU in Negotiations on the Cartagena Protocol on Biosafety' in Wouters J., Bruyninckx H., Basu S., Schunz S. (eds.), *The European Union and Multilateral Governance. Assessing EU Participation in United Nations Human Rights and Environmental Fora*, Basingstoke, Palgrave Macmillan, pp. 214–231.

Delreux T., Van den Brande K. (2013), 'Taking the lead: informal division of labour in the EU's external environmental policy-making' in *Journal of European Public Policy*, 20(1): pp. 113–131.

Delreux T. (2014), 'EU actorness, cohesiveness and effectiveness in environmental affairs' in *Journal of European Public Policy*, 21(7): pp. 1017–1032.

Demmke C. (2001), *Towards Effective Environmental Regulation: Innovative Approaches in Implementing and Enforcing European Environmental Law and Policy*, Jean Monnet Working Paper 5/01, Harvard Law School, European Union Jean Monnet Chair.

DeSombre E. (2011), 'The United States and Global Environmental Politics: Domestic Sources of U.S. Unilateralism' in Axelrod R., VanDeveer S., Downie D. (eds.), *The Global Environment: Institutions, Law, and Policy*, Washington, CQ Press, pp. 192–212.

Dijkstra H. (2009), 'Commission Versus Council Secretariat: An Analysis of Bureaucratic Rivalry in European Foreign Policy' in *European Foreign Affairs Review*, 14(3): pp. 431–450.

Dobbs M. (2011), 'Excluding Coexistence of GMOs? The Impact of the EU Commission's 2010 Recommendation on Coexistence' in *Review of European Community & International Environmental Law*, 20(2): pp. 180–193.

Dreger J. (2014), *The European Commission's Energy and Climate Policy. A Climate for Expertise?*, Basingstoke, Palgrave Macmillan.

Drieskens E., van Schaik L. (eds.) (2014), *The EU and Effective Multilateralism: Internal and External Reform Practices*, Abingdon, Routledge.

Dupont C., Oberthür S. (2012), 'Insufficient climate policy integration in EU energy policy: the importance of the long-term perspective' in *Journal of Contemporary European Research*, 8(2): pp. 228–247.

Dür A. (2008), 'Interest Groups in the European Union: How Powerful Are They?' in *West European Politics*, 31(6): pp. 1212–1230.

Dür A., Bernhagen P., Marshall D. (2015), 'Interest Group Success in the European Union: When (and Why) Does Business Lose?' in *Comparative Political Studies*, 20(1): pp. 1–33.

Eeckhout P. (2011), *EU External Relations Law*, Oxford, Oxford University Press.

Egeberg M., Schaefer G., Trondal J. (2003), 'The Many Faces of EU Committee Governance' in *West European Politics*, 26(3): pp. 19–40.

EIPA and IEEP (2003), *Evaluation of the European Environment Agency. Report to DG Environment*, EIPA and IEEP, Brussels and Maastricht.

Eising R. (2004), 'Multilevel governance and business interests in the European Union' in *Governance*, 17(2): pp. 211–245.

Elgström O. (2007), 'Outsiders' Perceptions of the European Union in International Trade Negotiations' in *Journal of Common Market Studies*, 45(4): pp. 949–967.

Elgström O., Jönsson C. (2000), 'Negotiation in the European Union: bargaining or problem-solving?' in *Journal of European Public Policy*, 7(5): pp. 684–704.

Eliassen K., Sjøvaag Marino M., Peneva P. (2010), *The Role of the European Commission in Concluding an Agreement on EU Climate Change Package in 2008*, paper presented at the 'European Union in International Affairs' Conference, Brussels.

Elliott L. (2004), *The Global Politics of the Environment*, Basingstoke, Palgrave Macmillan.

Entine J. (2014), *The Debate About GMO Safety Is Over, Thanks To A New Trillion-Meal Study*, http://www.forbes.com/sites/jonentine/2014/09/17/the-debate-about-gmo-safety-is-over-thanks-to-a-new-trillion-meal-study (consulted March 2015).

Euractiv (2014), *Election of Donald Tusk puts EU climate position in doubt*, http://www.euractiv.com/sections/sustainable-dev/election-donald-tusk-puts-eu-climate-position-doubt-308291 (consulted September 2014).

European Commission (1988), *Communication to the Council. The Greenhouse Effect and the Community. Commission Work Programme concerning the Evaluation of Policy Options to Deal With the 'Greenhouse Effect'*, COM(88) 656.

European Commission (1996), *Future Noise Policy. European Commission Green Paper*, COM(96) 540.

European Commission (2000), *Communication from the Commission on the precautionary principle*, COM(2000) 1.

European Commission (2001a), *European Governance - A White Paper*, COM(2001) 428.

European Commission (2001b), *Communication from the Commission. A Sustainable Europe for a Better World: A European Union Strategy for Sustainable Development (Commission's proposal to the Gothenburg European Council)*, COM(2001) 264.

European Commission (2005a), *EU Waste Policy – The Story behind the Strategy*, http://ec.europa.eu/environment/waste/pdf/story_book.pdf.

European Commission (2005b), *Communication from the Commission to the Council, the European Parliament, the European Economic and Social Committee and The Committee of the Regions. Taking sustainable use of resources forward – A Thematic Strategy on the prevention and recycling of waste*, COM(2005) 666.

European Commission (2010a), *Green Public Procurement*, Brussels, DG Environment.

European Commission (2010b), *Europe 2020. A strategy for smart, sustainable and inclusive growth*, COM(2010) 2020.

European Commission (2010c), *Commission Recommendation on guidelines for the development of national co-existence measures to avoid the unintended presence of GMOs in conventional and organic crops*, Official Journal, C200, 22/07/2010, pp. 1–5.

European Commission (2011a), *Special Eurobarometer 365. Attitudes of European citizens towards the environment*, http://ec.europa.eu/public_opinion/archives/ebs/ebs_365_en.pdf.

European Commission (2011b), *Communication from the Commission to the European Parliament, the Council, the European Economic and Social Committee and the Committee of the Regions. A Roadmap for moving to a competitive low carbon economy in 2050*, COM(2011) 112.

European Commission (2011c), *Communication from the Commission to the European Parliament, the Council, the European Economic and Social Committee and the Committee of the Regions. Roadmap to a Resource Efficient Europe*, COM(2011) 571.

European Commission (2011d), *Communication from the Commission to the European Parliament, the Council, the European Economic and Social Committee and the Committee of the Regions. Energy Roadmap 2050*, COM(2011) 885.

European Commission (2011e), *White Paper. Roadmap to a Single European Transport Area – Towards a competitive and resource efficient transport system*, COM(2011) 144.

European Commission (2011f), *Communication from the Commission to the European Parliament, the Council, the Economic and Social Committee and the Committee of the Regions. Our life insurance, our natural capital: an EU biodiversity strategy to 2020*, COM(2011) 244.

European Commission (2011g), *Report from the Commission to the European Parliament and the Council on the implementation of the Environmental Noise Directive in accordance with Article 11 of Directive 2002/49/EC*, COM(2011) 321.

European Commission (2011h), *Emissions trading: Commission welcomes vote to ban certain industrial gas credits*, http://europa.eu/rapid/press-release_IP-11-56_en.htm (consulted August 2014).

European Commission (2012a), *EU Cohesion Policy 2014-2020. Targeting Investments on Key Growth Priorities*, http://ec.europa.eu/regional_policy/sources/docgener/informat/2014/fiche_low_carbon_en.pdf (consulted July 2014).

European Commission (2012b), *Flash Eurobarometer 344. Attitudes of Europeans towards water-related issues*, http://ec.europa.eu/public_opinion/flash/fl_344_en.pdf.

European Commission (2013a), *Report from the Commission. 30th Annual Report on Monitoring the Application of EU Law (2012)*, COM(2013) 726.

European Commission (2013b), *Commission staff working document accompanying the report from the Commission. 30th Annual Report on Monitoring the Application of EU Law (2012)*, SWD(2013) 433.

European Commission (2013c), *European environmental NGOs. LIFE operating grants 2013*, http://ec.europa.eu/environment/life/funding/ngos/pdf/ngos2013.pdf.

European Commission (2013d), *Proposal for a Directive of the European Parliament and of the Council on the reduction of national emissions of certain atmospheric pollutants and amending Directive 2003/35/EC*, COM(2013) 920.

European Commission (2014a), *Human Resources Key Figure Card. Staff Members*, http://ec.europa.eu/civil_service/docs/hr_key_figures_en.pdf.

European Commission (2014b), *Communication from the Commission on the European Citizens' Initiative 'Water and sanitation are a human right! Water is a public good, not a commodity!'*, COM(2014) 177.

European Commission (2014c), *Consultations - Environment*, http://ec.europa.eu/environment/consultations_en.htm (consulted July 2014).

European Commission (2014d), *Register of Expert Groups and Other Similar Entities*, http://ec.europa.eu/transparency/regexpert/ (consulted July 2014).

European Commission (2014e), *Report from the Commission on the Working of Committees during 2012*, COM(2013) 701.

European Commission (2014f), *Legal Enforcement. Statistics on environmental infringements*, http://ec.europa.eu/environment/legal/law/statistics.htm (consulted October 2014).

European Commission (2014g), *The LIFE Programme*, http://ec.europa.eu/environment/life/about/index.htm#life2014 (consulted July 2014).

European Commission (2014h), *Supporting climate action through the EU budget*, http://ec.europa.eu/clima/policies/budget/index_en.htm (consulted July 2014).

European Commission (2014i), *What is GPP*, http://ec.europa.eu/environment/gpp/what_en.htm (consulted July 2014).

European Commission (2014j), *2030 framework for climate and energy policies*, http://ec.europa.eu/clima/policies/2030/index_en.htm (consulted July 2014).

European Commission (2014k), *Review of the Environmental Impact Assessment (EIA) Directive*, http://ec.europa.eu/environment/eia/review.htm (consulted July 2014).

European Commission (2014l), *Communication from the Commission to the European Parliament, the Council, the European Economic and Social Committee and the Committee of the Regions. Towards a circular economy: A zero waste programme for Europe*, COM(2014) 398.

European Commission (2014m), *Review of Waste Policy and Legislation*, http://ec.europa.eu/environment/waste/target_review.htm (consulted July 2014).

European Commission (2014n), *Soil*, http://ec.europa.eu/environment/soil/index_en.htm (consulted April 2014).

European Commission (2014o), *Daily news 21/05/2014. Commission withdraws 53 legislative proposals*, http://europa.eu/rapid/press-release_MEX-14-0521_en.htm (consulted July 2014).

European Commission (2014p), *Glossary*, http://europa.eu/legislation_summaries/glossary/genetically_modified_organisms_en.htm (consulted August 2014).

European Commission (2014q), *Transatlantic Trade and Investment Partnership (TTIP): Questions and answers*, http://ec.europa.eu/trade/policy/in-focus/ttip/questions-and-answers/ (consulted August 2014).

European Commission (2014r), *European Climate Change Programme*, http://ec.europa.eu/clima/policies/eccp/index_en.htm (consulted August 2014).

European Commission (2014s), *EU ETS 2005-2012*, http://ec.europa.eu/clima/policies/ets/pre2013/index_en.htm (consulted August 2014).

European Commission (2014t), *Structural reform of the European carbon market*, http://ec.europa.eu/clima/policies/ets/reform/index_en.htm (consulted August 2014).

European Commission (2014u), *International carbon market*, http://ec.europa.eu/clima/policies/ets/linking/index_en.htm (consulted September 2014).

European Commission (2014v), *EU legislation to control F-gases*, http://ec.europa.eu/clima/policies/f-gas/legislation/index_en.htm (consulted December 2014).

European Commission (2014w), *EU greenhouse gas emissions and targets*, http://ec.europa.eu/clima/policies/g-gas/index_en.htm (consulted January 2015).

European Commission (2015a), *Proposal for a Regulation of the European Parliament and of the Council amending Regulation (EC) No 1829/2003 as regards the possibility for the Member States to restrict or prohibit the use of genetically modified food and feed on their territory*, COM/2015/177.

European Commission (2015b), *EU Register of authorised GMOs*, http://ec.europa.eu/food/dyna/gm_register/index_en.cfm (consulted April 2015).

European Commission (2015c), *Communication from the Commission to the European Parliament, the Council, the European Economic and Social Committee, the Committee of the Regions and the European Investment Bank. A Framework Strategy for a Resilient Energy Union with a Forward-Looking Climate Change Policy*, COM(2015) 80.

European Commission (2015d), *Communication from the Commission to the European Parliament and the Council. Achieving the 10% electricity interconnection target Making Europe's electricity grid fit for 2020*, COM(2015) 82.

European Commission (2015e), *Communication from the Commission to the European Parliament and the Council. The Paris Protocol – A blueprint for tackling global climate change beyond 2020*, COM(2015) 81.

European Commission (2015f), *Reducing emissions from the shipping sector*, http://ec.europa.eu/clima/policies/transport/shipping/index_en.htm (consulted March 2015).

European Commission (2015g), *Multilateral environmental agreements to which the EU is a contracting party or a signatory*, http://ec.europa.eu/environment/international_issues/pdf/agreements_en.pdf.

European Communities (1972), 'Statement from the Paris Summit' in *Bulletin of the European Communities*, 10, October 1972, pp. 14–26.

European Council (2007), *Presidency conclusions European Council 8–9 March*, EUCO 7224/1/07.

European Council (2014), *Conclusions European Council 23 and 24 October*, EUCO 169/14.

European Council on Foreign Relations (2015), *European Foreign Policy Scorecard 2015*, http://www.ecfr.eu/page/-/ECFR125_ SCORECARD_2015.pdf

European Environment Agency (2010), *The European Environment. State and Outlook 2010*, Copenhagen, European Environment Agency.

European Environment Agency (2011), *BLOSSOM – Bridging long-term scenario and strategy analysis: organisation and methods. A cross-country analysis*, EEA Technical Report 5, Copenhagen, European Environment Agency.

European Environment Agency (2012), *Key observed and projected climate change and impacts for the main regions in Europe*, http://www. eea.europa.eu/data-and-maps/figures/key-past-and-projected-impacts-and-effects-on-sectors-for-the-main-biogeographic-regions-of-europe-3 (consulted July 2014).

European Environment Agency (2014a), *Progress towards 2008–2012 Kyoto targets in Europe*, EEA Technical Report 18/2014, Copenhagen, European Environment Agency.

European Environment Agency (2014b), *Trends and projections in Europe 2014. Tracking progress towards Europe's climate and energy targets for 2020*, EEA Report 6/2014, Copenhagen, European Environment Agency.

European Environment Agency (2015), *The European environment – state and outlook 2015: synthesis report*, Copenhagen, European Environment Agency.

European Parliament (2012), *Activity report 14 July 2009 - 31 December 2011 (7th parliamentary term)*, http://www.europarl.europa.eu/code/ information/activity_reports/activity_report_2009_2011_en.pdf

European Parliament (2014a), *Committee on the Environment, Public Health and Food Safety (ENVI). Activity report for the 7th parliamentary term 2009-2014*, http://www.europarl.europa.eu/document/activities/ cont/201406/20140618ATT85502/20140618ATT85502EN.pdf.

European Parliament (2014b), *Activity Report on Codecision and Conciliation 14 July 2009 - 30 June 2014 (7th parliamentary term)*, http://www.europarl.europa.eu/code/information/activity_reports/ activity_report_2009_2014_en.pdf.

European Parliament (2014c), *Statistics on concluded codecision procedures (by signature date)*, http://www.europarl.europa.eu/code/about/ statistics_en.htm (consulted July 2014).

European Parliament (2015), *Member States' bans on GMO cultivation*, http://www.europarl.europa.eu/EPRS/EPRS-AaG-545708-Member-State-bans-on-GMOs-FINAL.pdf.

European Resource Efficiency Platform (2014), *Manifesto & Policy Recommendations*, http://ec.europa.eu/environment/resource_efficiency/documents/erep_manifesto_and_policy_recommendations_31-03-2014.pdf.

European Union (2014), *Transparency Register*, http://ec.europa.eu/transparencyregister (consulted October 2014).

Eurostat (2014), *Waste generation and management*, http://epp.eurostat.ec.europa.eu/portal/page/portal/waste/waste_generation_and_management/generation (consulted August 2014).

Falkner R. (2000), 'Regulating biotech trade: the Cartagena Protocol on Biosafety' in *International Affairs*, 76(2): pp. 299–313.

Falkner R. (2007), 'The political economy of "normative power" Europe: EU environmental leadership in international biotechnology regulation' in *Journal of European Public Policy*, 14(4): pp. 507–526.

Falkner G., Treib O. (2008), 'Three Worlds of Compliance or Four? The EU-15 Compared to New Member States' in *Journal of Common Market Studies*, 46(2): pp. 293–313.

Falkner G., Treib O., Hartlapp M., Leiber S. (2005), *Complying with Europe. EU harmonization and soft law in the member states*, Cambridge, Cambridge University Press.

Farrell H., Héritier A. (2004), 'Interorganizational Negotiation and Intraorganizational Power in Shared Decision Making. Early Agreements Under Codecision and Their Impact on the European Parliament and the Council' in *Comparative Political Studies*, 37(10): pp. 1184–1212.

Favoino M., Knill C., Lenschow A. (2000), 'New structures for environmental governance in the European Commission: the institutional limits of governance change' in Knill C., Lenschow A. (eds.), *Implementing EU environmental policy. New directions and old problems*, Manchester, Manchester University Press, pp. 39–61.

Finke D. (2012), 'Proposal stage coalition-building in the European Parliament' in *European Union Politics*, 13(4): pp. 487–512.

Fischer C. (2011), 'The development and achievements of EU waste policy' in *Journal of Material Cycles and Waste Management*, 13: pp. 2–9.

Food and Agriculture Organization (2003), *Weighing the GMO arguments: for*, http://www.fao.org/english/newsroom/focus/2003/gmo7.htm (consulted August 2014).

Food and Agriculture Organization (2015), *The Role of Technology*, http://www.fao.org/docrep/004/y3557e/y3557e09.htm (consulted March 2015).

Franchino F. (2000), 'Control of the Commission's Executive Functions. Uncertainty, Conflict and Decision Rules' in *European Union Politics*, 1(1): pp. 63–92.

Franchino F., Mariotto C. (2013), 'Explaining negotiations in the conciliation committee' in *European Union Politics*, 14(3): pp. 345–365.

Frieden J. (2004), 'One Europe, One Vote?' in *European Union Politics*, 5(2): pp. 261–276.

Friends of the Earth (2006), *US did not win transatlantic GM trade dispute*, https://www.foe.co.uk/resource/press_releases/us_did_not_win_transatlant_11052006 (consulted August 2014).

Georgiev V. (2013), 'Too much executive power? Delegated law-making and comitology and perspective' in *Journal of European Public Policy*, 20(4): pp. 535–551.

Goho A. (2008), *Corn Primed for Making Biofuel*, http://www.technology-review.com/news/409913/corn-primed-for-making-biofuel/ (consulted March 2015).

Gornitzka Å., Sverdrup U. (2008), 'Who Consults? The Configuration of Expert Groups in the European Union' in *West European Politics*, 31(4): pp. 725–750.

Gornitzka Å, Sverdrup U. (2011), 'Access of Experts: Information and EU Decision-Making' in *West European Politics*, 34(1): pp. 48–70.

Grant W. (2012), 'Business' in Jordan A., Adelle C. (eds.), *Environmental Policy in the EU: Actors, Institutions and Processes. Third edition*, Abingdon, Routledge, pp. 170–188.

Gravey V. (2014), *Are EU environmental policies at risk? Learning from the 1990s subsidiarity crisis and the 2000s Better Regulation agenda*, paper prepared for the 2014 UACES Student Forum Conference, Birmingham.

Green 10 (2014), *Letter to President-elect of the European Commission Jean-Claude Juncker. New Commission sidelining environment*, http://www.green10.org/app/download/9792387493/20140911_OpenlettertoJuncker.pdf.

Greenpeace (2014), *What's wrong with genetic engineering (GE)?*, http://www.greenpeace.org/international/en/campaigns/agriculture/problem/genetic-engineering/ (consulted April 2015).

Greenwood J. (2011), *Interest Representation in the European Union. Third edition*, New York, Palgrave.

Groen L., Niemann A. (2013), 'The European Union at the Copenhagen climate negotiations: A case of contested EU actorness and effectiveness' in *International Relations*, 27(3): pp. 308–324.

Groen L., Niemann A., Oberthür S. (2012), 'The EU as a Global Leader? The Copenhagen and Cancun UN Climate Change Negotiations' in *Journal of Contemporary European Research*, 8(2): pp. 173–191.

Groen L., Oberthür S. (2012), 'Global environmental institutions' in Jørgensen K., Laatikainen K. (eds.), *Routledge Handbook on the European Union and International Institutions*, Abingdon, Routledge, pp. 282–293.

Groenleer M. (2009), *The Autonomy of European Union Agencies. A Comparative Study of Institutional Development*, Delft, Eburon.

Groenleer M., van Schaik L. (2007), 'United We Stand? The European Union's International Actorness in the Cases of the International Criminal Court and the Kyoto Protocol' in *Journal of Common Market Studies*, 45(5): pp. 969–998.

Gupta J. (2010), 'A history of international climate change policy' in *Climate Change*, 1(5): pp. 636–653.

Gupta A., Falkner R. (2006), 'The Influence of the Cartagena Protocol on Biosafety: Comparing Mexico, China and South Africa' in *Global Environmental Politics*, 6(4): pp. 23–55.

Haas P. (1992), 'Introduction: Epistemic Communities and International Policy Coordination' in *International Organization*, 46(1): pp. 1–35.

Häge F. (2013a), 'Coalition Building and Consensus in the Council of the European Union' in *British Journal of Political Science*, 43(3): pp. 481–504.

Häge F. (2013b), *Bureaucrats as Law-makers. Committee decision-making in the EU Council of Ministers*, Abingdon, Routledge.

Häge F., Kaeding M. (2007), 'Reconsidering the European Parliament's Legislative Influence: Formal vs Informal Procedures' in *Journal of European Integration*, 29(3): pp. 341–361.

Hagemann S., Høyland B. (2010), 'Bicamercal Politics in the European Union' in *Journal of Common Market Studies*, 48(4): pp. 811–833.

Hallstrom L. (2004), 'Eurocratising Enlargement? EU Elites and NGO Participation in European Environmental Policy' in *Environmental Politics*, 13(1): pp. 175–193.

Halpern C. (2010), 'Governing Despite its Instruments? Instrumentation in EU Environmental Policy' in *West European Politics*, 33(1): pp. 39–57.

Halpern C., Jacquot S., Le Galès P. (2008), *A Mainstreaming: Analysis of a Policy Instrument*, NewGov Policy Brief 33, San Domenico di Fiesole, European University Institute.

Hanrahan C. (2010), *Agricultural Biotechnology: The U.S.-EU Dispute*, Congressional Research Service Report 69, University of Nebraska.

Hansen S., Carlsen L., Tickner J. (2007), 'Chemicals regulation and precaution: does REACH really incorporate the precautionary principle?' in *Environmental Science & Policy*, 10: pp. 395–404.

Happaerts S. (2014), *International Discourses and Practices of Sustainable Materials Management*, Research Paper 5, Leuven, Policy Research Centre on Sustainable Materials Management.

Happaerts S. (2015), 'Rising powers in global climate governance. Negotiating inside and outside the UNFCCC' in Lesage D., Van de Graaf T. (eds.), *Rising Powers and Multilateral Reform*, Basingstoke, Palgrave Macmillan, pp. 238–257.

Happaerts S. (2016), 'Discourse and Practice of Transitions in International Policy-making on Resource Efficiency in the EU' in Brauch H., Oswald Spring U., Grin J., Scheffran J. (eds.), *Handbook of Sustainability Transitions and Sustainable Peace*, Heidelberg, Springer (forthcoming).

Happaerts S., Bruyninckx H. (2014), 'Sustainable development: the institutionalization of a contested policy concept' in Betsill M., Hochstetler K., Stevis D. (eds.), *Advances in International Environmental Politics*, Basingstoke, Palgrave, pp. 300–327.

Harris K. (2014), *Trouble ahead with TTIP?*, http://sustainablefoodtrust. org/articles/trouble-ahead-with-ttip/ (consulted March 2015).

Hartlapp M., Metz J., Rauh C. (2013), 'Linking Agenda Setting to Coordination Structures: Bureaucratic Politics inside the European Commission' in *Journal of European Integration*, 35(4): pp. 425–441.

Hartley T. (1998), *The Foundations of European Community Law*, New York, Oxford University Press.

Haverland M. (2000), 'National Adaptation to European Integration: The Importance of Institutional Veto Points' in *Journal of Public Policy*, 20(1): pp. 83–103.

Haverland M., Liefferink D. (2012), 'Member State interest articulation in the Commission phase. Institutional pre-conditions for influencing "Brussels"' in *Journal of European Public Policy*, 19(2): pp. 179–197.

Hayes-Renshaw F., Wallace H. (2006), *The Council of Ministers*, New York, Palgrave Macmillan.

Heard-Laureote K. (2010), *European Union Governance: Efficiency and Legitimacy in European Commission Committees*, Abingdon, Routledge.

Heisenberg D. (2005), 'The institution of "consensus" in the European Union: Formal versus informal decision-making in the Council' in *European Journal of Political Research*, 44(1): pp. 65–90.

Hendriks C. M. (2009), 'Policy design without democracy? Making democratic sense of transition management' in *Policy Sciences*, 42(4): pp. 341–368.

Héritier A. (2007), *Explaining Institutional Change in Europe*, Oxford, Oxford University Press.

Héritier A. (2013), 'Twenty years of legislative codecision in the European Union: experience and implications' in *Journal of European Public Policy*, 20(7): pp. 1074–1082.

Héritier A., Reh C. (2012), 'Codecision and Its Discontents: Intra-Organisational Politics and Institutional Reform in the European Parliament' in *West European Politics*, 35(5): pp. 1134–1157.

Hertin J., Berkhout F. (2003), 'Analysing Institutional Strategies for Environmental Policy Integration: The Case of EU Enterprise Policy' in *Journal of Environmental Policy & Planning*, 5(1): pp. 39–56.

Hildebrand P. (1993), 'The European Community's Environmental Policy, 1957 to "1992": From Incidental Measures to an International Regime?' in Judge D. (ed.), *A Green Dimension for the European Community. Political Issues and Processes*, Abingdon, Frank Cass, pp. 13–44.

Hillion C., Koutrakos P. (eds.) (2010), *Mixed Agreements Revisited. The EU and Its Member States in the World*, Oxford, Hart.

Hix S., Høyland B. (2011), *The Political System of the European Union. Third edition*, New York, Palgrave Macmillan.

Hix S., Noury A., Roland G. (2007), *Democratic Politics in the European Parliament*, Cambridge, Cambridge University Press.

HM Government (2011), *Transposition guidance: how to implement European Directives effectively*, London, Department for Business, Innovation and Skills.

Holzinger K., Knill C. (2005), 'Causes and conditions of cross-national policy convergence' in *Journal of European Public Policy*, 12(5): pp. 775–796.

Holzinger K., Knill C., Schäfer A. (2006), 'Rhetoric or Reality? "New Governance" in EU Environmental Policy' in *European Law Journal*, 12(3): pp. 403–420.

Holzinger K., Sommerer T. (2011), '"Race to the Bottom" or "Race to Brussels"? Environmental Competition in Europe' in *Journal of Common Market Studies*, 49(2): pp. 315–339.

Howlett M., Ramesh M. (2003), *Studying Public Policy. Policy Cycles and Policy Subsystems*, Don Mills, Oxford University Press.

Hulme M., Neufeldt H., Colyer H., Ritchie A. (2009), *Adaptation and Mitigation Strategies: Supporting European Climate Policy*, The Final Report from the ADAM Project, University of East Anglia, Tyndall Centre for Climate Change Research.

Hurka S. (2013), 'Changing the output: The logic of amendment success in the European Parliament's ENVI Committee' in *European Union Politics*, 14(2): pp. 273–296.

Institute for Responsible Technology (2015), *Health Risks*, http://www.responsibletechnology.org/health-risks (consulted March 2015).

International Centre for Trade and Sustainable Development (2014), *EU Environment Ministers Agree to National GMO Bans*, http://www.ictsd.org/bridges-news/bridges/news/eu-environment-ministers-agree-to-national-gmo-bans (consulted August 2014).

James C. (2013), *Global Status of Commercialized Biotech/GM Crops: 2013*, Brief 46, Ithaca, International Service for the Acquisition of Agri-biotech Applications.

Jänicke M. (1992), 'Conditions for Environmental Policy Success: An International Comparison' in *The Environmentalist*, 12(1): pp. 47–58.

Jänicke M., Weidner H. (eds.) (1997), *National Environmental Policies. A Comparative Study of Capacity-Building*, Berlin, Springer.

Jans J., Squintini L. (2009), 'Gold plating of European environmental measures?' in *Journal for European Enviromental & Planning Law*, 6(4): pp. 417–436.

Jans J., Vedder H. (2012), *European Environmental Law. After Lisbon*, Groningen, Europa Law Publishing.

Jehliaka P., Tickle A. (2004), 'Environmental Implications of Eastern Enlargement: The End of Progressive EU Environmental Policy?' in *Environmental Politics*, 13(1): pp. 77–95.

Jordan A. (1998), 'Step Change or Stasis? EC Environmental Policy after the Amsterdam Treaty' in *Journal of Environmental Politics*, 7(1): pp. 53–60.

Jordan A. (1999), 'The Implementation of EU Environmental Policy: A Policy Problem without a Political Solution?' in *Environment and Planning C*, 17(1): pp. 69–90.

Jordan A., van Asselt H., Berkhout F., Huitema D., Rayner T. (2012), 'Understanding the Paradoxes of Multilevel Governing: Climate Change Policy in the European Union' in *Global Environmental Politics*, 12(2): pp. 43–66.

Jordan A., Bauer M., Green-Pedersen C. (2013), 'Policy dismantling' in *Journal of European Public Policy*, 20(5): pp. 795–805.

Jordan A., Benson D., Wurzel R., Zito A. (2013), 'Governing with multiple policy instruments?' in Jordan A., Adelle C. (eds.), *Environmental Policy in the EU: Actors, Institutions and Processes. Third edition*, Abingdon, Routledge, pp. 309–325.

Jordan A., Brouwer R., Noble E. (1999), 'Innovative and responsive? A longitudinal analysis of the speed of EU environmental policy-making 1967–1997' in *Journal of European Public Policy*, 6(3): pp. 376–398.

Jordan A., Lenschow A. (2010), 'Environmental Policy Integration: a State of the Art Review' in *Environmental Policy and Governance*, 20(3): pp. 147–158.

Jordan A., Liefferink D. (2004), 'Europeanization and convergence. Comparative conclusions' in Jordan A., Liefferink D. (eds.), *Environmental Policy in Europe*, London, Routledge, pp. 224–245.

Jordan A., Wurzel R., Zito A. (eds.) (2003), *'New' Instruments of Environmental Governance? National Experiences and Prospects*, London, Frank Cass.

Jørgensen K., Oberthür S., Shahin J. (2011), 'Introduction: Assessing the EU's Performance in International Institutions – Conceptual Framework and Core Findings' in *Journal of European Integration*, 33(6): pp. 599–620.

Jupille J., Caporaso J. (1998), 'States, Agency, and Rules: The European Union in Global Environmental Politics' in Rhodes C. (ed.), *The European Union in the World Community*, London, Lynne Rienner Publishers, pp. 213–229.

Kaeding M. (2004), 'Rapporteurship Allocation in the European Parliament. Information or Distribution?' in *European Union Politics*, 5(3): pp. 353–371.

Kaeding M. (2006), 'Determinants of Transposition Delay in the European Union' in *Journal of Public Policy*, 26(3): pp. 229–253.

Kassim H., Peterson J., Bauer M., Connolly S., Dehousse R., Hooghe L., Thompson A. (2013), *The European Commission of the Twenty-First Century*, Oxford, Oxford University Press.

Kassiola J. (1990), *The Death of Industrial Civilization*, Albany, State University of New York Press.

Kelemen D. (2010), 'Globalizing European Union environmental policy' in *Journal of European Public Policy*, 17(3): pp. 335–349.

Kelemen D., Vogel D. (2010), 'Trading Places: The Role of the United States and the European Union in International Environmental Politics' in *Comparative Political Studies*, 43(4): pp. 427–456.

Keukeleire S., Delreux T. (2014), *The Foreign Policy of the European Union. Second edition*, Basingstoke, Palgrave.

Kirsop B. (2002), 'The Cartagena (Biosafety) Protocol' in *Journal of Commercial Biotechnology*, 8(3): pp. 214–218.

Klümper W., Qaim M. (2014), 'A Meta-Analysis of the Impacts of Genetically Modified Crops' in *PLoS ONE*, 9(11): pp. 1–7.

Klüver H. (2011), 'The contextual nature of lobbying: Explaining lobbying success in the European Union' in *European Union Politics*, 12(4): pp. 483–506.

Knill C. (2006), 'Implementation' in Richardson J. (ed.), *European Union. Power and policy-making*, New York, Routledge, pp. 351–375.

Knill C., Lehmkuhl D. (2002), 'The national impact of European Union regulatory policy: Three Europeanization mechanisms' in *European Journal of Political Research*, 41(2): pp. 255–280.

Knill C., Lenschow A. (2000), 'Do new brooms really sweep cleaner? Implementation of new instruments in EU environmental policy' in Knill C., Lenschow A. (eds.), *Implementing EU Environmental Policy. New Directions and Old Problems*, Manchester, Manchester University Press, pp. 251–286.

Knill C., Liefferink D. (2007), *Environmental Politics in the European Union*, Manchester, Manchester University Press.

Knill C., Liefferink D. (2012), 'The establishment of EU environmental policy' in Jordan A., Adelle C. (eds.), *Environmental Policy in the EU: Actors, Institutions and Processes. Third edition*, Abingdon, Routledge, pp. 13–31.

Knill C., Tosun J. (2009), 'Hierarchy, networks, or markets: how does the EU shape environmental policy adoptions within and beyond its borders?' in *Journal of European Public Policy*, 16(6): pp. 873–894.

Kollman K. (1998), *Outside lobbying: Public opinion and interest group strategies*, Princeton, Princeton University Press.

Koppen I. (1993), 'The Role of the European Court of Justice' in Liefferink J., Lowe P., Mol A. (eds.), *European Integration and Environmental Policy*, Chichester, John Wiley & Sons, pp. 126–149.

Kramer J. (2004), 'EU Enlargement and the Environment: Six Challenges' in *Environmental Politics*, 13(1): pp. 290–311.

Krämer L. (2012a), *EU Environmental Law*, London, Sweet & Maxwell.

Krämer L. (2012b), 'The European Court of Justice' in Jordan A., Adelle C. (eds.), *Environmental Policy in the EU: Actors, Institutions and Processes. Third edition*, Abingdon, Routledge, pp. 113–131.

Kuijper P., Wouters J., Hoffmeister F., De Baere G., Ramopoulos T. (2013), *The Law of EU External Relations. Cases, Materials, and Commentary on the EU as an International Legal Actor*, Oxford, Oxford University Press.

Kulosevi K. (2012), 'Climate change in EU external relations: please follow my example (or I might force you to)' in Morgera E. (ed.), *The External Environmental Policy of the European Union. EU and International Law Perspectives*, Cambridge, Cambridge University Press, pp. 115–148.

Kulovesi K., Morgera E., Muñoz M. (2011), 'Environmental integration and multi-faceted international dimensions of EU law: Unpacking the EU's 2009 climate and energy package' in *Common Market Law Review*, 48: pp. 829–891.

Laïdi Z. (2010), 'Is Europe a Risk Averse Actor?' in *European Foreign Affairs Review*, 15: pp. 411–426.

Larsson T., Murk J. (2007), 'The Commission's relations with expert advisory groups' in Christiansen T., Larsson T. (eds.), *The Role of Committees in the Policy-Process of the European Union*, Cheltenham, Edward Elgar, pp. 64–95.

Lavenex S., Schimmelfennig F. (2009a), 'Special issue: European Union external governance' in *Journal of European Public Policy*, 16(6): pp. 791–949.

Lavenex S., Schimmelfennig F. (2009b), 'EU rules beyond EU borders: theorizing external governance in European politics' in *Journal of European Public Policy*, 16(6): pp. 791–812.

Lee B., Preston F., Kooroshy J., Bailey R., Lahn G. (2012), *Resource Futures*, London, Chatham House.

Lee M. (2014), *EU Environmental Law, Governance and Decision-Making. Second edition*, Portland, Hart Publishing.

Lelieveldt H., Princen S. (2011), *The Politics of the European Union*, New York, Cambridge University Press.

Lempert R., Popper S., Min E., Dewar J. (2009), *Shaping Tomorrow Today. Near-Term Steps Towards Long-Term Goals*, Santa Monica, Arlington, RAND.

Lempp J., Altenschmidt J. (2008), 'The Prevention of Deadlock through Informal Processes of "Supranationalization": The Case of Coreper' in *Journal of European Integration*, 30(4): pp. 511–526.

Lenschow A. (2002), 'New Regulatory Approaches in "Greening" EU Policies' in *European Law Journal*, 8(1): pp. 19–37.

Lenschow A. (2005), 'Environmental Policy. Contending Dynamics of Policy Change' in Wallace H., Wallace W., Pollack M. (eds.), *Policy-Making in the European Union*, New York, Oxford University Press, pp. 305–327.

Lenschow A. (2010), 'Environmental Policy: Contending Dynamics of Policy Change' in Wallace H., Pollack M., Young A. (eds.), *Policy-Making in the European Union. Sixth edition*, New York, Oxford University Press, pp. 307–330.

Lenschow A., Liefferink D., Veenman S. (2005), 'When the birds sing. A framework for analysing domestic factors behind policy convergence' in *Journal of European Public Policy*, 12(5): pp. 797–816.

Lewis J. (2005), 'The Janus Face of Brussels: Socialization and Everyday Decision Making in the European Union' in *International Organization*, 59(4): pp. 937–971.

Lidskog R., Sundqvist G. (2002), 'The Role of Science in Environmental Regimes: The Case of LRTAP' in *European Journal of International Relations*, 8(1): pp. 77–101.

Lightfoot S. (2012), 'The EU in the World Summit on Sustainable Development' in Wouters J., Bruyninckx H., Basu S., Schunz S. (eds.), *The European Union and Multilateral Governance. Assessing EU Participation in United Nations Human Rights and Environmental Fora*, Basingstoke, Palgrave Macmillan, pp. 232–250.

Lightfoot S., Burchell J. (2005), 'The European Union and the World Summit on Sustainable Development: Normative Power Europe in Action?' in *Journal of Common Market Studies*, 43(1): pp. 75–95.

Locwin B. (2014), *Should GMO drugs be perceived differently than GMO food?*, http://geneticliteracyproject.org/2014/08/should-gmo-drugs-be-perceived-differently-than-gmo-food/ (consulted March 2015).

Long T., Lörinczi L. (2009), 'NGOs as Gatekeepers: A Green Vision' in Coen D., Richardson J. (eds.), *Lobbying the European Union: Institutions, Actors, and Issues*, New York, Oxford University Press, pp. 169–185.

Lowery D. (2013), 'Lobbying influence: Meaning, measurement and missing' in *Interest Groups & Advocacy*, 2(1): pp. 1–26.

Majone G. (1994), 'The rise of the regulatory state in Europe' in *West European Politics*, 17(3): pp. 77–101.

Mak G. (2004), *In Europa. Reizen door de twintigste eeuw.*, Amsterdam, Atlas.

Martens M. (2008), 'Administrative Integration through the Back Door? The Role and Influence of the European Commission in Transgovernmental Networks within the Environmental Policy Field' in *Journal of European Integration*, 30(5): pp. 635–651.

Martens M. (2010), 'Voice or Loyalty? The Evolution of the European Environment Agency (EEA)' in *Journal of Common Market Studies*, 48(4): pp. 881–901.

Martens M. (2012), 'Executive power in the making: the establishment of the European Chemicals Agency (ECHA)' in Busuioc M., Groenleer M., Trondal J. (eds.), *The Agency Phenomenon in the European Union. Emergence, Institutionalisation and Everyday Decision-making*, Manchester, Manchester University Press, pp. 42–62.

Mastenbroek E. (2005), 'EU compliance: still a "black hole"?' in *Journal of European Public Policy*, 12(6): pp. 1103–1120.

Mazey S., Richardson J. (2006), 'Interest groups and EU policy-making. Organisational logic and venue shopping' in Richardson J. (ed.), *European Union. Power and Policy-making*, New York, Routledge, pp. 247–268.

McCormick J. (2001), *Environmental Policy in the European Union*, New York, Palgrave.

McElroy G. (2006), 'Committee Representation in the European Parliament' in *European Union Politics*, 7(5): pp. 5–29.

Meadowcroft J. (2007), 'National Sustainable Development Strategies: Features, Challenges and Reflexivity' in *European Environment*, 17: pp. 152–163.

Medarova-Bergstrom K., Volkery A., Schiellerup P., Withana S., Baldock D. (2011), *Strategies and Instruments for Climate Proofing the EU Budget*, Brussels, Institute for European Environmental Policy.

Meunier S. (2005), *Trading Voices. The European Union in International Commercial Negotiations*, Princeton, Princeton University Press.

Meyer K. (2005), 'Air' in Scheuer S. (ed.) *EU Environmental Policy Handbook. A Critical Analysis of EU Environmental Legislation*, Brussels, European Environmental Bureau, pp. 46–76.

Mol A. (2006), 'Environment and Modernity in Transitional China: Frontiers of Ecological Modernization' in *Development and Change*, 37(1): pp. 29–56.

Mol A., Spaargaren G. (2000), 'Ecological Modernization Theory in Debate: A Review' in *Environmental Politics*, 9(1): pp. 17–49.

Mol A., Buttel F., Spaargaren G. (2005), *Governing Environmental Flows*, Cambridge, MIT Press.

Momtaz D. (1996), 'The United Nations and the protection of the environment: from Stockholm to Rio de Janeiro' in *Political Geography*, 15(3/4): pp. 261–271.

Moreau D. (2014), 'Ecological Risk Analysis and Genetically Modified Salmon: Management in the Face of Uncertainty' in *Annual Review of Animal Biosciences*, 2: pp. 515–533.

Morris S., Spilane C. (2012), 'EU GM Crop Regulation: A Road to Resolution or a Regulatory Roundabout?' in *European Journal of Risk Regulation*, 4: pp. 359–369.

Mupotola M. (2005), 'Trade Policy' in Were Omamo S., von Grebmer K. (eds.), *Biotechnology, Agriculture, and Food Security in Southern Africa*, Washington, DC, International Food Policy Research Institute, pp. 187–198.

Najam A. (2011), 'The View from the South: Developing Countries in Global Environmental Politics' in Axelrod R., VanDeveer S., Downie D. (eds.), *The Global Environment: Institutions, Law, and Policy*, Washington, CQ Press, pp. 239–258.

Neuhold C., Settembri P. (2007), 'The role of the European Parliament committees in the EU policy-making process' in Christiansen T., Larsson T. (eds.), *The Role of Committees in the Policy-Process of the European Union*, Cheltenham, Edward Elgar, pp. 152–181.

Niederhafner S. (2013), *The Governance Modes of the Tokyo Metropolitan Government Emissions Trading System*, Hitotsubashi Invited Fellow Program Discussion Paper 26, Seoul, Seoul National University.

Niemann A., Mak J. (2010), '(How) do norms guide Presidency behaviour in EU negotiations?' in *Journal of European Public Policy*, 17(5): pp. 727–742.

Novak S. (2013), 'The Silence of Ministers: Consensus and Blame Avoidance in the Council of the European Union' in *Journal of Common Market Studies*, 51(6): pp. 1091–1107.

Nugent N. (2010), *The Government and Politics of the European Union*, Basingstoke, Palgrave Macmillan.

Oberthür S. (2009), 'The role of the EU in global environmental and climate governance' in Telò M. (ed.), *The European Union and Global Governance*, London, Routledge, pp. 192–209.

Oberthür S. (2011), 'The European Union's Performance in the International Climate Change Regime' in *Journal of European Integration*, 33(6): pp. 667–682.

Oberthür S., Dupont C. (2011), 'The Council, the European Council and international climate policy. From symbolic leadership to leadership by example' in Wurzel R., Connelly J. (eds.), *The European Union as a Leader in International Climate Change Politics*, Abingdon, Routledge, pp. 74–91.

Oberthür S., Gehring T. (2006), 'Institutional Interaction in Global Environmental Governance: The Case of the Cartagena Protocol and the World Trade Organization' in *Global Environmental Politics*, 6(2): pp. 1–31.

Oberthür S., Pallemaerts M. (2010), 'The EU's Internal and External Climate Policies: an Historical Overview' in Oberthür S., Pallemaerts M. (eds.), *The New Climate Politics of the European Union*, Brussels, VUB Press, pp. 27–63.

Oberthür S., Rabitz F. (2014), 'On the EU's performance and leadership in global environmental governance: the case of the Nagoya Protocol' in *Journal of European Public Policy*, 21(1): pp. 39–57.

Oberthür S., Roche Kelly C. (2008), 'EU Leadership in International Climate Policy: Achievements and Challenges' in *The International Spectator*, 45(3): pp. 35–50.

Olivier J., Janssens-Maenhout G., Muntean M., Peters, J. (2013), *Trends in Global CO2 Emissions: 2013 Report*, *The Hague*, PBL Netherlands Environmental Assessment Agency/EU Joint Research Centre.

Olson M. (1965), *The Logic of Collective Action. Public Goods and the Theory of Groups*, Cambridge, Harvard University Press.

O'Riordan T., Cameron J. (eds.) (1994), *Interpreting the Precautionary Principle*, London, Earthscan.

Palmer D. (2010), *U.S. farmers urge sanctions against EU's GM crop ban*, http://in.reuters.com/article/2010/07/27/idINIndia-50441920100727 (consulted March 2015).

Parker C., Karlsson C. (2010), 'Climate Change and the European Union's Leadership Moment: An Inconvenient Truth?' in *Journal of Common Market Studies*, 48(4): pp. 923–943.

Pavese C., Torney D. (2012), 'The contribution of the European Union to global climate change governance: explaining the conditions for EU actorness' in *Revista Brasileira de Política Internacional*, 55: pp. 125–143.

Pearsall D. (2013), 'GM crop co-existence. A question of choice, not prejudice' in *GM Crops & Food: Biotechnology in Agriculture and the Food Chain*, 4(3): pp. 143–150.

Persson T. (2007), 'Democratizing European Chemicals Policy: Do Consultations Favour Civil Society Participation?' in *Journal of Civil Society*, 3(3): pp. 223–238.

Poli S. (2013), 'Member States' Long and Winding Road to Partial Regulatory Autonomy in Cultivating Genetically Modified Crops in the EU' in *European Journal of Risk Regulation*, 2013(2): pp. 143–158.

Pollack M. (1997), 'Representing diffuse interests in EC policy-making' in *Journal of European Public Policy*, 4(4): pp. 572–590.

Pollack M., Shaffer G. (2010), 'Biotechnology Policy: Between National Fears and Global Disciplines' in Wallace H., Pollack M., Young A. (eds.), *Policy-Making in the European Union*, New York, Oxford University Press, pp. 331–355.

Pollitt C., Bouckaert G. (2011), *Public Management Reform. A Comparative Analysis New Public Management, Governance, and the Neo-Weberian State*, Oxford, Oxford University Press.

Poppelaars C. (2009), *Steering a Course between Friends and Foes. Why Bureaucrats Interact with Interest Groups*, Delft, Uitgeverij Eburon.

Porter M., van der Linde C. (1995), 'Green and Competitive. Ending the stalemate' in *Harvard Business Review*: pp. 120–134.

Puetter U. (2014), *The European Council and the Council. New Intergovernmentalism and Institutional Change*, Oxford, Oxford University Press.

Quittkat C. (2011), 'The European Commission's Online Consultations: A Success Story?' in *Journal of Common Market Studies*, 49(3): pp. 653–674.

Quittkat C., Finke B. (2008), 'The EU Commission consultation regime' in Kohler-Koch B., De Bièvre D., Maloney W. (eds.), *Opening EU-Governance to Civil Society: Gains and Challenges*, Mannheim, CONNEX Report Series No 5, pp. 183–222.

Quittkat C., Kotzian P. (2011), 'Lobbying via Consultation – Territorial and Functional Interests in the Commission's Consultation Regime' in *Journal of European Integration*, 33(4): pp. 401–418.

Radaelli C., Meuwese A. (2010), 'Hard Questions, Hard Solutions: Proceduralisation through Impact Assessment in the EU' in *West European Politics*, 33(1): pp. 136–153.

Randour F., Janssens C., Delreux T. (2014), 'The Cultivation of Genetically Modified Organisms in the European Union: A Necessary Trade-Off?' in *Journal of Common Market Studies*, 52(6): pp. 1307–1323.

Rasmussen A. (2010), 'Early conclusion in bicameral bargaining: Evidence from the co-decision legislative procedure of the European Union' in *European Union Politics*, 12(1): pp. 41–64.

Rasmussen A., Reh C. (2013), 'The consequences of concluding codecision early: trilogues and intra-institutional bargaining success' in *Journal of European Public Policy*, 20(7): pp. 1006–1024.

Rasmussen M. (2012), 'Is the European Parliament still a policy champion for environmental interests?' in *Interest Groups & Advocacy*, 1(2): pp. 239–259.

Rasmussen M. (2015), 'The Battle for Influence: The Politics of Business Lobbying in the European Parliament' in *Journal of Common Market Studies*, 53(2): pp. 365–382.

Reh C., Héritier A., Bressanelli E., Koop C. (2013), 'The Informal Politics of Legislation: Explaining Secluded Decision Making in the European Union' in *Comparative Political Studies*, 46(9): pp. 1112–1142.

Rehbinder E., Steward R. (1985), *Environmental Protection Policy. Volume 2, Integration Through Law: Europe and the American federal experience*, Florence, European University Institute.

Reuters (2013), *EU court annuls approval of BASF's Amflora GMO potato*, http://www.reuters.com/article/2013/12/13/eu-gmo-potato-idUSL6N0JS1TH20131213 (consulted August 2014).

Rhinard M., Kaeding M. (2006), 'The International Bargaining Power of the European Union in "Mixed" Competence Negotiations: The Case of the 2000 Cartagena Protocol on Biosafety' in *Journal of Common Market Studies*, 44(5): pp. 1023–1050.

Rigby D. (2004), *GM food, risk, regulation and the EU-US trade dispute*, School of Economic Studies Discussion Paper Series No 0410, Manchester, The University of Manchester.

Sanchez Salgado R. (2014), 'Rebalancing EU Interest Representation? Associative Democracy and EU Funding of Civil Society Organizations' in *Journal of Common Market Studies*, 52(2): pp. 337–353.

Savaresi A. (2012), 'EU external action on forests: FLEGT and the development of international law' in Morgera E. (ed.), *The External Environmental Policy of the European Union. EU and International Law Perspectives*, Cambridge, Cambridge University Press, pp. 149–173.

Sbragia A. (1998), 'Institution-Building from below and above: The European Community in Global Environmental Politics' in Sandholz W., Stone Sweet A. (eds.), *European Integration and Supranational Governance*, New York, Oxford University Press, pp. 283–303.

Sbragia A., Damro C. (1999), 'The changing role of the European Union in international politics: institution building and the politics of climate change' in *Environment and Planning C: Government and Policy*, 17(1): pp. 53–68.

Schalk J., Torenvlied R., Weesie J., Stokman F. (2007), 'The Power of the Presidency in EU Council Decision-making' in *European Union Politics*, 8(2): pp. 229–250.

Scheffran J., Brzoska M., Brauch H., Link P., Schilling J. (eds.) (2012), *Climate Change, Human Security and Violent Conflict. Challenges for Societal Stability*, Heidelberg, Springer.

Scheipers S., Sicurelli D. (2007), 'Normative Power Europe: A Credible Utopia?' in *Journal of Common Market Studies*, 45(2): pp. 435–457.

Schiffino N., Varone F. (2005), 'La régulation politique des OGM' in *Courrier hebdomadaire du CRISP*, 35(1900): pp. 5–34.

Schmidt S. (2000), 'Only an Agenda Setter? The European Commission's Power over the Council of Ministers' in *European Union Politics*, 1(1): pp. 37–61.

Schoenefeld J. (2014a), *The Politics of the Rise of DG Climate Action*, http://environmentaleurope.ideasoneurope.eu/2014/02/24/the-politics-of-the-rise-of-dg-climate-action (consulted November 2014).

Schoenefeld J. (2014b), *Does the European Commission's Climate Change Department Make a Difference?*, http://environmentaleurope.ideasoneurope.eu/2014/03/03/does-the-european-commission's-climate-change-department-make-a-difference (consulted July 2014).

Schön-Quinlivan E. (2012), 'The European Commission' in Jordan A., Adelle C. (eds.), *Environmental Policy in the EU: Actors, Institutions and Processes. Third edition*, Abingdon, Routledge, pp. 95–112.

Schout A., Vanhoonacker S. (2006), 'Evaluating Presidencies of the Council of the EU: Revisiting Nice' in *Journal of Common Market Studies*, 44(5): pp. 1051–1077.

Schreurs M. (2004), *Environmental Politics in Japan, Germany and the United States*, Cambridge, Cambridge University Press.

Schreurs M., Tiberghien Y. (2007), 'Multi-Level Reinforcement: Explaining European Union Leadership in Climate Change Mitigation' in *Global Environmental Politics*, 7(4): pp. 19–46.

Schulze K., Tosun J. (2013), 'External dimensions of European environmental policy: An analysis of environmental treaty ratification by third states' in *European Journal of Political Research*, 52(5): pp. 581–607.

Schunz S. (2014), *European Union Foreign Policy and and the Global Climate Regime*, Brussels, Peter Lang.

Scott J., Rajamani L. (2013), 'Contingent Unilateralism – International Aviation in the European Emissions Trading Scheme' in Van Vooren B., Blockmans S., Wouters J. (eds.), *The EU's Role in Global Governance: The Legal Dimension*, Oxford, Oxford University Press, pp. 209–223.

Shackleton M. (2006), 'The European Parliament' in Peterson J., Shackleton M. (eds.), *The Institutions of the European Union*, New York, Oxford University Press, pp. 104–124.

Shah A. (2010), *Causes of Hunger are Related to Poverty*, http://www.globalissues.org/article/7/causes-of-hunger-are-related-to-poverty (consulted March 2015).

Skjærseth J., Bang G., Schreurs M. (2013), 'Explaining Growing Climate Policy Differences Between the European Union and the United States' in *Global Environmental Politics*, 13(4): pp. 61–80.

Skogstad G. (2011), 'Contested Accountability Claims and GMO Regulation in the European Union' in *Journal of Common Market Studies*, 49(4): pp. 895–915.

Smeets S., Vennix J. (2014), 'How to make the most of your time in the Chair: EU presidencies and the management of Council debates' in *Journal of European Public Policy*, 21(10): pp. 1435–1451.

Smith A. (2014), 'How the European Commission's Policies Are Made: Problematization, Instrumentation and Legitimation' in *Journal of European Integration*, 36(1): pp. 55–72.

Smith M. (2008), 'All Access Points are Not Created Equal: Explaining the Fate of Diffuse Interests in the EU' in *British Journal of Politics and International Relations*, 10(1): pp. 64–83.

Soroos M. (2011), 'Global Institutions and the Environment: An Evolutionary Perspective' in Axelrod R., VanDeveer S., Downie D. (eds.), *The Global Environment: Institutions, Law, and Policy*, Washington, CQ Press, pp. 24–47.

Spangenberg J. (2010), 'A European Methodology for Sustainable Development Strategy Reviews' in *Environmental Policy and Governance*, 20: pp. 123–134.

Spence D. (2006), 'The Directorates General and the services: structures, functions and procedures' in Spence D., Edwards G. (eds.), *The European Commission*, London, John Harper Publishing, pp. 128–155.

Spendzharova A., Versluis E. (2013), 'Issue salience in the European policy process: what impact on transposition?' in *Journal of European Public Policy*, 20(10): pp. 1499–1516.

Sprinz D. (2009), 'Long-Term Environmental Policy: Definition, Knowledge, Future Research' in *Global Environmental Politics*, 9(3): pp. 1–8.

Sprinz D. (2012), 'Long-Term Environmental Policy: Challenges for Research' in *The Journal of Environment Development*, 21(1): pp. 67–70.

Steunenberg B., Kaeding M. (2009), '"As time goes by": Explaining the transposition of maritime directives' in *European Journal of Political Research*, 48(3): pp. 432–454.

Steunenberg B., Rhinard M. (2010), 'The transposition of European law in EU member states: between process and politics' in *European Political Science Review*, 2(3): pp. 495–520.

Steunenberg B., Toshkov D. (2009), 'Comparing transposition in the 27 member states of the EU: the impact of discretion and legal fit' in *Journal of European Public Policy*, 16(7): pp. 951–970.

Steurer R., Hametner M. (2013), 'Objectives and Indicators in Sustainable Development Strategies: Similarities and Variances across Europe' in *Sustainable Development*, 21(4): pp. 224–241.

Tallberg J. (2003), 'The agenda-shaping powers of the EU Council Presidency' in *Journal of European Public Policy*, 10(1): pp. 1–19.

Tallberg J. (2004), 'The Power of the Presidency: Brokerage, Efficiency and Distribution in EU Negotiations' in *Journal of Common Market Studies*, 42(5): pp. 999–1022.

Tallberg J. (2008), 'Bargaining Power in the European Council' in *Journal of Common Market Studies*, 46(3): pp. 685–708.

Tanasescu I. (2006), 'The Political Process Leading to the Development of the EU Sustainable Development Strategy' in Pallemaerts M., Azmanova A. (eds.), *The European Union and Sustainable Development*, Brussels, VUBPress, pp. 53–77.

Thomson J. (2012), 'A Member State's perspective on the post-Lisbon framework for the EU's representation in multilateral environmental negotiations' in Morgera E. (ed.), *The External Environmental Policy of the European Union. EU and International Law Perspectives*, Cambridge, Cambridge University Press, pp. 96–112.

Thomson R. (2009), 'Same effects in different worlds: the transposition of EU directives' in *Journal of European Public Policy*, 16(1): pp. 1–18.

Thomson R., Hosli M. (2006), 'Who Has Power in the EU? The Commission, Council and Parliament in Legislative Decision-making' in *Journal of Common Market Studies*, 44(2): pp. 391–417.

Tiberghien Y. (2009), 'Competitive Governance and the Quest for Legitimacy in the EU: The Battle over the Regulation of GMOs since the mid-1990s' in *Journal of European Integration*, 31(3): pp. 389–407.

Tolentino E. (2013), 'Ramsar Convention. Cultural Values of Wetlands' in *Environmental Policy and Law*, 43(2): pp. 87–90.

Torney D. (2014a), 'Challenges of European Union Climate Diplomacy: The Case of China' in *European Foreign Affairs Review*, 19: pp. 119–134.

Torney D. (2014b), 'External Perceptions and EU Foreign Policy Effectiveness: The Case of Climate Change' in *Journal of Common Market Studies*, 52(6): pp. 1358–1373.

Torney D. (2015), 'Bilateral Climate Cooperation: The EU's Relations with China and India' in *Global Environmental Politics*, 15(1): pp. 105–122.

Toshkov D. (2008), 'Embracing European Law. Compliance with EU Directives in Central and Eastern Europe' in *European Union Politics*, 9(3): pp. 379–402.

Trondal J. (2001), 'Is there any social constructivist-institutionalist divide? Unpacking social mechanisms affecting representational roles among EU decision-makers' in *Journal of European Public Policy*, 8(1): pp. 1–23.

Trondal J. (2010), *An Emergent European Executive Order*, New York, Oxford University Press.

Trondal J., Veggeland F. (2003), 'Access, voice and loyalty: the representation of domestic civil servants in the EU committees' in *Journal of European Public Policy*, 10(1): pp. 59–77.

Tsebelis G. (1994), 'The Power of the European Parliament as a Conditional Agenda Setter' in *American Political Science Review*, 88(1): pp. 128–142.

United Nations Conference on the Human Environment (1972), *Declaration of the United Nations Conference on the Human Environment*, http://www.unep.org/Documents.multilingual/Default.asp?DocumentID=97&ArticleID=1503 (consulted May 2015).

United Nations General Assembly Special Session, *Programme for the further implementation of Agenda 21*, New York, United Nations Department of Economic and Social Affairs.

Van de Velde C. (2014), 'Environmental and consumer protection' in Bussière E., Dujardin V., Dumoulin M., Ludlow P., Brouwer J., Tilly P. (eds.), *The European Commission 1973–86. History and Memories of an Institution*, Luxembourg, Publications Office of the European Union, pp. 385–391.

Van den Brande K. (2012), 'The European Union in the Commission on Sustainable Development' in Wouters J., Bruyninckx H., Basu S., Schunz S. (eds.), *The European Union and Multilateral Governance: Assessing EU Participation in United Nations Human Rights and Environmental Fora*, Basingstoke, Palgrave Macmillan, pp. 171–190.

Van der Wee H. (1986), *Prosperity and Upheaval. The World Economy 1945–1980*, Berkeley, University of California Press.

Van Deth J., Maloney W. (2011), *New 'Participatory' Dimensions in Civil Society: Professionalization and Individualized Collective Action*, Abingdon, Routledge.

van Schaik L. (2012), *The EU and the progressive alliance negotiating in Durban: saving the climate?*, Climate and Development Knowledge Network working paper 354, London.

van Schaik L. (2013), *EU Effectiveness and Unity in Multilateral Negotiations. More than the Sum of its Parts?*, Basingstoke, Palgrave Macmillan.

van Schaik L., Schunz S. (2012), 'Explaining EU Activism and Impact in Global Climate Politics: Is the Union a Norm- or Interest-Driven Actor?' in *Journal of Common Market Studies*, 50(1): pp. 169–186.

Van Tatenhove J., Mak J., Liefferink D. (2006), 'The Inter-play between Formal and Informal Practices' in *Perspectives on European Politics and Society*, 7(1): pp. 8–24.

Varela J. (2012), 'The New Strategy on Coexistence in the 2010 European Commission Recommendation' in *European Journal of Risk Regulation*, 4: pp. 353–358.

Vedder H. (2010), 'The Treaty of Lisbon and European Environmental Law and Policy' in *Journal of Environmental Law*, 22(2): pp. 285–299.

Versluis E., van Keulen M., Stephenson P. (2011), *Analyzing the European Union Policy Process*, Houndmills, Palgrave MacMillan.

Vig N., Faure M. (eds.) (2004), *Green Giants? Environmental Policies of the United States and the European Union*, Cambridge, The MIT Press.

Vogler J. (2005), 'The European contribution to global environmental governance' in *International Affairs*, 81(4): pp. 835–850.

Vogler J. (2011), 'The European Union as a global environmental policy actor' in Wurzel R., Connelly J. (eds.), *The European Union as a Leader in International Climate Change Politics*, Abingdon, Routledge, pp. 21–37.

Vogler J., Stephan H. (2007), 'The European Union in global environmental governance: leadership in the making?' in *International Environmental Agreements*, 7(4): pp. 389–413.

von Homeyer I. (2009), 'The Evolution of EU Environmental Governance' in Scott J. (ed.) *Environmental Protection: European Law and Governance*, Oxford, Oxford University Press, pp. 1–26.

Voss J., Smith A., Grin J. (2009), 'Designing long-term policy: rethinking transition management' in *Policy Sciences*, 42(4): pp. 275–302.

Votewatch (2014), *VoteWatch Europe*, http://www.votewatch.eu (consulted July 2014).

Warleigh A. (2000), 'The hustle: citizenship practice, NGOs and "policy coalitions" in the European Union – the cases of Auto Oil, drinking water and unit pricing' in *Journal of European Public Policy*, 7(2): pp. 229–243.

Warntjen A. (2008), 'The Council Presidency. Power Broker or Burden? An Empirical Analysis' in *European Union Politics*, 9(3): pp. 315–338.

Webster, R. (2002), *Greening Europe together: the collaborative strategies of the European environmental NGOs*. Paper presented at the Paper prepared the Political Studies Association's 52nd Annual Conference, Making Politics Count, University of Aberdeen.

Weale A., Pridham G., Cini M., Konstadakopulos D., Porter M., Flynn B. (2000), *Environmental Governance in Europe*, New York, Oxford University Press.

Weidner H., Jänicke M. (2002), *Capacity Building in National Environmental Policy. A Comparative Study of 17 Countries*, Berlin, Springer.

Weimer M. (2010), 'Applying precaution in EU Authorisation of Genetically Modified Products – Challenges and Suggestions for Reform' in *European Law Journal*, 16(5): pp. 624–657.

Wessel R. (2011), 'The EU as a party to international agreements: shared competences, mixed responsibilities' in Dashwood A., Maresceau M. (eds.), *Law and Practice of EU External Relations. Salient Features of a Changing Landscape*, Cambridge, Cambridge University Press, pp. 152–187.

Wettestad J. (2002), 'The Convention on Long-Range Transboundary Air Pollution (CLRTAP)' in Miles E., Underdal A., Andresen S., Wettestad

J., Skjærseth J., Carlin E. (eds.), *Environmental Regime Effectiveness. Confronting Theory with Evidence*, Cambridge, MIT Press, pp. 197–221.

Wettestad J. (2014), 'Rescuing EU Emissions Trading: Mission impossible?' in *Global Environmental Politics*, 14(2): pp. 64–81.

Wilkinson D. (1992), 'Maastricht and the environment: the implications for the EC's environment policy of the Treaty on the European Union' in *Journal of Environmental Law*, 4(2): pp. 221–239.

Winham G. (2009), 'The GMO Panel: Applications of WTO Law to Trade in Agricultural Biotech Products' in *Journal of European Integration*, 31(3): pp. 409–429.

Wonka A., Rittberger B. (2010), 'Credibility, Complexity and Uncertainty: Explaining the Institutional Independence of 29 EU Agencies' in *West European Politics*, 33(4): pp. 730–752.

Woolcock S. (2012), *European Union Economic Diplomacy. The Role of the EU in External Economic Relations*, Surrey, Ashgate.

World Commission on Environment and Development (1987), *Our Common Future*, Oxford, Oxford University Press.

Wright S., Fritsch O. (2011), 'Operationalising active involvement in the EU Water Framework Directive: Why, when and how?' in *Ecological Economics*, 70: pp. 2268–2274.

Wurzel R. (2012), 'Member states and the Council' in Jordan A., Adelle C. (eds.), *Environmental Policy in the EU: Actors, Institutions and Processes. Third edition*, Abingdon, Routledge, pp. 75–94.

Wurzel R., Connelly J. (eds.) (2011), *The European Union as a Leader in International Climate Change Politics*, Abingdon, Routledge.

Wurzel R., Zito A., Jordan A. (2013), *Environmental Governance in Europe. A Comparative Analysis of New Environmental Policy Instruments*, Cheltenham, Edward Elgar.

Ydersbond I. (2014), 'Multilevel "venue shopping": The case of EU's Renewables Directive' in *Interest Groups & Advocacy*, 3(1): pp. 30–58.

Yordanova N. (2009), 'The Rationale behind Committee Assignment in the European Parliament. Distributive, Informational and Partisan Perspectives' in *European Union Politics*, 10(2): pp. 253–280.

Yordanova N. (2013), *Organising the European Parliament. The Role of Committees and their Legislative Influence*, Colchester, ECPR Press.

Yoshinaka A., McElroy G., Bowler S. (2010), 'The Appointment of Rapporteurs in the European Parliament' in *Legislative Studies Quarterly*, 35(4): pp. 457–486.

Zito A. (1999), 'Task Expansion: A Theoretical Overview' in *Environment and Planning C*, 17(1): pp. 19–35.

Zito A. (2005), 'The European Union as an Environmental Leader in a Global Environment' in *Globalizations*, 2(3): pp. 363–375.

Index

Note: page numbers in **bold** are major entries